SYSTEMS OF HIGHER EDUCATION: CANADA

Edward Sheffield
Duncan D. Campbell
Jeffrey Holmes
B. B. Kymlicka
James H. Whitelaw

ICED — International Council for Educational Development

First edition 1978
Second edition 1982

Copyright © 1982 by International Council for Educational Development

ISBN Number: 0-89192-204-0

Printed in the United States of America

Distributed by Interbook Inc., 611 Broadway
New York, N.Y. 10012

CONTENTS

FOREWORD

PREFACE

1	**THE NATIONAL SCENE** Edward Sheffield	1
2	**THE ATLANTIC PROVINCES** Jeffrey Holmes	37
3	**POSTSECONDARY SYSTEMS IN QUEBEC** James H. Whitelaw	65
4	**ONTARIO** B. B. Kymlicka	101
5	**WESTERN CANADA** Duncan D. Campbell	133
6	**SUMMARY AND COMMENT** Edward Sheffield	189
	SELECTED BIBLIOGRAPHY	211
	LIST OF COUNTRY DIRECTORS	218

FOREWORD

An important and largely unexamined development in higher education is the emergence of systems of institutions, which are planned and managed by advisory, coordinating, or governing bodies poised between institutions and governments. Countries with highly centralized governments now seek to devolve responsibility on such organizations, while in other countries the effort is to move from individual autonomous institutions to more central planning and controls. In both cases, a balance is sought between the values of institutional independence and public responsibility. Problems of organization and procedure are similar but patterns of solution vary widely. The design and management of the systems are, therefore, of universal interest and merit comparative study.

The central issue is easy to state but extremely difficult to answer: How can systems of higher education be designed and managed so as to assure maximum flexibility for institutions with responsible monitoring of the public interest?

Everywhere on the international scene, institutions of higher education are seeing their autonomy challenged—their right to decide their own methods of operation in management, in teaching, and in setting their own goals and purposes. Whether the institutions are public or private, this independence is directly threatened. Public funds and planning call for accountability and service in the national interest as government and society may see it.

The International Council for Educational Development has, for some years, watched this development. It produced what was, to our knowledge, the first collection of essays on the subject in 1972 under the title *Higher Education: From Autonomy to Systems*. So we welcomed the opportunity provided through a generous grant from the Krupp Foundation of the Federal Republic of Germany to make a three-year comparative analysis of how different countries are adjusting their higher education systems to meet the new demands.

Twelve countries were invited to participate. Guidelines were given for the study with the admonition that they were not to be inflexibly followed: each country needed latitude to explain its own context, development, and unique characteristics. Some problems would be more pertinent to one country than another. Further, we asked for a frank evaluation. Aside from the first section requesting a description of the system with data on institutions, enrollment, and various patterns of governance, the body of each study rests on the informed opinion of leaders in the higher education of the country.

In this respect the study differs from many preceding efforts to draw comparisons based on quantifiable facts. Seldom has that approach yielded more than a collection of data presented in a series of separate descriptions. So we have endeavored to go one step further and provide critical analysis of the issues being faced and the solutions being tried.

The study, in its entirety, comprises: twelve books, one for each country; a volume, crossing national lines, which explores the five major topics selected for analysis—planning, administration, and management; coordination; effectiveness of the system in meeting its social purposes; the effectiveness of the system to change and adjust; and the efficiency of the system—and, finally, a concluding report.

On a broad scale this study offers a statement about how different countries are dealing with critical problems of educational planning and operations. It speaks to social scientists and public officials who are necessarily concerned with problems of social unrest and cohesion as well as finance and changing priorities. It further holds the prospect of learning from the experience of others. Most educational systems have imported ideas from abroad, or at least they have been stimulated frequently by others to think creatively about their own systems. Also the study provides the means to learn of others' successes as well as difficulties. Finally, there is the possibility of discovering some general rules of governance that, with due caution, should be studied carefully by all those concerned with macroplanning of higher education.

We urge a careful reading of this study on Canada. It will be enlightening to the intracountry audience as a comment on their present situation. For interested parties in other countries, it is a critique that will illuminate their own efforts and stage of development. And those working at the frontier of international, comparative studies in higher education will discover, we trust, a valuable piece in an international puzzle.

We are indebted to the Canada Council for the major part of the financial contribution to make this study possible. We are also grateful to Duncan D. Campbell, James H. Whitelaw, B. B. Kymlicka, and Jeffrey Holmes for preparing the regional case studies, and especially to Edward Sheffield who directed the project.

January 1978   James A. Perkins
  Nell P. Eurich

PREFACE

The Study

In Canada, as elsewhere, in the years since World War II opportunities for higher education have been greatly extended and diversified. Existing institutions were expanded and new ones founded on the established models, new types of institutions were created, enrollments increased manyfold. Costs rose dramatically and governments became much more heavily involved in financing higher education. Not surprisingly, they showed increasing interest in the coordination and control of institutions of higher education. "Systems" came into being.

While the sixties were still years of expansion, the seventies were a period of consolidation. Therefore, the mid-seventies present an especially good context for a review of the structures, processes, and effectiveness of higher education in Canada. In order that this review might be undertaken within the brief period of time allotted, it seemed wise to arrange for simultaneous studies of the several Canadian systems of higher education. A 1974–75 review of Canadian educational policies undertaken by the Organization for Economic Cooperation and Development (OECD) focused on five areas: the Atlantic region, Quebec, Ontario, the Western region, and the government of Canada. A similar approach was chosen for this study, except that we will devote a section to discussing the national scene in general rather than the government of Canada alone.

In our discussion of the national scene in the first chapter we will describe the setting, summarize the rudimentary developments of systems of higher education from the beginning of World War II to the eve of the period of rapid expansion in the sixties, and then examine recent developments and the current situation with particular attention to the characteristics and problems of federalism. The following four chapters will be devoted to provincial and regional systems, one each on the Atlantic region (the provinces of Newfoundland, Prince Edward Island, Nova Scotia, and New Brunswick), Quebec, Ontario, and the West (Manitoba, Saskatchewan, Alberta, and British Columbia). We should mention that June 30, 1977 was our cut-off date and changes which have occurred since then have not been taken into account.

Those who comprised the Canadian study team were: Jeffrey Holmes, executive director of the Association of Atlantic Universities and former director of information for the Association of Universities and Colleges of Canada, who also contributed to the OECD review of educational policies; James H. Whitelaw, associate vice-rector, Academic Planning, and former professor and chairman of the Department of French and Modern Languages, Concordia University, Montreal; B. B. Kymlicka, professor of Political Science and dean of the Faculty of Social Science, University of Western Ontario, London, formerly director of research of the Hurtubise-Rowat Commission on the Relations between Universities and Governments, 1968-69, and the Wright Commission on Post-Secondary Education in Ontario, 1969-71; Duncan D. Campbell, professor of higher education, University of Alberta, Edmonton; and Edward Sheffield, professor of higher education and chairman of the Higher Education Group, University of Toronto (Professor Emeritus from July 1, 1977).

Responsibility for the national scene had been assumed by David Monroe, former special advisor in the Department of Secretary of State, Ottawa, and also a contributor to the 1974-75 OECD review. At the time of his death, in July 1976, I became responsible for the national scene as well as for coordination of the project. The first and last chapters are based in part on the notes David Munroe prepared. Patrick W. Naughton, a graduate student in the Higher Education Group at the University of Toronto, was my research assistant and the cartographer.

Though the five members of the team drew heavily on their own experience and on available documents, much of the review depended on interviews with and comments by officers of government departments and agencies concerned directly or indirectly with higher education and research, officers of voluntary associations in the field of higher education, and members of universities and community colleges. To all of those who helped — our thanks.

Definitions

We use the term higher education to encompass all types of formal postsecondary education, including that pursued in or under the aegis of universities, community colleges, institutes, and specialized schools, although we refer also to related, mostly informal, types of postsecondary and continuing education. For the Canadian study, the term postsecondary education would do as well as higher education (with reference to Quebec it would be better, as you will see) and we use it to mean the same thing. Occasionally institutions are classed as postsecondary because this term applies literally to the highest level courses they offer, even though they may also offer courses below that level.

The word college is used in Canada in many ways, sometimes referring to a subdivision or an affiliate of a university, sometimes to an independent university-level institution, sometimes to a community college without the power to grant degress, or to an adult education extension program. (The same word is used in Canada, though not in this study, to refer to a private secondary school or vocational training establishment.) Recognizing the possibility of confusion when we refer to colleges, we shall try to indicate clearly which meaning is intended.

It is more difficult to say precisely what we mean by system and subsystem. We do not use the word system in the technical sense employed in systems analysis, implying input-process-output-feedback. Rather we use it in the same loose sense as when one speaks of the school system or the political system. Implied, however, are structure, articulation, relations between the parts or subsystems, planning, and coordination. Also implied, therefore, are authority and the process by which it is exercised. In place of system we could have used such terms as network (as Campbell does in the chapter on the western provinces), pattern, organization, administration, but none seemed to have the general usefulness of system. It will be noted, however, that we have felt it necessary on occasion to speak of "system," implying that the phenomenon referred to is not as systematic or centralized as is sometimes suggested by the word.

An Aspect of Public Administration

The design and management of a system of higher education is an activity within the field of social policy and administration. To the extent that it is a concern of public bodies, of which the chief is government, it is an aspect of public policy and administration. Modern Canadian systems of higher education are government-centered so it is relevant to treat them in political terms and to analyze them in terms of what we know about Canadian governmental structures and processes in general.

Central to our theme, of course, are the politics of confederation, expressed primarily in the realm of federal-provincial relations. Throughout this report it should be remembered that the role of a democratic government is to express the will of the people. It may do so imperfectly, and occasionally seem to members of the academic community to be mistaken. Indeed it may seem at times that the people are mistaken. Nevertheless, the politics of Canadian systems of higher education reflect the government's conception of its role and its current assessment of what the voters want.

January 1978   Edward Sheffield

PREFACE TO THE SECOND EDITION

This second edition allows us to correct a number of errors that eluded the authors, the copy editor and the proof reader in the first. We have attempted little more than that. A thorough updating of the report would have involved many minor changes, but none of real consequence: the trends observable when we wrote nearly five years ago have continued, notably the trend toward increased government control, but the patterns of Canada's systems of higher education remain essentially as they were then.

There have been more studies of the situation—by at least three provincial governments, by the federal government, by voluntary associations, and by individual scholars. So far, however, none of these has resulted in substantive reform. One province (British Columbia) has established a separate ministry for higher education, and another (Manitoba) has rejoined its separate ministry to the ministry of education. British Columbia has new legislation governing colleges and institutes, including provision for three new intermediary bodies, and Quebec now has an intermediary council for the colleges of general and vocational education (CEGEPs). The Federal-Provincial Fiscal Arrangements and Established Programs Financing Act of 1977 expired at the end of March 1982 and was succeeded immediately by an amended version that made relatively little difference in the financing of postsecondary education. In sum: no major changes.

Ottawa, April 1982   E.S.

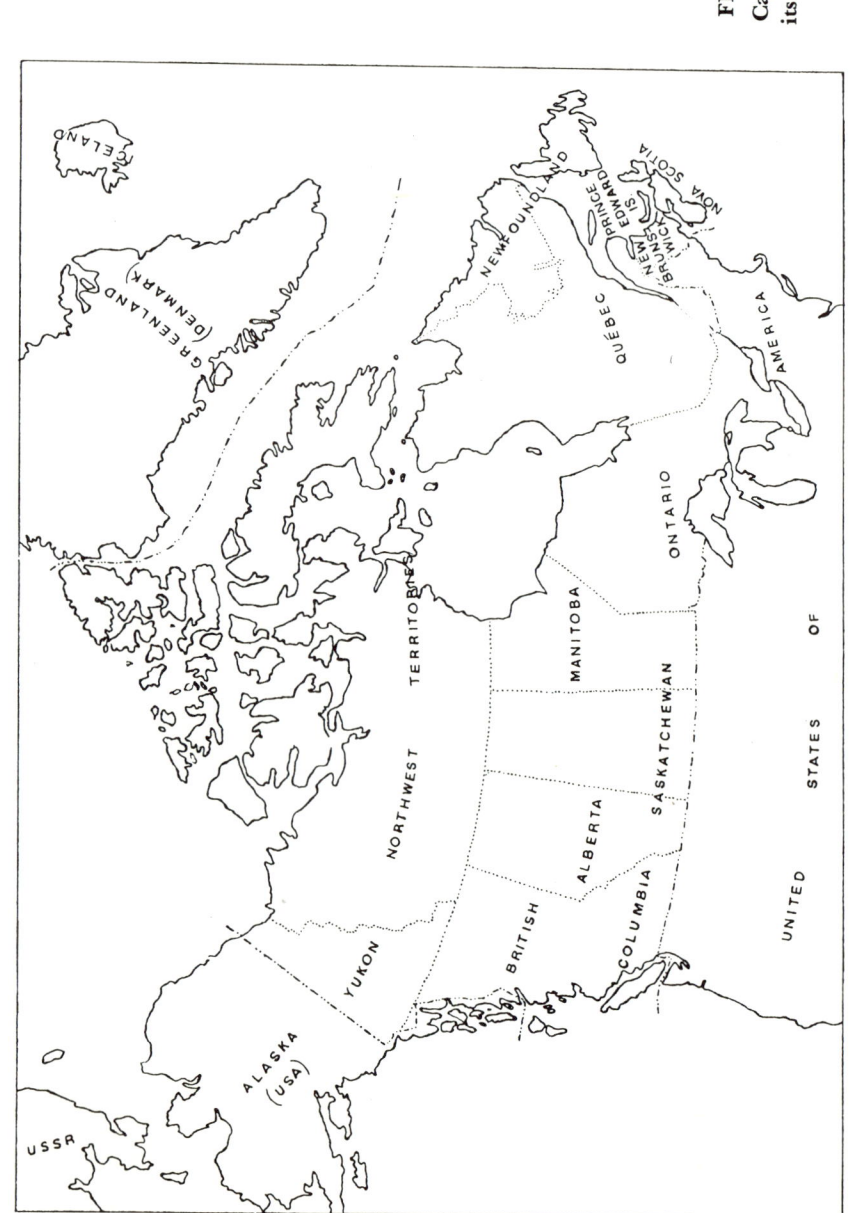

FIGURE 1
Canada and its Provinces

THE NATIONAL SCENE
Edward Sheffield

The Setting

Canada is a large country with a small population. It is exceeded in land mass only by the USSR, but its people number only twenty-three million—less than half the population of Great Britain—and most of them live within one-hundred miles of the U.S. border. For a little more than one hundred years, it has been a federal state, now consisting of ten provinces and two territories. The basis of its Constitution is the British North America (BNA) Act of 1867 which allocated responsibilities and powers to the Parliament of Canada and the legislatures of the provinces. Among the fields consigned to provincial jurisdiction was that of education: "In and for each Province the Legislature may exclusively make laws in relation to Education." Consequently, each province in Canada has its own system of education.

The federal Parliament, however, has responsibility for the national interest, which is not necessarily, and often is not, the same as that of any one or more of the provinces. The federal government has spending power not only in areas in which, according to the Constitution, it has specific jurisdiction but also in others in which only the provinces have legislative power. In addition, under the clause giving the federal Parliament authority "to make Laws for the Peace, Order, and good Government of Canada" it has power to legislate regarding matters which are in the interest of more than one of the provinces or of the nation as a whole. Actually, the Constitution is as often interpreted by federal-provincial negotiation as by judicial decision, giving Canada *de facto* what Donald Smiley calls constitutional flexibility.[1] Nevertheless, federal intervention is often resisted by the provinces, especially in the field of education.

Two other characteristics of Canadian government are worth mentioning in this context. The first concerns form. Canadian government is called cabinet or responsible government: ministers are involved with both legislation and operation in their fields. The other is that the Canadian government depends heavily upon ad hoc commissions, often called "royal commissions," for study and recommendations regarding current social problems. These commissions are major sources for innovation in government policy.

Canada is essentially a society of two cultures. Each of the two main cultural groups, francophone and anglophone, has its own institutions of higher education and uses its own language as the medium of instruction. Most of the francophone universities and community colleges are in the province of Quebec where French is the predominant language, but there are a few in other provinces, including some which use both French and English. English is the medium in almost all institutions of higher education outside Quebec, and also in those serving the anglophone minority in that province. Throughout Canada, roughly three-quarters of the students in higher education are in English-language institutions, one-quarter in French.

Though nominally there are both public and private institutions of higher education in Canada, the real difference in recent years has been between church-related institutions on one hand and nondenominational institutions (whether public or private foundations) on the other. The significance of this distinction has been that in some provinces church-related universities and colleges have not been eligible for provincial government grants or, as in the case of private church-related community colleges in Quebec, they have received provincial support at a rate below that which applies to public colleges.

Such discrimination has never been practiced in Quebec so far as the universities are concerned, nor for many years in Nova Scotia. It was the practice in Ontario, however, from 1868 to 1973. During that time most of the church-related institutions in that province gave up their religious affiliation and went public in order to qualify for provincial government grants, and since 1973 church-related colleges in Ontario get provincial grants indirectly through the public universities with which they are (if they are) affiliated. Most of the formerly church-related universities in the provinces of Manitoba, New Brunswick, and Prince Edward

Island also have become public institutions in the past fifteen years, while the remaining church colleges in those provinces are associated with public universities and now receive public support. In the remaining provinces of Newfoundland, Saskatchewan, Alberta, and British Columbia, all but one of the universities—Notre Dame of Nelson in British Columbia—were public foundations. Some affiliated colleges in these provinces remain outside the range of provincial support, but they account for small numbers of students. From 1951 to 1966 when the federal government made direct grants to universities, it did not distinguish between denominational and nondenominational institutions. Also, with few exceptions (all of which are in British Columbia, Alberta, and Quebec), community colleges are public institutions. Generally speaking, therefore, as members of the provincial systems and of the national "system" of higher education, public and private institutions receive the same treatment.

For the reader who is not acquainted with the general arrangements for schooling in Canada, here is a brief outline, omitting reference to the many exceptions which could be mentioned—some of which are noted in the following chapters. Most children enter kindergarten at the age of five and attend elementary school and secondary school for eleven to thirteen years, with transition from one level to the other after the sixth, seventh, or eighth year. Some secondary schools are comprehensive (called "composite" or "polyvalent" in Canada), with both university preparatory and vocational courses, while others are confined to one or the other of these functions. There are postsecondary community colleges and institutes offering programs lasting from a few months to one, two, and three years for entry to the labor market, programs of two years for entry (usually with advanced standing) to the university, and community-oriented programs of adult education.

Bachelor's degree programs usually require three to four years of study at a university. Those who pursue postgraduate studies in the arts and sciences spend at least one additional year (usually two) for the master's degree and at least two (often as many as four) more for the doctorate. Courses leading to specific professions—engineering, education, and pharmacy, for example—may be entered upon directly after graduating from secondary school. In others (e.g. law, dentistry, and medicine) students will usually spend at least two (more often three or four) years in an arts and science program. School teachers, once trained in separate institutions, are now usually trained in the universities, and the initial training of nurses, formerly undertaken in hospital schools, now takes place in community colleges. Opportunities for adult or continuing education are provided by almost all universities and colleges—some leading toward degrees or diplomas, some offering no certification. In addition, there are correspondence programs and occasional use is made of radio and television.

Although Canadian universities reflect the early influence of French, English, Scottish, and American institutions, they have become uniquely Canadian, especially in this century.[2] The technical institutes owe much to British models and some community college subsystems are patterned on American prototypes, but others, notably the CEGEPs of Quebec, are purely Canadian inventions.

Figure 2 shows the distribution of university and other institutions of postsecondary education across the land, underscoring the fact that the population is concentrated in a small portion of the country. Table 1, which follows, presents basic statistics on the system, for each province and region and for Canada as a whole. Only about two-thirds of the sixty-nine university institutions counted are multifaculty establishments, having professional schools as well as faculties of arts and science. Most in the other postsecondary category are community colleges, including institutes of technology, agricultural colleges, schools of art, teachers' colleges, and regional and hospital schools of nursing. With respect to students it will be noted that the estimates of part-time students in other postsecondary institutions are incomplete and include students studying in vocational courses below the postsecondary level. If there were, say, 100,000 part-time students in nonuniversity postsecondary institutions (including the CEGEPs) in Quebec, the total for Canada for 1975-76 was probably on the order of 234,000—roughly equal to the number of full-time students enrolled in these institutions. On the whole, full-time students outnumber part-time by about three to two, but there are notable provincial variations. The number of part-time students in noncredit courses probably numbered more than 500,000 during 1975-76.

Participation rates also vary from province to province. Only 10 percent (half the national average) of the eighteen- to twenty-

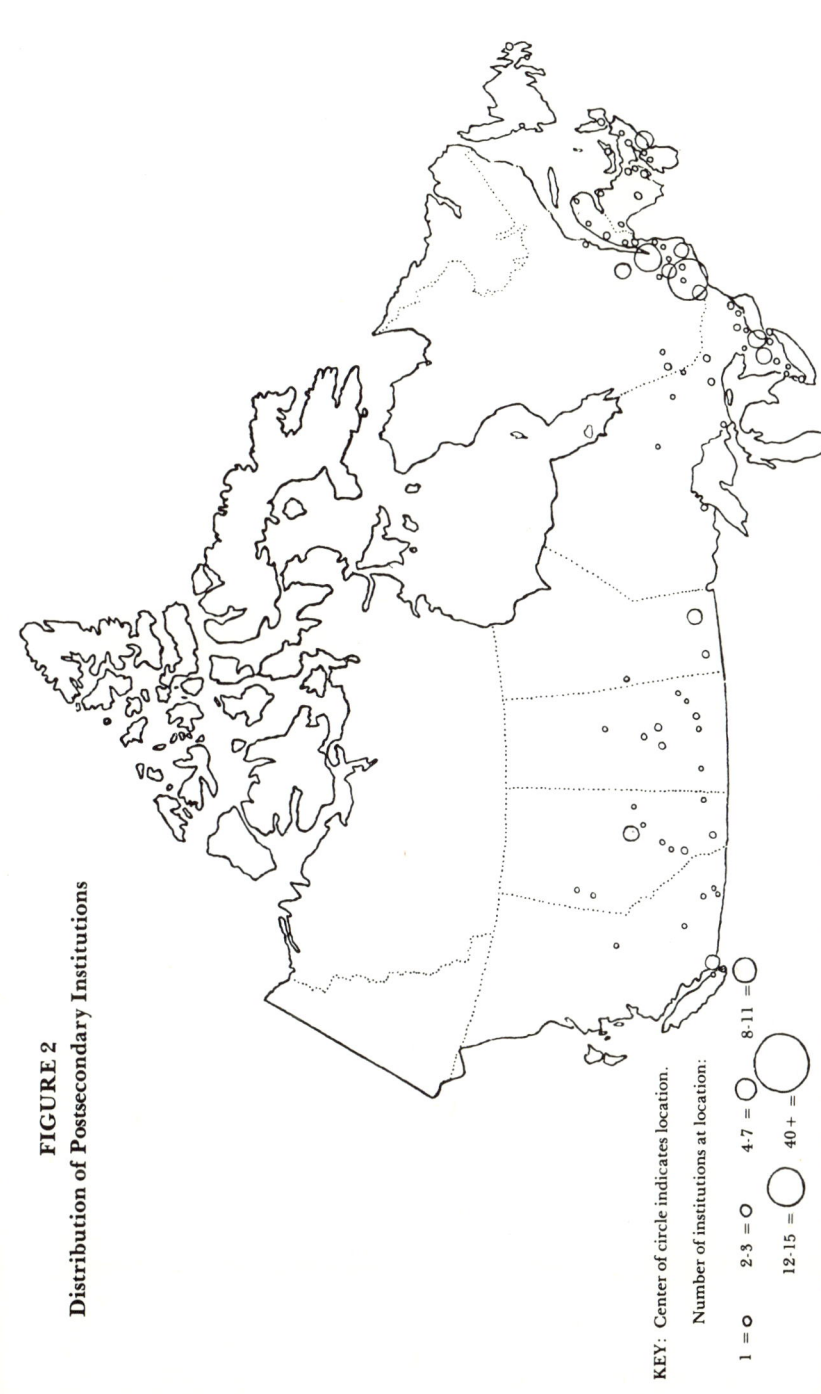

FIGURE 2
Distribution of Postsecondary Institutions

KEY: Center of circle indicates location.
Number of institutions at location:

1 = o   2-3 = ○   4-7 = ◯   8-11 = ◯
12-15 = ◯   40+ = ◯

Source: Based on 1976 data from Statistics Canada.

four-year old population is enrolled full-time in Newfoundland. Nova Scotia comes close to the national average in terms of enrollment and Ontario, Quebec, and Alberta are above the nationwide rate which, at 20 percent, is the second highest in the world— topped only by the United States.[3]

Total expenditures (operating and capital) for higher education exceeded $1 billion in Quebec and $1.5 billion in Ontario, and amounted to more than $4 billion in the whole of Canada for 1976-77. Per capita expenditures for higher education average $182 for the nation, ranging from $111 in one province to nearly twice that in another. As an indication of priorities, total expenditures on postsecondary education are shown as a percentage of gross provincial product (gross national product in the case of Canada). That percentage varied from 3.0 in Newfoundland, the poorest province, to 1.6 in British Columbia, one of the richest. For Canada as a whole, expenditures on postsecondary education equaled 2.2 percent of the GNP.

It will be noted that there are no postsecondary institutions in the North—the Yukon and Northwest Territories. The climate is severe and the population, including the Indians and the Inuit (Eskimo) is small. The expenditures for higher education in these areas have allowed residents of the territories to study in institutions in the provinces.

Loose National System Era, 1939-59

In the sixties, when increased enrollment created the need for more institutions and provincial expenditure on higher education began to soar, the era of provincial systems began. In the twenty years before that, however, the universities related to one another and to the government of Canada in what might be called a loose national system.

When Canada entered World War II in 1939, among the many problems facing the federal government was how to treat university personnel, both staff and students, within the provisions of the National Selective Service Act. To the government's credit, it chose to consult the universities before making any decision, and turned to the National Conference of Canadian Universities (NCCU) for guidance. At that time, the executive committee of the NCCU comprised the heads of the most prestigious universities of the

TABLE 1
Basic Statistics of Postsecondary Education in Canada, 1976–77
(preliminary or estimated)

Province or Region	Institutions Universities	Institutions Other[1]	Full-Time Teachers Universities	Full-Time Teachers Other[1]	Students in Credit Courses Full-Time Universities	Students in Credit Courses Full-Time Other[1]	Participation Rate[3]	Part-Time Universities	Part-Time Other[2]	Total Expenditures[4] Thousands of Dollars	Per Capita $	% of GPP (GNP)
Newfoundland	1	5	765	175	6,640	2,060	10.3	3,220	2,180	79,433	142	3.0
Prince Edward Is.	1	2	120	70	1,480	760	13.2	850	770	13,108	111	2.9
Nova Scotia	11	13	1,608	285	18,720	2,660	18.5	6,020	3,300	147,997	179	2.9
New Brunswick	4	9	1,102	170	11,230	1,470	12.4	4,120	1,940	85,391	126	2.2
Total Atlantic	17	29	3,595	700	38,070	6,950	14.1	14,210	8,190	325,929	149	2.7
Quebec	7	76	7,140	8,990	79,920	121,410	22.6	65,500	—	1,278,002	205	2.8
Ontario	22	30	12,697	4,930	164,350	64,090	21.3	72,990	82,250	1,532,688	185	2.0
Manitoba	5	8	1,627	340	18,680	3,480	16.3	11,590	3,600	160,295	157	2.0
Saskatchewan	4	3	1,380	210	15,290	2,360	13.1	6,860	4,870	133,195	145	1.9
Alberta	6	19	2,660	1,480	33,260	16,600	20.1	9,020	9,000	349,927	190	1.7
British Columbia	8	22	2,864	1,390	32,490	16,170	15.3	8,720	26,120	346,264	140	1.6
Total Western	23	52	8,531	3,420	99,720	38,610	16.6	36,190	43,590	989,681	158	1.7
Yukon, NWT, and Undistributed	—	—	—	—	—	—	—	—	320	60,367	922	—
Total Canada	69	187	31,963	18,040	382,060	231,060	19.6	188,890	—	4,186,667	182	2.2

Source: Statistics Canada

1. Other postsecondary education, including community colleges, etc.
2. These estimates are for 1975–76 and include unknown numbers of students below the postsecondary level.
3. Participation rate: Total of full-time students in universities and other institutions of postsecondary education as percent of the population eighteen- to twenty-four years old.
4. Total expenditure (operating and capital) on postsecondary education, per capita of the population, and as percent of the Gross Provincial Product (Gross National Product for Total Canada).

country. The committee had the trust of the member institutions of the conference and it served them and the government energetically and effectively. Details of the selective service arrangements worked out by the committee need not concern us here but it is relevant to note that these activities brought university and government leaders into closer contact than ever before and also consolidated the university community by giving it a new sense of purpose.

Comparable discussions took place between representatives of the federal government and the executive committee of the NCCU with regard to plans for what was euphemistically called the "university training" of veterans after their war service. (The more appropriate term, "university education," was thought to imply federal intrusion into provincial jurisdiction.) These plans included the provision of financial aid to student veterans and also grants to the universities to help them meet the costs of increased enrollment of veterans. Thus, in the name of defense, the federal government became involved in financing higher education. In this case, as in the matter of selective service, the government of Canada dealt directly with the universities as elements of a national system of higher education.

Due to the restrictions imposed by the BNA Act, the government of Canada had no ministry of education. There was, however, an education statistics division in the Dominion Bureau of Statistics.

As a result of the influx of veterans, university enrollments reached a peak of 83,882 full-time students during 1947-48. But as the number of veterans enrolling declined, so did the universities' revenues. When the government launched a Royal Commission on National Development in the Arts, Letters, and Sciences (the Massey Commission) in 1949, the universities sought and received authorization to submit a plea for support to the commission. In its report (1951), the commission responded with warm appreciation:[4]

> The universities are provincial institutions; but they are much more than that. It would be a grave mistake to underestimate or to misconceive the wider and indeed universal functions of these remarkable institutions. . . . They are local centres for education at large and patrons of every movement in aid of the arts, letters, and sciences. They also serve the national cause in so many ways, direct and indirect, that theirs must be regarded as the finest of contributions to national strength and unity.

In keeping with this endorsement, the commission recommended that the federal government make direct, unrestricted grants to the universities. It also recommended a program of national scholarships and the creation of a council for the encouragement of the arts, humanities, and social sciences.

The Parliament approved the recommendation of university grants and the government implemented the program immediately for the academic year 1951-52. The premier of the province of Quebec protested, however, that this was interference in provincial affairs. He permitted the universities of the province to accept the grants for that year, but forbade them to do so thereafter. (It is said, though not officially recorded, that he threatened withdrawal of provincial grants.) In 1956, hoping to break the deadlock, the Prime Minister of Canada announced that the per capita amount of the federal grants to universities would be doubled and invited the National Conference of Canadian Universities to act as the distributing agent—with authority to hold unclaimed funds in trust until they were requested. Even this did not work, and it was not until 1959 that an optional formula was devised (instituted in 1960-61) which met Quebec's criteria—essentially the transfer of taxing power from the federal government to any province preferring that option. Quebec was the only province choosing the option, but its stance from 1952 to 1959 presaged the end of what we have called the era of a loose national system.

The NCCU was not the only nationwide voluntary education association. In 1926 the National Federation of Canadian University Students (NFCUS) was established, and its campaign for aid to students was reflected in the Massey Commission's recommendation of a program of national scholarships—which was to be adopted only in an oblique way when, in 1964, a Canada Student Loans Program was launched. The NFCUS and its successors, the Canadian Union of Students (1963-69) and the National Union of Students (1972—), have had a national office and a secretariat from time to time since 1951.

It was not until 1951 that the professors organized. They formed the Canadian Association of University Teachers (CAUT), devoted primarily to improving salaries and fringe benefits, permitting faculty membership on university governing boards, and assuring academic freedom. The CAUT opened a national office in 1958. (Although it had been in existence since 1911, the NCCU did not have a national office with a paid secretariat until 1957.) All three associations chose Ottawa, the national capital, for their headquarters. So far, we have referred to the federal government's role in higher education with respect to providing aid to veterans and operating grants to universities. However, long before either of these programs was adopted, the federal government had promoted the cause of research. The National Research Council was established in 1916 and by the end of the fifties had developed a significant program of pure and applied research in the natural sciences and engineering in its own laboratories and grants-in-aid for university research, including bursaries for science students. It had spawned two independent research bodies: the Defence Research Board (a researching and granting agency) in 1947, and the Medical Research Council (to promote, assist, and undertake basic, applied, and clinical research in the health sciences) in 1960. In 1957 the Canada Council for the Encouragement of the Arts, Humanities, and Social Sciences was established—for support of the arts and research in the humanities and social sciences. The creation of such a council had been recommended six years earlier by the Massey Commission. By 1960, therefore, the national government had programs of support for university research in all fields. Although more funds were provided for natural science than for the social sciences and humanities, there was systematic provision for research in institutions of higher education.

Meanwhile, provincial systems of higher education were developing slowly. Most universities founded in the seventeenth, eighteenth, and nineteenth centuries were the result of private initiative, usually of the churches. In Ontario, however, the "provincial" University of Toronto was incorporated in 1827 on government initiative, and in the four western provinces—Manitoba, Saskatchewan, Alberta and British Columbia—provincial universities were established, one in each, between 1877 and 1915. After confederation in 1867, new universities received official incorporation through the enactment of provincial legislation. Also, universities that had been established earlier by the Crown (the British Parliament) or the Pope (by papal decree) sought and received changes in their constitution through provincial legislation. As a result, by 1960 virtually all of the legally recognized universities were creatures of the provinces. To that extent, the provincial governments were responsible for the universities, but although government support comprised a significant proportion of the universities' budgets, it amounted to little of the total government expenditure and, with few exceptions, neither the provincial nor the federal governments interfered with the universities' autonomy. Universities were not yet considered to be "affected with a public interest," and the few junior colleges spotted here and there had not yet been succeeded by the networks of community colleges which were to appear in the sixties.

During this time, then, there was a loose national system of higher education and incipient provincial systems. There were also (and still are) systems or minisystems of another sort—those that have been called university families, some of which date back to the nineteenth century, such as the University of Toronto family. It consists of the public University of Toronto proper with which are federated Victoria University (United Church), the University of Trinity College (Anglican), and the University of St. Michael's College (Roman Catholic). All three church-related institutions are legally empowered to grant university degrees, but while they are in federation with the University of Toronto, they hold that power in abeyance, except with respect to degrees in theology. Their students, and those enrolled in the University of Toronto proper, prepare for and receive degrees from the University of Toronto. (York University joined the family when it was incorporated in 1959 and affiliated with the University of Toronto. It became independent, however, in 1965.)

Before the reform of the system of education which took place in the province of Quebec in the mid-sixties, the family of the Université Laval consisted of more than forty church-related *collegès classiques* and *séminaires* which prepared students for the bachelor's degree of the university. The students of the various departments of the university itself were candidates for the other degrees awarded by Laval. The Université de Montreal (which began as a branch of Laval) and the Université de Sherbrooke also were family institutions in Quebec, the former much the larger, indeed rivaling the size and scope of the Université Laval. In addition to those just mentioned, the larger university families included the University of Western Ontario, and the universities of Manitoba, Saskatchewan, Alberta, and British Columbia.

These minisystems of university families served to group weak institutions around the strong, small around the large, and often, though not in all cases, church-related institutions around public universities. It was characteristic of the university families that the central or parent institution controlled the academic programs of all members of the family, while each member was responsible for its own financing, staffing, and administration.

During the two decades between 1939-40 and 1959-60 higher education was a relatively small enterprise in Canada. The number of university families (some with one institution) only increased from twenty-seven to thirty-eight, and the number of full-time undergraduate students from 37,000 to 102,000. Nonuniversity establishments consisted of roughly 300 small teacher-training institutions, hospital nursing schools, and technical institutes (few of these), with total enrollment over that period increasing from 12,000 to 46,000.[5]

All this was to change in the next decade. In 1955 an NCCU-commissioned projection of full-time university enrollment suggested that enrollment would double in ten years.[6] (Indeed, it more than doubled in eight years, and continued to rise dramatically for another eight.) Both universities and governments, especially the governments of the provinces, heeded the warning. For the first time, higher education was recognized as a service to be provided to more than a small percentage of the population. Consequently, facilities for higher education had to be expanded. This would cost money, public money, and lots of it. The provincial governments organized for the task, and the development of provincial systems proceeded posthaste.

The era of the loose national system was soon to end. The next decade would be characterized by the provincialization of higher education, as the center of power shifted from the central to the provincial governments.

The Development Of Provincial Systems, 1960—

This section has two main parts. In the first, we will focus on the three sectors of the national higher education scene—the federal government, the provincial governments, and the academic community—and describe the components, roles, and internal relations of each. In the second section we will examine the relations, on a national scale, of these sectors with one another during the period since 1960.

The Government of Canada

In spite of the fact that the provinces have been assigned constitutional responsibility for legislation dealing with education, the federal government is interested — must be interested — in many aspects of higher education.[7] Given the constitutional situation, it would be inappropriate for the federal government to have, or at any rate to articulate, clear-cut general goals for higher education. However, one can identify particular goals which *are* appropriate to the central government and which have implications for higher education. These goals can be achieved only with the assistance of the provincial governments and the institutions of higher education themselves.

Federal Goals

In opening the 1966 federal-provincial conference on financing higher education, the Prime Minister of Canada asserted the federal government's interests in higher education:[8]

> Education is obviously a matter of profound importance to the economic and social growth of the country as a whole. This is particularly true of higher education. Apart altogether from the general interest in fostering equality of opportunity for Canadians, wherever they may live or wherever they may be brought up, the federal government has specific and particular responsibilities to which higher education is relevant. While education itself is provincial, the federal government accepts primary responsibility for employment and economic activity generally in the country. We recognize that provincial governments share our concern in these matters and pursue these common aims in the conduct of their own affairs. It is, however, the responsibility of the federal government to devise and apply national policies and measures that are necessary to ensure that the economy of Canada will continue to expand and will become increasingly productive, in order that there may be full employment and an increasing level of prosperity for all our citizens. The preparation of our young people for productive participation in the labor force of the country is a matter of vital concern to all Canadians. We have also to keep in mind that young peo-

ple of a particular province do not necessarily receive their education and training in their home province, and that people, after graduation, do not necesssarily live out their lives and take up employment in the province where they received their education.

Later, with respect to adult occupational training, he claimed that:[9]

The training and retraining of adults for participation in the labour force are well within the scope of federal jurisdiction. They are manifestations of the federal government's responsibility for national economic development. Once the normal process of education for an individual has been completed and that individual is established in the labour force, measures of training thereafter to fit him to the constantly changing requirements of a rapidly changing technological world are not "education" in the constitutional sense. They are measures designed to ensure the maximum possibility of effective participation in production. They are measures to reduce unemployment; to increase the productivity and earnings of Canadian workers; and to maintain and improve the competitive position of Canada in relation to other countries. In short, the federal government believes that it has a constitutional and necessary role in the training and development of our adult labour force for economic growth and full employment.

He also discussed research: "In our view, research, as the means by which we expand the frontier of knowledge, is today one of the most important factors in the economic and social growth of any modern political society" and "governments at any level must feel free to sponsor and support research of any kind."[10]

Two years later, in a White Paper published by the government of Canada for the Constitutional Conference of February 1968,[11] the Prime Minister asserted that the areas of federal responsibility for higher education included formulation of economic policy, equalization of opportunity, technological and cultural development, international affairs. (The provincial governments also have responsibilities in these areas.) He also stated: "The federal government must remain responsible to Parliament, and the provincial governments to their legislatures; federal-provincial conferences must, it seems to us, occupy themselves with the art of influence rather than the power of decision-making."

In 1972, when he was deputy secretary (for planning) of the Treasury Board, Douglas G. Hartle addressed the Canadian Society for the Study of Higher Education, stating, in part: "Governments attempt to reflect social consensus regarding the overall value of education to society by influencing, via financial and other policies, the size and structure of the total educational sector." He suggested that the purposes to be served by the federal government with respect to higher education were: to correct for "market 'imperfections' which prevent the individual from investing sufficiently in higher education to maximize *his own wellbeing*" in the belief that "higher education produces benefits for society which cannot be appropriated by the individuals who undertake higher education"; and to achieve "equity in treatment of the federation's component regions."[12]

A little more than two years later, the secretary of state addressed the Association of Universities and Colleges of Canada,[13] noting what he called the "imperatives" — areas which required federal involvement. (These became "concerns" in a later version, and were slightly refined for the secretary of state's submission to OECD.) He said that a "major concern of the government is the process of matching up the skills of persons produced by the educational system with the manpower requirements of the Canadian economy." Then he identified "the three major national concerns which remain foremost in our mind. They are: advancement of knowledge; equality of opportunity; and cultural development." Elaborating on the second of these he restated the most commonly held objective for education in Canada: "In our country, it is widely accepted that everyone should have an equal opportunity to obtain the kind of education that his capacities will permit — this, not only to enable him to compete more successfully on the job market, but also to achieve a higher degree of self-fulfillment."

As a summing-up to date (1975), the secretary of state's contribution to the OECD review of education policies included notes on "concerns" which have led to federal involvement in education (chiefly postsecondary education):[14]

> The first of these was the emergence of research and scholarship. An area of activity not envisaged at the time of confederation, it was only some sixty years ago that research and scholarship began to emerge as a parallel responsibility of Canadian universities. This was a responsibility which carried

with it attendant requirements for graduate studies and for national and international commitments. These needs resulted in the creation of federal research support programs.

The second concern prompting federal involvement emerged during the late fifties and early sixties. At that time, the sudden expansion of education expenditures across the country reached crisis proportions. Drawn into assuming some capital costs on behalf of Canadian universities and more particularly in relation to technical and vocational facilities at the secondary level, the Government of Canada also assumed half of all operating costs of the postsecondary sector.

Almost simultaneously a third concern called for action. It had become apparent that it was in the interest of all Canadians to involve a national input in education — an input capable of correcting some of the interregional and interpersonal inequities in educational opportunities that would otherwise prevail. This requirement led to the creation of the student aid program and influenced the program of fiscal transfers.

From these statements we can cull a number of federal objectives which have implications for higher education. Some are much broader than others, and obviously they are not mutually exclusive.
- to enhance our national life (cultural development, Canadianism);
- to achieve greater national unity (improved intercultural and interregional relations);
- to develop the economy (manpower supply and training, technological advance);
- to improve accessibility to postsecondary education (equality of opportunity);
- to encourage the discovery of new knowledge and ways of applying it;
- to assume appropriate international responsibilities.

Most federal government programs affecting higher education — for the most part supporting higher education — can be related to one or more of these general objectives. In point of fact, it could be demonstrated that all activities in higher education help in the achievement of the first and third objectives, that is, to promote cultural and economic development.

Fiscal Transfers

We have seen above how the federal government's program of direct grants to universities began and how the Quebec universities were excluded from 1952-53 to 1959-60. The notion of transferring tax revenues to the provinces in lieu of grants to universities was worked out for Quebec beginning in 1960-61. The other provinces were offered this option too but Quebec was the only one to choose it. Until 1966-67, therefore, universities in the other provinces continued to receive grants based on the population of each province and divided within each province in proportion to the enrollment of full-time undergraduate and graduate students (in 1966-67 a weighted enrollment formula was substituted for the simple head count which had been used in previous years).

For the next ten years, all provinces were put on a basis similar in principle to the tax transfer scheme which had been initiated in Quebec in 1960-61. Then in 1977 the arrangements were changed again to make the federal influence on provincial spending for postsecondary education even more indirect. (The negotiations which went on between the federal and provincial governments during that decade will be discussed later in this chapter under the heading "Intersector Relations.") At this time, it is appropriate to note the value of federal payments and fiscal transfers of this kind since 1960 (see Table 2).

TABLE 2
Federal Grants to Universities 1960-61 to 1966-67 and Fiscal Transfers and Payments to the Provinces for Postsecondary Education, 1967-68 to 1976-77
(thousands of dollars)

1960-61[1]	$26,708	1968-69	$527,364
1961-62	27,249	1969-70	650,912
1962-63[2]	37,062	1970-71[5]	789,891
1963-64	37,714	1971-72	930,673
1964-65	38,388	1972-73	1,012,784
1965-66	39,062	1973-74	1,161,773
1966-67[3]	99,859	1974-75	1,336,038
1967-68[4]	422,680	1975-76	1,529,732
		1976-77	1,759,198

Source: Department of the Secretary of State, November 1976.
1. Base for 1960-61 and 1961-62: $1.50 per capita of the provincial population.
2. Base for 1962-63 to 1965-66: $2.00 per capita.
3. Base for 1966-67: $5.00 per capita.
4. Base for 1967-68 to 1976-77: 50 percent of eligible expenditures on postsecondary education or $15 (escalating annually) per capita of the population.
5. Amounts for 1970-71 to 1976-77 not finally settled.

This program is clearly intended to supplement the provinces' financial resources for postsecondary education and to assure equitable regional distribution of such resources. Thus it can be considered as related to the goal of increasing the accessibility of higher education.

Research

From the founding of the National Research Council in 1916 to passage of the Government Organization (Scientific Activities) Act in 1977, Canada has been slowly developing a national science policy.[15] The 1977 Act modified arrangements for the support of university research by providing for a social sciences and humanities research council, a natural sciences and engineering research council, and a medical research council, the first two of which are new bodies with functions formerly assigned to other agencies. The National Research Council and a number of operating departments of government engage in their own research, commission research, support research initiated by university personnel, and in some cases contribute to the costs of professional training in their fields. Examples are the departments of agriculture, the environment, national defence (which operates three military colleges), energy, mines and resources, communications, national health and welfare, and atomic energy of Canada, a crown (government-owned) corporation.

The estimated federal expenditures on research and development totaled $1,000 million for 1976-77. Of this, $173 million (17 percent) was for research in universities, $228 million (23 percent) for research in industry, and $522 million (52 percent) represented the cost of research undertaken by the government itself in its various departments and agencies. Another $77 million (8 percent) was spent in other settings.[16]

The Ministry of State for Science and Technology was established in 1971 "for the purpose of formulating and developing policies in relation to the activities of the government of Canada that affect the development and application of science and technology." It advises the Cabinet on policies that may affect supply and demand for highly qualified manpower, including, of course, graduates of the universities, and engages in studies of related problems, and it advises on the organization and management of all federal programs in the fields of science and technology, including the coordination of research support. To aid in the latter task provision was made in 1977 for an Inter-Council Coordinating Committee, comprising the heads of the three granting councils with the secretary of the ministry as chairman, reporting to the minister of state for science and technology. Since 1966, independent advice on science policy has been provided by the Science Council of Canada. According to the Scientific Activities Act, the Science Council is to play a larger role in informing the public on scientific and related issues, including those in the domain of the human sciences.

These activities in the realm of science, technology, and research are related particularly to the federal government's concern for the development of the economy, the discovery, dissemination, and application of knowledge, and the preparation, in appropriate numbers, of highly qualified manpower.

Vocational Training

In the second decade of the twentieth century the federal government offered aid to the provinces to encourage vocational training. Through one program or another, this assistance continued until 1967. At that time, the government of Canada terminated the Technical and Vocational Training Act which had provided for federal contributions to the costs of training and facilities for training in provincial establishments. In its place, the Canada Manpower Training Program — designed to improve the earning potential or employability of adult workers in industrial establishments or provincial educational institutions — was launched under the Adult Occupational Training Act of 1967. Program planning is undertaken cooperatively by the federal government and the provinces, with the former paying the costs. The provincial community colleges supply some of the needed facilities.

These vocational training programs are directly related to the central government's responsibility for the economy, for manpower supply, for the welfare of the unemployed, and for accessibility to education, including postsecondary education.

Bilingualism

One result of the Royal Commission on Bilingualism and Biculturalism, which reported over the period 1965-1969,[17] was the federal creation, with provincial cooperation, of a number of programs "to promote, facilitate, and encourage the acquisition and use of the two official languages in Canadian society [English and French], thereby reinforcing the equality of status of the two official languages."[18] These programs include: federal support of minority-language and bilingual institutions of postsecondary education (10.85 percent of provincial payments); fellowships for second-language monitors (native-speaker teaching assistants); capital funds for language-training centers; contributions to the costs of French-language teachers' colleges; assistance to voluntary associations; and research and special projects related to bilingualism, among others. Federal expenditures on these programs at the postsecondary level amount to approximately $40 million a year.

External Aid and Exchanges

Canada takes its obligations as a member of the international community seriously. In this connection it provides assistance in the education of personnel from less-favored nations in Canadian universities and colleges, and in applied research in developing nations. The two bodies chiefly concerned with these activities are the Canadian International Development Agency (CIDA) and the International Development Research Centre (IDRC). CIDA is a wholly Canadian governmental body though it supports voluntary associations such as the Canadian University Service Overseas. IDRC has its headquarters in Ottawa and its finances are provided by the Canadian government, but it is run by a board whose members are chosen from many countries. In addition, through its Department of External Affairs (frequently in collaboration with the Council of Ministers of Education), Canada takes part in numerous cultural and academic exchanges with other nations.

Student Aid

In keeping with its desire to improve accessibility to postsecondary education (from the level of the community college to that of doctoral studies) the federal government has provided financial assistance to students since the National Research Council was founded in 1916. In 1977 the chief vehicles of such assistance were the Canada Manpower Training Program (providing weekly allowances for trainees), the Canada Student Loans Program (launched

1964), the bursaries, scholarships, and fellowships awarded by the research councils, and several small programs run by individual government departments in connection with their own missions.

Central Services

Among the central services concerned in part with higher education is the country's national statistical service, Statistics Canada, which has had a division for gathering statistics on education since 1919, and for education, science, and culture since 1973. Mention should be made, too, of the Economic Council of Canada, established by the government in 1963 to study and make recommendations on the economy. Several of its annual reviews and a number of its special studies have offered analyses of the roles and state of postsecondary education in relation to the economic health of the nation. A relatively new body which has potential for the field of higher education but has not yet turned its attention to that study is the Institute for Research on Public Policy which was formed by the government in 1972.

Coordination

We have mentioned the coordinating role of the Ministry of State for Science and Technology with respect to scientific research. The Department of the Secretary of State has a comparable role with respect to postsecondary education:[19]

> In 1966 the secretary of state was assigned the task of advising Cabinet on postsecondary education. An Education Support Branch was established in the Department of the Secretary of State, and within a year it became responsible for the administration of that part of the Federal-Provincial Fiscal Arrangements Act, 1967, which related to postsecondary education.
>
> In 1973 the Department of the Secretary of State was designated by Cabinet as the agency within the federal government responsible for coordinated development, formulation, implementation and review of federal policies and programs relating to education. In addition to administering the program of fiscal transfers for postsecondary education, the Department of the Secretary of State is also responsible for: federal policies and programs in support of postsecondary education generally; communication with provincial governments, the academic community, and national organizations,

on matters of education; cooperating with the Department of External Affairs in the coordination of Canada's effective participation in international forums on educational questions; and evaluating the effectiveness of federal policies and programs in support of education against national goals.

In the period before 1960 the closest Canada came to having a national ministry or office of education was the Education Division of the Dominion Bureau of Statistics. This division continues to function, but the Education Support Branch of the Secretary of State's department is now the agency which most resembles, though is not really much like, an office of education.

Centers of Power

It would be a mistake not to draw attention to the fact that — in spite of elaborate provisions for the allocation of responsibility for coordination to such departments as the Ministry of State for Science and Technology and that of the Secretary of State — the real power remains in the Department of Finance, the Treasury Board, the Privy Council Office (of which the Federal-Provincial Relations Office is an important subdivision), and the Prime Minister's Office. These are the centers in which the crucial decisions are made, subject, of course, to the will of Parliament.

Provincial Governments

Many people think it is nonsense to speak now of a national system of higher education in Canada, though it is generally agreed that provincial systems have existed since the mid-sixties. The provincial governments have been the key factors in these systems; the role of the federal government has been supportive, especially in terms of finance.

Our interest here is in the provincial governments' role in higher education on a national scale. Since 1967 the chief medium through which the provincial governments have played a national role is the Council of Ministers of Education, Canada (CMEC). Modeled on the *Kultusministerkonferenz* (Standing Conference of Ministers of Culture and Education) of the eleven West German Länder, it succeeded the Standing Committee of Ministers of Education of the Canadian Education Association. The new pattern of federal-provincial fiscal relations with respect to postsecondary education implemented in 1967 created problems for the provincial governments, especially in connection with the adult occupational training program which was to be administered by the provinces at federal expense. Although this was the immediate reason for formalizing the Council of Ministers of Education, they had many other common concerns. A statement issued by the council in 1974 described its structure and role as follows:[20]

> The council is an interprovincial educational agency set up for coordination, information and liaison purposes, operating at the interprovincial, provincial-federal, and international levels, under the direction of the departments of education. Its basic aim is to enable the ministers to consult on such matters as are of common interest, and to provide a means for the fullest cooperation among provincial governments in areas of mutual interest and concern in education. Each provincial department of education continues to be autonomous within the council; no recommendations or decisions of the council are binding on provincial ministries with respect to their jurisdictions.

According to the record of the December 1975 meeting between the Canadian delegation and OECD's Education Committee, the Manitoba minister of colleges and universities affairs, who later became chairman of the CMEC, reviewed the role and function of the council in part as follows:[21]

> When the ministers meet in council, it acts merely as a forum for the exchange of views, information, and ideas interprovincially, but at no time does it assume the posture of a body acting on behalf of the ministers of education of the provinces of Canada. The council meets, and consensus of view may be arrived at, but that is then taken back to the provinces and each minister of education assumes the responsibility for dealing with it — whether it be within the province or interprovincially, or between a particular province and the federal government.

In its annual report for 1975-76 the council listed the following matters related to postsecondary education which engaged the attention of its secretariat, its committees, and the council itself. Note that in all cases these concerns were being undertaken jointly with appropriate representatives of federal departments or agencies.[22]

- the federally financed Summer Language Bursary Program, launched in 1971 "to provide young Canadians with the opportunity to increase their knowledge of the second official language and their understanding and appreciation of the culture of the other official language group;"
- the provincially administered Interprovincial Second-Language Monitor Program (1973), also financed by the government of Canada through the Department of the Secretary of State, "to promote the learning and use of Canada's official languages by sending anglophone and francophone postsecondary students to act as second-language monitors in another province;"
- the federal-provincial fiscal arrangements for the financing of postsecondary education (agreement was reached in December 1976 on new arrangements which began in 1977);
- the OECD review of Canada's educational policies, including those for higher education (the OECD's report was published in 1976);
- joint federal-provincial discussions regarding the cost and financing of university research (this led in 1976 to announcement of the formation of the Canadian Committee on Financing University Research);
- development of a new national student assistance plan to replace the Canada Student Loans Program; and
- statistics of education, including postsecondary education.

One might conclude that the Council of Ministers of Education is in a position to play a role of national leadership in higher education, but, in fact, it seems reluctant to assume this role. It is a creature of the provincial governments, and they do not and perhaps will not delegate to it any of the decision-making powers regarding higher education which they so jealously guard.

One other aspect of the national role of the provincial governments with respect to higher education should be noted: both students and staff may move freely from one province to another. Preparation for admission to university, college, or technical institutions in one province is recognized in the others; degrees and diplomas have Canadian-wide currency. Although two provinces have required their universities and colleges to inaugurate differential fees for foreign students — that is, those who are neither Canadian citizens nor landed immigrants — such discrimination does not operate against students from other Canadian provinces.

The Academic Community

The universities have a natural affinity for each other, regardless of provincial boundaries. This is expressed by their administrators, their members of faculty, and their students, and is reflected in a host of voluntary associations, most of them national in scope. Among the most significant are the three already mentioned — the Association of Universities and Colleges of Canada (AUCC), the Canadian Association of University Teachers (CAUT), and the National Union of Students (NUS). Community colleges, too, have much in common although they are obviously local institutions under the close control of the provincial governments. Nevertheless, they have a national organization, the Association of Canadian Community Colleges (ACCC). To the list of national associations concerned with higher education policy at least another three score can be added, ranging from the Association of Canadian Faculties of Dentistry to the World University Service of Canada. In addition, there are at least as many societies for scholars: the Royal Society of Canada, the Social Science Federation of Canada, the Humanities Research Council of Canada, the Association of the Scientific, Engineering, and Technological Community of Canada (SCITEC), and others related to particular disciplines.

Most of these organizations have national concerns and membership from throughout the country. Many of them publish bulletins or journals which are distributed from coast to coast, and a considerable proportion of these are bilingual, with articles in both English and French. Examples are *University Affairs,* published ten times a year by the AUCC, the CAUT *Bulletin* (published six times a year), *College Canada* (published nine times a year by the ACCC), and several other journals, usually published quarterly, in economics, chemistry, history, Canadian studies, psychology, public administration, medicine, and so on. These publications maintain communication between members and almost every society holds an annual conference, ordinarily in a different part of the country each year. Truly, the scholarly community is national in scope.

These, then, are the three sectors — the principal groups of actors on the national stage: the federal government (represented by a score of departments and agencies whose interests in higher education are loosely coordinated by the Department of the Secretary of State and the Ministry of State for Science and Technology), the provincial governments (represented on program matters by the Council of Ministers of Education, Canada, but separately, and seemingly without the participation of CMEC, on matters of higher policy and finance by their colleagues—the premiers and ministers of finance), and the academic community (represented by its many national associations).

Intersector Relations

When the decade of expansion and change in the sixties began, the universities (except those in Quebec) enjoyed a fruitful relationship with the government of Canada. That is to say they were receiving direct federal support for almost all classes of expenditure: unrestricted annual grants which could be and were used to help meet general operating costs, grants for construction of facilities for the arts, humanities, and social sciences, loans for the construction of student housing, and grants in aid of research. And in 1964 a program providing loans to students was introduced. Although the federal government's share in the costs of higher education amounted to only 20 percent in 1960-61, it represented a significant portion of university income. Accordingly, one of the roles of the National Conference of Canadian Universities, later named the AUCC, was that of lobbying—seeking continuation or improvement of federal programs in support of higher education—and in this the NCCU (AUCC) received complementary support from the CAUT.

So, for the first few years of the decade the most significant intersector relations on the national scene involved those between the universities and the federal government. (The community colleges had not yet been established.) The federal-provincial conference on university finance in October 1966, however, shifted the focus to relations between the federal government and the provincial governments.

Playing its role as spokesman for and servant of the universities, the AUCC had commissioned a study of the financing of higher education in Canada. The report from the study appeared in 1965[23] and recommended an immediate increase, from $2.00 to $5.00 per capita of the population of the provinces, in the federal grants to universities (increasing annually thereafter by $1.00), a capital grants fund of $5.00 per capita, and more support for research. It also recommended that the provincial governments establish grants commissions, and determine financing on the basis of weighted enrollment.

The timing was fortunate, since the provisions established by the Federal-Provincial Fiscal Arrangements Act (FAA) were due to expire on March 31, 1967. With the AUCC commission report as background and the immediate necessity of continuing or revising the FAA, the federal minister of finance invited his provincial counterparts to Ottawa in October 1966 to discuss how the federal government could most usefully (and feasibly) help to support the universities for the next five years. Since 1951-52 the federal government had raised its grants to universities from a base of 50¢ per capita of the population of the provinces to an average of $5.00. Should that amount escalate as recommended by the AUCC?

To the surprise of the provincial ministers and even of many of the federal representatives at that 1966 conference, the Prime Minister announced that the federal government would no longer make grants to universities through the AUCC. Instead, it would extend the program by which, since 1960, it had surrendered taxing power in Quebec, to allow that province to support its universities in a fashion comparable to other provinces. In other words, the federal government would yield part of its share of tax income to the provinces in order that they might be better able to discharge their constitutional responsibility for postsecondary education.

But the federal government was not ready to let go entirely. It proposed a shared-cost program, with the federal government matching eligible expenditures on postsecondary education in each province — adding a cash adjustment to the value of the transferred taxing power to yield the calculated 50 percent. The basis of the calculations would be $15 per capita, based on the 1967-68 population (a per capita amount which would escalate annually thereafter) rather than 50 percent of eligible expenditures, if the $15 calculation was more beneficial to the province. Three provinces were assisted on the per capita basis: Newfoundland, Prince Edward Island, and New Brunswick.

This was the formula designated for the next five years (1967-72) by the Federal-Provincial Fiscal Arrangements Act. The program cost the federal government much more than had been estimated, partly because the definition of "postsecondary" education, arrived at by negotiation with the provinces, was much broader than had been anticipated. Discussions prior to the renewal of the Act in 1972 led to no change except that the federal government imposed an overall limit of 15 percent in the annual increase of its share. In addition to the problems already mentioned, the program had other disadvantages:

- Expenditure on postsecondary education in the provinces, up to the amount claimed for sharing, was subject to audit by the federal government and this could be interpreted as a form of intrusion in provincial affairs.
- Although the federal share in the financing of postsecondary education exceeded that of the provincial governments, it was seldom acknowledged because the provinces made "provincial" grants for postsecondary education without identifying the sources of the funds. Thus the universities became more dependent on a single source—the provincial government—for the major portion of their income. (Some would argue, though not legally, that the federal government did no more than restore to the provinces some of the tax money which was really theirs.)
- The formula did not assure equitable distribution of federal contributions among the provinces. In 1976-77, for example, the estimated per capita contribution ranged from $53 for the province of British Columbia to $98 for the province of Quebec (see Table 3).

As April 1, 1972 (the next date for renewal of the Federal-Provincial Fiscal Arrangements Act) approached, a number of studies seeking ways to improve the program were carried out, without notable effect. As the subsequent renewal date drew near there were briefs and conferences with similar intent. The universities wanted more money and less provincial control.

TABLE 3
Estimated Per Capita Federal Contributions to the Provinces for Postsecondary Education, 1976–77

Newfoundland	$56	Ontario	$53
Prince Edward Island	59	Manitoba	64
Nova Scotia	72	Saskatchewan	65
New Brunswick	59	Alberta	77
Quebec	98	British Columbia	53
Average for Canada 76			

Source: Department of the Secretary of State, June 1977

The provinces wanted more money and less federal control. The federal government wanted to spend less money and at the same time to assure equality of access to postsecondary education for all citizens in all parts of the country. And it wanted out of shared-cost programs.

Before the end of 1976 details of the revised arrangements had been agreed upon. By a combination of tax-point transfers and adjustment payments the federal government would increase and equalize provincial fiscal resources. Though postsecondary education was still of interest to the government of Canada, there would be no more direct sharing of its costs. Health costs were linked to those of postsecondary education and the new arrangement was that, for both fields, federal contributions (equal per capita payments for all provinces) would be related to changes in the GNP. The federal government had retreated to the basic stand it had taken in 1966, in favor of enabling the provinces to discharge their own constitutional responsibility for postsecondary education. It was the end of an era—a quarter century of federal aid to higher education which began with the university grants of 1951-52 and ended with the transfer payments for postsecondary education of 1976-77.

The federal government would no longer audit and match expenditures on postsecondary education in the provinces, but its contribution would appear in the federal government *Estimates* for all to see. In addition, it would seek "provision for continuing federal participation with the provinces in the consideration and development of policies of national significance in the fields of health and postsecondary education."[24] (Discussions between the federal and provincial governments which could lead to pursuit of the objectives of both—in short, a forum such as the Council of Ministers of Education, Canada could provide—was recommended by the OECD examiners in their 1976 review of national policies for education in Canada.) Once again the federal government had almost let go, but not quite. At the June 1976 conference of federal and provincial first ministers at which the new federal policy was announced, the Prime Minister of Canada mentioned the following as areas of common interest: accessibility to postsecondary education, "the development of our national life, our economy and technology," the extent to which it is desirable and practicable to rationalize on a national basis the use of existing postsecondary education resources, "bilingualism in education," and "the introduction into appropriate academic disciplines of a greater knowledge and understanding of Canada."[25]

How could "continuing federal participation" be assured? Presumably by inclusion of these two clauses in the new act:[26]

— The secretary of state shall, as an essential and continuing indication of the interest of the government of Canada expressed by the funding arrangements in respect of the postsecondary education financing program provided under this part, consult with the governments of the provinces with regard to the relationship between the programs and activities of the Government of Canada and of the governments of the provinces that relate to post-secondary education.

— The secretary of state shall, in his annual report to Parliament pursuant to section six of the *Department of State Act*, report on the proceedings, transactions, and affairs of the Department of the Secretary of State under this section in the year to which the report relates.

The CMEC invited the secretary of state to its next meeting (in September 1976) to review the suggestion of federal participation, but it was reluctant to settle on any formal structure which would be tantamount to admitting the federal government's right to take part in policy making for postsecondary education. Instead, the council indicated its willingness to discuss particular problems, from time to time, with appropriate federal officials. Its end-of-meeting communiqué concluded as follows:[27]

The council has also been seriously considering its relations with the federal government. Because the concerns of the CMEC cover all aspects of education, the council sees the need to exchange views with the federal government from time to time, depending on the subject, for the purpose of discussing the interface between education policies as determined by the provinces, and various federal programs. It is agreed that the council is the mechanism for such discussions and it will provide further opportunites for them to take place in the future.

The council received federal officials at its January 1977 meeting to discuss student aid and bilingual programs. Earlier, discussions by a joint federal-provincial study group on research, which had been meeting since 1974, led to an announcement in October 1976 by the chairman of CMEC and the federal minister of state for science and technology that a Canadian Committee on Financing University Research "to exchange information and to develop recommendations on policies, programs and procedures affecting the financing of research in universities" would be created.

Although the provinces and the Council of Ministers of Education were obviously cautious, there was evidence in 1976-77 that fruitful communication between them and the federal government on matters relating to postsecondary education would be increased.

The universities sought to participate in the new relations being worked out between the federal and the provincial governments. After all, were they not the instruments of governmental policies for higher education? The AUCC tried on several occasions to engage the CMEC in discussion, only to be informed that its members should take their case to their own provincial ministers at home. As the date of expiry of the Federal-Provincial Fiscal Arrangements Act of 1972-77 approached, the AUCC launched a campaign for a two-year extension of the Act and tripartite consultation on national policy for higher education — seeking to bring the federal government, the provincial governments, and the universities together for this purpose. With this objective, the association submitted a brief to the Prime Minister of Canada and the premiers of the provinces in January 1976,[28] and in March arranged a "Seminar on Canadian Universities"[29] to discuss admission policies, part-time education, foreign students, models for university financing, and graduate studies and research. Of the roughly 115 persons in attendance, there were about twenty from federal departments and agencies, twenty from provincial governments (most of them instructed to act as observers only), and seventy-five from the universities and their organizations. In terms of its main objective, the seminar was not a success. Obviously, the provinces were not prepared either to acknowledge AUCC sponsorship of such consultation or to appear to share responsibility for higher education with either of the other sectors.

Almost concurrently with this conference, the Canadian Association of University Teachers was lobbying members of the Canadian Parliament, with special attention to members of the Cabinet, in the hope that recent cuts in research funds could be restored (some were), and proposing a three-year extension of the Fiscal Arrangements Act and a joint federal-provincial commission to investigate the funding of higher education. In November, the National Union of Students added its voice to those speaking out in favor of a review of the financing of postsecondary education. As we have seen, their efforts, like those of the AUCC, failed to influence the political negotiations between the two levels of government which concluded in December 1976.

Meantime, however, the Council of Ministers of Education was reexamining its role and the relations between it and agencies interested in education. The concluding paragraph of its September 1976 communiqué was quoted earlier. The previous paragraph gave new encouragement to the academic community:[30]

> The council has been reviewing its method of operation with regard to such matters as cooperation among the provinces, its relationship to nongovernment educational organizations and agencies and its relationship with the federal government. Emanating from this review, the council decided to increase its emphasis on interprovincial cooperation. The council will meet with nongovernment education organizations to discuss major problems in their respective spheres of operation.

Soon after that statement was released, the council invited a score of national voluntary associations to express their views on issues with "national dimension" which were raised by the OECD examiners in their 1976 report on national policies for education in Canada.

Three other noteworthy events took place in the first half of 1977. In February the president of the AUCC wrote to the Prime Minister of Canada noting that, in the wake of the new Federal-Provincial Fiscal Arrangements and Established Programs Financing Act, a number of important questions not mentioned in the Act needed attention; the AUCC president offered the association's cooperation with the federal and provincial governments in whatever forum might develop for discussion of these matters. The Prime Minister replied in April, saying, in part, "The federal government is deeply interested in those questions you are raising.... It is however within the framework of the Council of Ministers of Education or the Canadian Committee on Financing

University Research [a joint federal-provincial body] that it intends to examine them."[31]

The second significant event was the tabling of a federal paper on exchange of information at the second meeting of the Canadian Committee on Financing University Research which proposed that "the committee should be informed of any major changes in policy and programs affecting university research in advance of the changes having been made."[32]

The third and final noteworthy event was the June CMEC meeting to which representatives of the AUCC, the Canadian Association of University Teachers, and the Association of Canadian Community Colleges were invited to discuss matters of mutual interest. Evidently, the discussions were productive.

Three days later, in his presidential address to the 1977 annual meeting of the AUCC, Dr. Harry Duckworth reported on these developments, concluding:[33]

> I believe that Federal-Provincial relations with respect to universities are extremely fluid right now and, with luck, could easily solidify into an improved mode. The current attempts to find a new equilibrium are tentative, but appear to be conciliatory, and undoubtedly could profit from creative university intervention—which, mainly and clearly, should be through provincial channels.

Indeed, this is an era of provincial systems. They are analyzed in the next four chapters. In the final chapter we will return to the national scene and an assessment of the system as a whole.

FOOTNOTES

1. See D. V. Smiley, *Canada in Question: Federalism in the Seventies,* Second Edition (Toronto: McGraw-Hill Ryerson, 1976), especially pp. 26-34. Also Pierre Elliott Trudeau, "Federal-Provincial Grants and the Spending Power of Parliament," in J. Peter Meekison, ed., *Canadian Federalism: Myth or Reality,* Second Edition (Toronto: Methuen, 1971), pp. 216-34.
2. This is documented by Robin S. Harris, *A History of Higher Education in Canada, 1663-1960* (Toronto: University of Toronto Press, 1976).
3. Canada, Statistics Canada: Education, Science, and Culture Division.
4. Canada, Royal Commission on National Development in the Arts, Letters and Sciences, *Report* (Ottawa: King's Printer, 1951), p. 132.
5. Canada, Statistics Canada: Education, Science, and Culture Division.
6. E. F. Sheffield, "Canadian University and College Enrolment Projected to 1965," *Proceedings, National Conference of Canadian Universities, 1955* (Ottawa: National Conference of Canadian Universities, 1956).
7. A detailed statement of the federal government's educational activities was prepared for the OECD review of educational policies in Canada in 1975: *Review of Educational Policies in Canada,* Submission of the Secretary of State.
8. The Right Honourable L. B. Pearson, "Opening Statement at the Conference on Financing Higher Education," Monday, October 24, 1966, pp. 7-8.
9. *Ibid.,* pp. 14-15.
10. *Ibid.,* p. 19.
11. Lester B. Pearson, *Federalism for the Future* (Ottawa: Queen's Printer, 1968).
12. Douglas G. Hartle, "The Financing of Higher Education in the '70's: A Viewpoint from Ottawa," *Stoa: The Canadian Journal of Higher Education,* Vol. 3, No. 2 (1973), pp. 114, 124-25.
13. Hugh Faulkner, "Notes for an Address by The Honourable Hugh Faulkner, Secretary of State, to the Association of Universities and Colleges of Canada, Chateau Laurier, Ottawa, November 6, 1974" (Ottawa: Department of the Secretary of State, 1974).
14. Canada, Secretary of State . . . for OECD review, p. 73.
15. Most influential in the achievements to date, and on the structures in place in 1977 or to be implemented soon after were these four reports: Canada, Royal Commission on Government Organization, J. Grant Glassco, chairman, *The Organization of the Government of Canada,* Vol. 5 (Ottawa: Queen's Printer, 1963); John B. Macdonald *et al., The Role of the Federal Government in Support of Research in Canadian Universities,* Special Study No. 7, prepared for The Science Council of Canada and The Canada Council (Ottawa: Queen's Printer, 1969); Organisation for Economic Cooperation and Development, *Review of National Science Policy: Canada* (Paris: OECD, 1969); and Canada, Senate Special Committee on Science Policy, Honourable Maurice Lamontagne, chairman, *A Science Policy for*

Canada (Ottawa: Information Canada, 1970-1974).
16. Canada, Ministry of State for Science and Technology, *Federal Science Expenditures 1976/77-1977/78*, Report No. 100-3 (Ottawa: The Ministry, 1977), Table 9. See also MOSST's report on *Federal Science Programs 1977/78* (Ottawa: Minister of Supply and Services Canada, 1977).
17. Canada, *Report of the Royal Commission on Bilingualism and Biculturalism* (Ottawa: Queen's Printer, 1965-1969).
18. Canada, Department of the Secretary of State, "The Language Programs Branch of the Department of the Secretary of State," unpublished memorandum, 1977.
19. Canada, Secretary of State . . . for OECD review, pp. 73-74. See also the statement of objectives and subobjectives for the Educational Support Program in the 1976-77 *Estimates* of the Secretary of State, pp. 24-28.
20. Council of Ministers of Education, Canada, "General Information" (Toronto: The Council, 1974).
21. Organisation for Economic Co-operation and Development, *Reviews of National Policies for Education: Canada* (Paris: OECD, 1976), p. 131.
22. Council of Ministers of Education, Canada, *Annual Report, 1975-1976* (Toronto: The Council, 1976).
23. Association of Universities and Colleges of Canada, Commission on the Financing of Higher Education, Vincent W. Bladen, chairman, *Report of the Commission* (Toronto: University of Toronto Press, 1965).
24. The Right Honourable Pierre Elliott Trudeau, "Established Program Financing: A Proposal regarding the Major Shared-Cost Programs in the Fields of Health and Post-Secondary Education," statement tabled by the Prime Minister of Canada at the Federal-Provincial Conference of First Ministers, June 14-15, 1976.
25. *Ibid.*
26. Canada, Federal-Provincial Fiscal Arrangements and Established Programs Financing Act, 1977, Part VI, Section 24, Subsections (3) and (4).
27. Council of Ministers of Education, Canada, "CMEC Position on Relations with the Federal Government," adopted by the Council at its 26th meeting, September 20-21, 1976.
28. Association of Universities and Colleges of Canada, "A Canadian Policy for Universities and their Financing: A Brief to the Prime Minister of Canada and to the Premiers of the Provinces of Canada" (Ottawa: The Association, 1976).
29. Association of Universities and Colleges of Canada, *Proceedings of the Seminar on Canadian Universities, McGill University, Montreal, March 25-26, 1976* (Ottawa: The Association, 1976).
30. Council of Ministers of Education, " . . . Relations with the Federal Government."
31. Quoted in Harry E. Duckworth, "President's Address," *Proceedings of the Annual Meeting of the Association of Universities and Colleges of Canada*, Vol. II (Ottawa: The Association, 1977), p. 35.
32. Quoted in *ibid.*, p. 36.
33. *Ibid.*, p. 37.

THE ATLANTIC PROVINCES
Jeffrey Holmes

Canada's four eastern provinces are known collectively as the Atlantic provinces—a designation dating from 1949 when Newfoundland joined the confederation. Neither Canada's newest province nor the three Maritime provinces (New Brunswick, Nova Scotia, Prince Edward Island) are comfortable with the title, and the region is far from being the integrated unit some Ottawa politicians and planners would like it to be. In their attitudes toward cooperation, traditional Maritime provinces have always reflected independent views, stemming from the distinct political, linguistic, religious, historical, and geographical facts of their settlement, which began around 1600.

Despite these differences, the Atlantic provinces do have some common features which justify a regional approach. All are heavily dependent upon the basic fishing, forestry, farming, and mining industries. All are low on the Canadian economic totem pole and usually "lead" the provinces in statistics such as those dealing with rates of unemployment. The region's population is appreciably more rural than the national average and there is only one metropolitan area, Halifax/Dartmouth, of more than 200,000 population.

The region has a narrow tax base, with an under-fifteen and over-sixty-years old population appreciably above the national proportions. It has few major industries and the per capita income is 20 percent or more below the national average. Within the region itself, there are significant variations, with Nova Scotia tending to be the richest province and Newfoundland the poorest.

However, the quality of life in these regions somewhat offsets the gloomy economic picture. The pace is slower than the sometimes frenetic pace of the major industrial regions. The air is fresher, and the sea is rarely more than an hour's drive away. And the region is poor only by comparison with the affluent regions of Canada and the United States. On a world scale, the investment in postsecondary education ranks high.

The four Atlantic provinces have the largest number of degree-granting institutions per capita in the world. The nondegree sector, however, is the weakest in Canada. And the majority of all postsecondary institutions in the region are found in Nova Scotia. As of July 1, 1977, the Atlantic region had seventeen degree-granting institutions and thirteen other postsecondary institutions to serve a population of little over two million.

The region has the oldest English-speaking universities in Canada and the great variety of institutions stems from religious differences of the nineteenth century. These differences have been replaced by local or regional jealousies which, although not as fierce as those of faith, have effectively hindered the development of any real system of postsecondary education. It is this variety, and its accompanying stress on institutional autonomy, which is the hallmark of the system, if one may be said to exist, in the region.

Design

There is no design of an Atlantic system as such. In fact, there is frequently open resistance to a regional approach which, combined with tradition and inertia, make an Atlantic system unattainable — and probably undesirable — in the foreseeable future. The Atlantic postsecondary links are all voluntary, with the Association of Atlantic Universities (AAU) the key element.

The links among the three Maritime provinces (excluding Newfoundland) are more formal, particularly since the formation of the Council of Maritime Premiers (CMP) in 1971. The Maritime Provinces Higher Education Commission (MPHEC), a creation of the CMP, came into existence in 1974, replacing the three grants commissions of the individual provinces. The institutions range in size from Université Sainte-Anne, with fewer than 200 full-time students, to Dalhousie University, with more than 7,000. Dalhousie, the University of New Brunswick (UNB), and Memorial have sizeable graduate schools but most universities are basically undergraduate liberal arts teaching institutions, or specialist colleges such as the Nova Scotia College of Art and Design. The University of Prince Edward Island is prohibited by its charter from offering graduate degrees.

Newfoundland

The Newfoundland system does have cohesion, with Memorial University the only degree-granting institution in the province. The university and two technical institutes are all in St. John's, the capital, on the southeast tip of a large island and far from the Labrador Coast which is the mainland of the province. There is a possibility that the two institutes will merge. Expansion at the university level is likely to come through the creation of additional regional colleges of Memorial, modeled on the first which opened at Corner Brook in 1975. Political and social pressure is for a rapid opening of two or three more regional colleges but each will require a major investment of provincial money. In the meantime, the Memorial extension service performs splendidly throughout the island and in Labrador.

Prince Edward Island

A Prince Edward Island system was established by the government in 1969, with the founding of the University of Prince Edward Island (UPEI) to replace the two existing degree-granting institutions. This change was accompanied by the opening of the region's first community college, Holland College. The Island's 120,000 inhabitants thus have the best of postsecondary worlds but many young islanders still leave the province for their education, even at the undergraduate level. And as the number of high school graduates begins to diminish early in the 1980s (due to the lower birth rates of the mid-1960s) the cooperative relationship between the university and the college is likely to suffer from the strain of competition.

New Brunswick

Beginning in the early 1960s, New Brunswick carried out a major organization of its postsecondary system. John Deutsch, who served as a commissioner or consultant to the government throughout the decade, was the primary architect of this effort. Further consolidation has been carried on by the MPHEC, particularly with regard to French-language institutions.

The province had a balanced university system in the late sixties, following the reforms based on Deutsch Commission recommendations:[1] Three French-language *collèges classiques* had been merged into, or became affiliated with, the new Université de Moncton; Mount Allison University, just across the border from Nova Scotia, offered a liberal arts education in the classic tradition to students drawn almost equally from the two provinces; St. Thomas University, a Catholic undergraduate institution, had moved some 100 miles from Chatham to Fredericton and lodged comfortably beside UNB, although still offering an independent undergraduate curriculum. The University of New Brunswick itself was the only institution offering graduate and professional work.

This happy balance was disturbed in the early seventies by the development (and calls for increased autonomy) of the UNB campus at Saint John, the province's largest city, and by the uncertain future of the three French-language colleges. These problems were exacerbated by the plateau in enrollments and cutback in funding increases that afflicted institutions across Canada. However, in 1976, the government accepted an MPHEC recommendation that one French-language college become part of the community college sector and that the other two become campuses of the Université de Moncton. The Saint John campus had been allowed to expand its programs, but its enrollment rate had slowed down.

In the nondegree sector, the two teacher training institutions joined UNB and Moncton respectively and the two technical institutes became part of the New Brunswick Community College.

Nova Scotia

In Nova Scotia, proliferation rather than consolidation has been the pattern—with the creation of specialist degree-granting institutions and the establishment of technical institutes in the 1960s. Although the presence of so many degree-granting institutions is occasionally deplored by the press and politicians, most of the increases are the results of political decisions.

In Halifax alone there are eight universities; although four of these are small and specialized. On the other hand, Cape Breton, the rugged eastern sector of the province, has no degree-granting institution—although Xavier College and the Nova Scotia Eastern Institute of Technology were combined in 1974 to form the College of Cape Breton, an interesting hybrid. Degrees are still granted by St. Francis Xavier University, as were those of Xavier College.

At the western end of the province, French-language Collège Sainte-Anne has just become Université Sainte-Anne, to emphasize its degree-granting status.

Halifax in the past ten years has seen both successes and failures in attempts at consolidation. The Maritime School of Social Work was taken into Dalhousie, with a regional advisory board appointed to oversee regional interests. The various theological institutions joined to form the Atlantic School of Theology. Another attempt at consolidation has fared less successfully. The Atlantic Institute of Education was created by the Nova Scotia government in the mid-sixties, conceived as an innovating and coordinating body in education for the Atlantic region. The other three provinces did not share this vision and the Nova Scotia institutions were not overjoyed to see another degree-granting body arrive on the scene.

An attempt to amalgamate Nova Scotia Technical College with Dalhousie was rejected by the government, despite positive recommendations from both institutions, and from the MPHEC and the AAU. However, Dalhousie, Nova Scotia Tech, Mount Saint Vincent, and the Nova Scotia College of Art and Design have entered into various five-year agreements. Dalhousie and Mount Saint Vincent, for example, offer a joint summer school program.

This review may confirm outsiders' opinions concerning the pettiness of Atlantic academic and "large P" politics. For example, the full-time enrollment of all the universities is not very much higher than that of the University of British Columbia or the University of Toronto. Yet events in other provinces suggest that proliferation—frequently an enemy of a systems approach—is spreading. Bifurcation has been a frequent means of creating new institutions in Canada and can result in competition between parent and offspring. No province, however, is likely to match the Atlantic region's per capita average of institutions.

Coordination

As we have seen, the skeleton of a system exists; but the hip bone is not connected to the thigh bone and the knee bone is not connected to the ankle bone and "dem bones" lie around, waiting to hear the word of the Lord. There is, however, no Lord. Only a small host of princes and chiefs, of varying power and influence, usually vying with each other.

Association of Atlantic Universities

The Association of Atlantic Universities (AAU), founded in 1964, comes closest to approximating an Atlantic system. But, as a voluntary association, it has no power over its constituents, whose presidents form the executive council. There are nineteen university and college members from the four Atlantic provinces, the great majority of them degree-granting institutions. The University of the West Indies is also a member, having joined in the mid-sixties to establish closer contact with Canadian universities. The link is more honorary than real, although there have been some useful exchanges of visits.

The association was founded "to assist the coordination of higher education, to ensure high academic standards in a period of rising costs, and to avoid unnecessary duplication of faculties and courses of study."[2] As noted in *Higher Education in the Atlantic Provinces for the 1970's* (an analysis prepared under the auspices of the AAU for the Maritime Union Study), "the first and possibly the most difficult task of the AAU was to create an atmosphere of frankness and trust between the institutions of higher learning. In their struggles to survive they had naturally been concerned almost exclusively with their own problems."[3] Some of the most significant AAU accomplishments in the 1960s were:

- a united approach to the Commission on the Financing of Higher Education in Canada[4] and to the federal government in regard to university operating grants;
- cooperation between university business officers to ensure comparable financial statistics;
- meetings at least annually, with provincial grants committees to discuss developments in higher education; and
- an agreement in 1965 that "in graduate work at the doctoral level, at the present time, the universities of the Maritime provinces would cooperate in doctoral work with the graduate schools of Dalhousie University and the University of New Brunswick, and in the special fields of the Nova Scotia Technical College." (It was understood "that a uni-

versity would consult with the other institutions before launching doctoral programs in any field.")[5]

Program consultation was expanded significantly by the creation of the Committee of Academic Vice-Presidents of the AAU in 1971. This committee has reviewed most proposals for new Maritime academic programs since the formation of MPHEC. Before that it reviewed only programs proposed for Nova Scotia.

There are some fifteen other Atlantic university groups of a basically administrative nature which are loosely linked to the AAU. These include the Association of Atlantic University Business Officers (AAUBO) and groups of librarians, registrars, computer center directors, and personnel responsible for student services and for continuing education.

In addition to these administrative associations, there are academic discipline groups covering most areas of study. Faculty from the science disciplines formed the Atlantic Provinces Inter-University Committee on the Sciences in 1962 and this continues to be an important voluntary coordinating body, with some dozen discipline subcommittees. Another important group is the Atlantic Universities Athletic Association.

Although faculty associations united in 1976 to form an Atlantic Conference of University Faculty Associations, they apparently have separated in 1977. An Atlantic Federation of Students appears to be firmly established, after a false start in the early 1970s. It has been active in areas related to student aid programs and student fees.

Maritime Provinces Higher Education Commission (MPHEC)

The Maritime provinces, through their premiers, are moving toward a regional approach, but the movement usually resembles the sideways advance of the crab which inhabits the region's serrated shoreline. Premiers and their cabinets do not always agree and in Nova Scotia there has been a public clash between one minister of education and the Council of Maritime Premiers.

Perhaps the most important, and certainly the most visible, of the CMP initiatives was the formation of MPHEC in 1974. The Maritime premiers made the decision to launch MPHEC at their first meeting. Although the AAU had recommended such a move, the announcement took the Maritime university presidents by surprise and created some consternation. They had assumed they would be consulted regarding the timing and terms of reference of the commission. The premiers, perhaps, had not thought the move through, although it is interesting that they seized on postsecondary education as the obvious point to initiate interprovincial cooperation/coordination. Presumably, although it was never stated officially, this was considered to be one area in which important financial savings could be realized. The premiers were obviously reflecting the public's opinion that a great deal of unnecessary duplication existed in the postsecondary system.

Choosing a commission chairman proved difficult and there was a long and quietly desperate search to find someone acceptable to all three provinces. The solution was to appoint an interim chairman charged with setting up the commission but with no commitment that he would head it. William Jenkins, former principal of the Nova Scotia Agricultural College, spent fifteen months laying the groundwork for the commission, consulting with the AAU and universities, with provincial ministers, and with other groups.

It was a stormy year. The Nova Scotia minister of education, in a public debate with Dr. Jenkins, took issue with the whole concept of the commission. It was clear that the minister was not prepared to let control of postsecondary education go out of the province, geographically and administratively. (An indication of the provincial politics of regionalism was the decision to locate the MPHEC in Fredericton, New Brunswick, not far from the geographic fringe of the Maritimes, presumably because the CMP headquarters had been established in Halifax, Nova Scotia.) The minister's stand represented the tip of the iceberg of provincial cabinet opposition to the three premiers "giving away" areas of ministerial responsibility to the regional body.

Another area of opposition surfaced during Dr. Jenkins' presentation to the Moncton University senate. A vocal and important sector of the Acadian (French-speaking) population was opposed to regionalism, reasoning that its 35 percent of New Brunswick's population gave it reasonable political power in that province but would count for little in the population of the whole Maritime region.

Given the overt and covert opposition to the proposal for a regional commission, it appeared several times as if the project would wither on the political vine. The task of finding a chairman acceptable to all parties, and with the courage and skill needed to create a viable commission, seemed insuperable. Happily, the appointment of Catherine Wallace, retiring president of Mount Saint Vincent University, solved the problem.

It is worth noting that, in the same session that the MPHEC Act was passed, the New Brunswich government passed an act establishing the New Brunswich Community College—an umbrella institution which does not appear on the schedule of institutions for which the commission has responsibility. At the same time, the Nova Scotia government was passing an Act to establish the College of Cape Breton, by merging the Sydney campus of St. Francis Xavier University (Xavier College) with the Nova Scotia Eastern Institute of Technology. A charitable interpretation would be that the governments of the two provinces did not wish to overburden the commission with responsibilities in its formative months.

If the universities felt snubbed at the time of the initial announcement, they had no cause to complain over the composition of the original commission. There are fifteen members, plus the chairman who[1] is the only full-time member. All fifteen are appointed by the Council of Maritime Premiers for a three-year term (staggered to allow for roughly one-third replacement annually). Five are chosen from the public at large, five are senior public servants or principals of nonuniversity institutions, and five are chosen from a list of ten submitted by a nominating committee of degree-granting institutions under AAU auspices. The large majority of the initial members had first-hand knowledge of higher education—including several nonuniversity men who had served on previous grants committees.

The legislated purpose of the MPHEC is "to assist the provinces and institutions in attaining a more efficient and effective utilization and allocation of resources in the field of higher education in the region." It is also mandated to carry out several tasks of a planning, advisory, and administrative nature:[6]

> The legislation assigns several duties to the commission. Those duties are, in or after consultation with the institutions and other parties involved:
> a) to advise the council [of Maritime premiers] with respect to existing needs in the field of higher education in the region;
> b) to formulate plans for the future structure and develop-

ment of higher education in the region, including an assessment of the cost of implementing such plans;

c) to make recommendations to the council as to the advisability of establishing or supporting new courses, programs and institutions, and of terminating support of existing programs;

d) to assist and encourage institutions in establishing or continuing cooperative arrangements among themselves;

e) to encourage and facilitate the establishment of regional centres of specialization in the field of higher education;

f) to facilitate the making of arrangements with agencies outside the region to supply higher educational services which are not available in the region or which can be obtained more economically from such agencies;

g) to recommend to the council formulas in relation to the respective contributions of funds to be made by the provinces and to the allocation of such funds among the institutions in the region;

h) to prepare for the council annually a comprehensive plan for financing higher education in the region, including provision for financing the operation of the commission;

i) to administer the funds paid to it by the provinces in accordance with the approved financial plan and formulas respecting allocation;

j) to recommend to the council programs of financial and other assistance to students in the region;

k) to recommend to the council additions to or deletions from Schedule A [the list of institutions for which the commission is responsible]; and

l) to undertake such other responsibilities within the scope of its purpose as the council shall assign to it.

The MPHEC reports to the Council of Premiers and, through it, to the regional and provincial treasury boards. Each premier takes the council's recommendations, based on MPHEC advice, to his own provincial legislature, which makes the final decision on funding. For the 1977-78 fiscal year, an agreement was made to fund on a regional basis, although the individual provincial legislatures still had to approve the amounts budgeted.

The MPHEC itself deals directly with individual institutions.

These are divided into two groups—degree-granting and non-degree-granting. The Commission's mandate does not, however, cover all postsecondary institutions: the most notable exception is the New Brunswick Community College which, as has been mentioned, comprises a number of vocational and technical institutions.

The AAU played no part in budgetary discussions until 1977 when it published a brief on financial needs and was allowed to send a delegation to present the brief directly to the CMP.

Functions

There is a paucity of statements by politicians or public servants on the functions of postsecondary institutions—and even fewer statements on the functions of a postsecondary education system.

Most postsecondary institutions in the region developed as private organizations, frequently with religious affiliation. Although essentially all institutions in the region are now public, they still retain more of the trappings of private institutions than similar institutions elsewhere in Canada. Dalhousie, thanks to its large endowment funds, has perhaps the highest percentage of private support of any institution in Canada. Tuitions at most Maritime universities are the highest in the country; the portion of government subsidies is, accordingly, below the national average. The "privateness" of the Maritime institutions made their provincial governments reluctant to interfere in their financing until the great surge in operating support of the late 1960s.

The situation changed slowly, in any event. Memorial, Moncton, and UPEI were all founded by provincial governments, as were the technical institutes, and the Nova Scotia Agricultural and Nova Scotia Teachers colleges. The religious character of all church-related universities has been appreciably diluted; there are many Protestant students and staff members at Saint Mary's (a Roman Catholic foundation), and many Catholics at Mount Allison (a United Church foundation). Now capital funds come very largely from government as private donations dry up and, for the region as a whole, governments account for some 80 percent of operating income.

A clear indication of governments' intention to intervene more directly came in 1968 when the government of Prince Edward Island (PEI) invited the province's two degree-granting institutions, one Catholic, one nondenominational, to a shotgun wedding. In his policy statement, Premier Alex Campbell noted: "I think the time has come when we, and the Government, as representatives of the taxpayers of the Province, must cease to merely serve the interests of institutions of higher education and ask ourselves *how these institutions can best serve the needs of the Province and, in particular, the needs of our youth.*"[7] He added:[8]

> In attempting to bring about a policy to serve the needs of the Province in the field of higher education, the government has had to consider two very important requirements. First, the need for a type of educational system to provide a base for future development in the Province, and in doing so, meet the direct educational needs of the community; and, as well, give an opportunity to those students who may choose to pursue occupations in other parts of Canada. Secondly, it was necessary to balance future development with past tradition — a tradition which has seen two separate universities develop over a period of years, each of which has struggled for survival independent of each other. Both of these institutions have served our Province and its people well. However, these services have developed in large measure along separate and unrelated paths. Consideration must now be given to the overall Provincial requirements.

The universities of the region have long been seen as a means of promoting social mobility. Despite this implicit function, the university was for years out of reach for most young men and women but was a natural training ground for the offspring of the wealthy and professional class. The Atlantic region population contains a higher proportion of "upper class" and "working class" than the Canadian average. The "middle class" form a relatively small proportion.[9]

St. Francis Xavier University, with its priests and a "parish" serving eastern mainland Nova Scotia and Cape Breton (where the Scottish ideal of university education for anyone with ability flourishes), made particular efforts to reach the sons of miners, woodworkers, and fishermen. But universities were basically an upper-class or upper-middle-class preserve. Women formed a very small percentage of enrollment.

The social situation has improved steadily since the late fifties, although there is still substantial under-representation of the working class. Female enrollment has increased at a faster rate than male, in accord with recent Canadian trends.

The establishment of the Université de Moncton, the development of the extension services of Memorial University, and the general expansion of enrollments have improved both the expectations and the opportunities of young people from the lower end of the socioeconomic scale. Although the opening of postsecondary technical institutes, and a community college in Prince Edward Island, increased educational opportunity, these institutions were widely regarded as places for students who were not good enough for university. It has only been in the mid-seventies that governments have actively begun encouraging students to attend such institutions, as a respectable alternative to university education.

Policy statements appear in the several major reports on postsecondary education produced in the various provinces since 1960. One interesting attitude is that expressed in the previously quoted 1968 PEI government White Paper, with its acknowledgment of the fact that many islanders with postsecondary education have to leave the province in search of suitable employment and should be educated so that they may succeed in that search.

Research and public service are two other functions of the universities. The region as a whole gets lower than average research grants but this is no doubt due to the limited amount of graduate work. Researchers at Dalhousie, Memorial, and UNB in particular, however, receive sizable individual or institutional grants.

Although much of the research is directly related to local or regional problems, the degree of contact with local industry that is found in Ontario does not exist in the Atlantic region. Most Atlantic industries are small and have no research staffs of their own; nor do most of them see a need to seek advice from academic consultants. Governments, however, do use economists and social scientists frequently as consultants — which is not to say they always follow their advice.

In the public service field, advice is given to the general public through such mechanisms as the Dalhousie storefront law service. In a more general sense, Atlantic institutions play a major role in the community's social and cultural life. In addition, most institutions make a major contribution to the economic well-being of the surrounding community. Such communities are frequently small towns — Sackville, for example, has a population hardly larger than the 1,400 full-time students of Mount Allison Univesity. In Antigonish, the univesity is a major "industry" and St. Francis Xavier University has been referred to by citizens as "the steel plant of Antigonish."

In his 1977 convocation address, the president of Memorial University drew attention to the multifaceted functions performed by the university and to the difficulty of assessing its value. His statements might well serve as a prototype, detailing the function of higher education in the Atlantic region:[10]

> It is difficult to assess in quantitative terms the value of Memorial University to this province. It constitutes in gross material terms a major industry whose contribution to the economic welfare of the area is, relatively speaking, enormous. Its gross operating budget is in excess of $50 million per year, and with external funds in support of research in excess of $5 million, it operates within itself a small research industry. It has brought some 32 million new dollars into the province in support of the construction of the Health Sciences Center and the new Engineering Building. Over and above the economic benefits, however, it brings to the community a diversity of people possessing diverse talents and skills who enliven and enrich our society. It serves to open doors and windows to the world of learning and scholarship, of art, music and ideas that would otherwise remain closed. It offers to our people the opportunities for higher education which would otherwise not be available, or else would be reserved for a particular economic group. It provides the education and training for professionals who serve the province in the delivery of a wide range of services in health, education and welfare, as well as in industry, government and business. It offers both the ways and the means whereby we may know ourselves better—where we came from, what we are, and where we are going.

Management Of The System

Formal attempts at planning on an Atlantic region basis have never succeeded. Both the AAU executive council and its Committee of Academic Vice-Presidents established academic planning committees in the early 1970s, at the urging of the association's executive director. However, since the committees were voluntary and could not really implement planning policies, the director recommended that they be disbanded in 1975. A more successful approach has been to engage in projects which may indirectly serve as planning instruments. Major projects undertaken in the 1970s include development of a joint financial information system, a study of computer resources, and the experimental introduction of a computerized library system.[11]

The financial information system was initiated by Statistics Canada and the Atlantic Association of University Business Officers. AAU and MPHEC have given it strong support. The other two projects, which were AAU initiatives, have also received significant MPHEC support. There is a possibility that these and other projects will gradually come together to form a plan for development. This approach seems much more suited to the needs and tastes of the region than a master plan.

As has been noted, there has been considerable provincial planning. The reorganizations in New Brunswick and PEI have already been mentioned and Newfoundland's developments follow a predictable course. Nova Scotia, by contrast, shows strong evidence of political ad hocery. The 1974 Graham Commission report is the only government-sponsored study of higher education, and it was prepared only as part of a massive inquiry into municipal taxation and related matters.[12] Postsecondary education, although it eventually formed a major section of the report, has shared the fate of the other sections in being virtually ignored by the provincial legislature.

The MPHEC is clearly the major regional instrument of planning. The regional commission, although more vigorous in its approach, is following in the footsteps of the three individual provincial commissions it replaced.

The MPHEC notes in *Higher Education in the Maritimes— 1976: An Overview* that:[13]

> One of the broad objectives of the commission since its inception has been to foster the progressive development of multi-year planning. In this context, the institutions have provided annually five-year projections to the MPHEC. As the commission progresses toward the development of multi-year plans, it appears timely to prepare and provide an overview of higher education in the region. As planning for higher education matures, the MPHEC intends to avail itself of a broad range of views.

According to the *Overview,* cooperative MPHEC arrangements at the regional level include: planning activities such as institutional five-year projections, a space study, and program inventories; computer networks, cooperative library development, and the advancement of a regional financial reporting system; program development and rationalization activities such as preparation of a master plan for physical education and recreation programs and studies of several program areas. In addition, the MPHEC has in progress, or planned, committees to study and make recommendations on admissions, accessibility, bilingualism, Canadian studies, centers of excellence, articulation between secondary and postsecondary education and among postsecondary institutions, summer school and extension courses, and other related matters.

Furthermore, MPHEC is now involved in developing a regional approach to the allocation of operating grants. The MPHEC considers such an approach essential to eliminate interprovincial inequities in support levels, to provide regional equity in postsecondary education, and to ensure the extension and effectiveness of regional cooperative planning.

In its *Overview* the MPHEC acknowledges that:[14]

> Prior to the establishment of the Maritime Provinces Higher Education Commission, a regional perspective already existed in higher education in the Maritimes.
>
> Cooperative efforts by both institutions and governments provide for regionwide educational services by such institutions as the medical, dental, and health science faculties of Dalhousie University, Nova Scotia Land Survey Institute, Nova Scotia Agricultural College, Nova Scotia College of Art and Design, the Atlantic Police Academy at Holland College, the School of Forestry at the University of New Brunswick, the Maritime Forest Ranger School, and other facilities wherein there are specialized programs offered in only one of the Maritime provinces.

Administration, Decision Making

There is no overt administration of a provincial Maritime or Atlantic system, although there is a clear management structure for the only postsecondary subsystem—the New Brunswick Community College. (The NBCC headquarters are in Fredericton, providing centralized administrative control over a number of vocational and postsecondary technical institutions, plus a French-language community college in Bathurst.)

The AAU itself has no legal or executive powers over the actions of its members. Even if it had, the presidents who form its executive council no longer have the freedom to commit their institutions that they might have had some twenty years ago. Presidential authority has been steadily eroded as institutions have grown in size and complexity: The department has emerged as a key decision-making center on each campus, particularly in matters relating to faculty hiring and curriculum. Changes in the composition of governing boards and senates have tended to further diffuse authority, as has collective bargaining between faculty unions and university administrators. Collective bargaining has burgeoned in the region since 1975 and there has been some talk of carrying this out at the provincial level. Institutional self-interest, already noted, is another powerful factor inhibiting centralized administration.

A form of covert system administration does occur, however, largely through the secretariats of the AAU and the MPHEC. The former exists to propose regional initiatives and to foster initiatives proposed by individual institutions or other bodies. The success or failure of regional schemes depends very largely upon the bureaucratic creativity of the secretariat. Similarly, the MPHEC secretariat, headed by its full-time chairman, plays a crucial role in any development in higher education, though the MPHEC, as a body, prefers not to impose regionalism upon the individual institutions. Its favored tactic is to encourage universities to take collective action through the AAU, and to stand ready to support such initiatives.

In these circumstances, decision making becomes a kind of dance—aimed at pleasing the political paymasters, the general public, and the disparate entities in some thirty individual institutions.

Finance and the Roles of Intermediaries

However, government interest in the universities increased noticeably in the sixties. In 1963 Nova Scotia became the first province in

Canada to appoint a grants committee. New Brunswick followed suit in 1967, in line with the recommendations of two major reports by Dr. Deutsch. The Prince Edward Island Commission was introduced in 1969 as part of a tradition-shattering reorganization of postsecondary education ordered by the government.

Newfoundland has never had a grants committee, although a cabinet committee was appointed in 1973 to review postsecondary expenditures.

The Prince Edward Island Commission was sponsored by a government (and especially by its premier) which has remained in office ever since. Once the initial reorganization was accomplished — with the help of two excellent individuals as president and principal of the university and the community college, respectively — the commission quickly withdrew to a part-time role and the system continued to work smoothly. Clearly, the planning and early spadework was top rate, including the government's wise appointment of E. F. Sheffield, a senior Canadian educator, as consultant and first commissioner.

New Brunswick chose to follow the advice of another of Canada's senior educators and government servants, John Deutsch, in organizing its own postsecondary system. The 1962 commission and the 1967 committee were both chaired by Dr. Deutsch. And the secretary of both bodies, J. F. O'Sullivan, became the first chairman of the New Brunswick Higher Education Commission. O'Sullivan and the commission quickly established a reputation for fairness and firmness and were backed to the hilt by successive premiers, despite a change of party in power.

Nova Scotia's committee, the first in Canada, was less fortunate. It had to deal with a far more complex situation than that facing the other provinces. History, geography, and politics had always played a strong role in the postsecondary affairs of the province. The committee's second chairman, Arthur Murphy,[15] was appointed in the fall of 1968, just before a change of government. The committee's influence was reduced overnight; in some cases, individual institutions were virtually encouraged to approach the finance minister directly, when the committee was unable to meet their needs. This situation began to change as the new government came to appreciate the impartiality of the advice given. When the MPHEC replaced the provincial commissions, the chairman and a staff member were appointed advisors to the minister of education.

The financing of education promises to become an increasingly effective (or at least increasingly used) tool for management. As noted earlier, before 1960 most Atlantic institutions relied heavily on private sources of funds, with Memorial the usual exception. Tuition comprised more than 30 percent of operating income, and local business provided both capital and scholarship assistance; endowments represented an important percentage of revenue, and, for the Catholic institutions, donated teaching services of priests and nuns were an invaluable but financially invisible support. Federal per capita grants, paid through the Association of Universities and Colleges of Canada, were important but provincial government support was negligible for most institutions.

The surge in enrollments and costs in the sixties revolutionized the situation. As a proportion of operating support, student fees fell steadily, although they still represent, for the Maritimes at least, the highest proportion of such income in the country. The portion of other income and contributed services also declined steadily. The need to increase staff to meet the demands of increased enrollment lead to a steady laicisation of faculty in the several denominational institutions. There were no longer enough clergy to go around.

The 1967 federal-provincial fiscal arrangement brought a major increase in provincial support on paper but, in fact, for the next three years none of the four provinces actually spent as much on postsecondary education as the additional federal assistance made possible. As has been noted, the new grants committees operated differently. For Prince Edward Island, with only two postsecondary institutions, the allocation of resources was a relatively simple matter. New Brunswick established a pattern of formula financing, with grants announced two or three years in advance, and this was generally recognized as the most equitable arrangement in the country. Windfall surpluses or unforeseen system deficits were handled jointly by the commission and the four university presidents and there were no individual arrangements. The political contrast in Nova Scotia was reflected in the allocation of resources. There was an understanding that the University Grants Committee worked on some kind of operating grants formula but the details were never revealed—nor could they be ascertained by analysis of actual grants. The provincial contribution increased substantially after 1970 on the operating side but this was accompanied by a moratorium on capital grants, only partially relaxed in 1973.

Anticipation that full-time enrollments will shrink in the eighties confirms the governments' reluctance to support major capital projects in the region. Although the private sector still provides support for building programs, the increasing preponderance of government on both the operating and capital sides tends to drive away private support. This, in turn, increases the institutions' dependence on government.

Reliance on government support is likely to increase — and to strain the relatively friendly operation of the system. The increasing tension was obvious early in 1977 when the AAU made a direct appeal to the CMP for operating funds. The AAU also appealed to the public through a press release explaining the regional need for a 12.5 percent increase. In a brief to the MPHEC itself, a few weeks later, the AAU noted its serious concern over:[16]

> ... the failure of the governments to come close to accepting the commission's advice on operating grants for 1977-78. Given the fact that the level of operating support has effectively shrunk in each of the three years the commission has advised the Council of Maritime Premiers on funding, the difference between the 7 percent global increase in operating funds and the 11.5 percent recommended by the commission makes us doubt that the governments are listening to the MPHEC. The grants for 77-78 will almost certainly mean fee increases for most institutions (when our fees are already the highest in the country) and some reduction in academic services. While we hope that academic standards can be preserved in the future, we believe that continued funding of this order will inevitably mean a reduction in the variety of programs and services, just as we were beginning to offer a range of programs comparable with those in other parts of the country.
>
> Our level of funding is still well below the national average. The gap is about to increase further.

The AAU recognizes that it must be more forceful as an association in making its case to the general public and to government, both directly and through the MPHEC. However, it looks to the MPHEC to make even stronger efforts to ensure that funding is adequate to meet increases in university costs which are frequently beyond the control of the universities themselves.

Related to this immediate concern is the long-term worry about the commission's efforts to standardize funding practices within the region. This desirable end might be achieved by bringing some institutions up to the average regional level of funding. At a time of real loss of purchasing power, there is a great danger that equalization means bringing some institutions down to the average regional level.

The AAU brief was one of a large number presented to MPHEC as a major public relations effort launched by the commission, which had been accused by faculty and students of operating in a secretive manner. The MPHEC held public meetings in the three Maritime provinces. The increasing tension between individual institutions and the commission is reflected in the following extract from the Dalhousie University submission:[17]

> Two aspects of our relations with the MPHEC continue to cause some concern — the relative responsibilities of universities and the commission, and the extent of consultation with the universities before major policies are adopted by the commission.
>
> Dalhousie sees itself as an autonomous institution, prepared to cooperate wherever feasible with others and to define and modify its own roles in and responsibilities to the region in ways that ensure the best level of higher education as efficiently and effectively as possible. But the ultimate decisions about its programs and responsibilities, and about its operations, are for Dalhousie to make and to meet. The board of governors of the university, on the advice of the senate in relation to all academic matters, is ultimately responsible under the university's statute for the functioning of Dalhousie.

Such tensions are bound to increase as the gap widens between the institutions' needs and the governments' ability, or willingness, to meet these. One senior public servant suggests that the absence of a spokesman for higher education in each Maritime provincial cabinet will put universities at a disadvantage. (In the Atlantic region the minister of education has traditionally concentrated on primary and secondary education.) The universities' financial problems will be exacerbated as the faculty ages and as the traditional pool of eighteen-year old entrants shrinks in the 1980s.

Despite criticisms of the kind leveled by Dalhousie—and increasing pressure by faculty and student groups for a greater part in MPHEC's work—the commission has made remarkable strides in its first three years. Its future will depend on politics as much as planning. Issues such as the consolidation of all French-language universities in New Brunswick under the Université de Moncton, the recommendation that a regional veterinary college be established at UPEI, and the establishment of a law school at Université de Moncton have all raised political issues and individual or group hackles. But the new commission has so far survived. It began life with a substantial body of experience and expertise at its command, and the political advantage of having a chairman who was well-known publicly but was not a former public servant.

On the universities' side, the banner of rampant individualism still floats over the ivory towers. Coordination and control are resisted instinctively. But the advance guard of provincial and regional bureaucracy is already laying siege. The fifteen university administrative groups meet once, twice, or more frequently each year, presumably creating the kind of soil in which a regional system can put down roots. The soil, however, is thin and frequently eroded by a downpour of internal or interinstitutional conflict. It may well become barren after the drought of funds expected over the next few years.

Effectiveness of the System

This review has concentrated on the fairly immediate past, but to evaluate the effectiveness of the "system" one has to look at development since World War II. Although, with few exceptions, goals have been implicit rather than explicit, one assumes that postsecondary institutions of the Atlantic region have had three main purposes:
- to contribute to scholarship and the spread of learning, within and outside the region;
- to offer postsecondary education to any student in the region capable of benefiting from it, and to students from outside the region who wish to study in Atlantic institutions;
- to use the scientific, economic, social, and humanistic expertise of the institutions to help solve the problems of the region—and, in some cases, of the world.

The distinction between a reasonable and an excessive commitment to any of these objectives is open to argument. The academic community and the sociopolitical community would presumably disagree on the amount of emphasis to be placed on each. But this outline will serve for the purpose of our discussion.

In regard to scholarship and learning, the system has achieved a large measure of success. The quality and variety of postsecondary programs has expanded enormously in the thirty years since the war. The numbers and types of institutions have almost doubled. Scholars and researchers in the Atlantic region enjoy national and international reputations and the region continues to attract first-class scholars.

Accessibility to postsecondary education has increased steadily since the early 1960s. The universities accommodated the immediate postwar influx of veterans and hardly had time to return to normalcy before the galloping increases in full-time enrollment began in the mid-1950s. The institutions managed to cope with five- or six-fold increases during the next fifteen years and are still showing an annual increase in enrollment, despite the relative plateau of the 1970s.

Postsecondary education, in both full- and part-time forms, is accessible to the great majority of the population in the region. In Nova Scotia, 70 percent of the population lives within thirty miles of a university. In Newfoundland, the extension service has brought university education into the scattered outports of the island and the Labrador coast.

Until recently, there were no explicit barriers to interprovincial movement except in New Brunswick, where a financial penalty operated against institutions with more than a 25 percent enrollment of out-of-province students. Less obvious barriers were introduced in Newfoundland, where a student does not qualify for a provincial bursary if he leaves the province, unless he can show that the program he is to follow is not offered in Newfoundland. Nova Scotia and PEI have recently made moves in the same direction. The foreign student question, which has become a major point of contention in Ontario and Alberta, is also surfacing in the region—although the percentage of foreign students is below the national average.

A combined system of federal and provincial student aid has made it much easier for students to take three or four years to achieve a bachelor's degree and then perhaps to pursue advanced studies. (New Brunswick and PEI generally favor a four-year undergraduate program; Nova Scotia generally favors a three-year program.) The establishment of the Université de Moncton, the development of the extension services of Memorial University, and the general expansion of enrollments have improved both the expectations and the opportunities of young people from the lower end of the economic scale. The opening of postsecondary technical institutes, and a community college in PEI facilitated additional changes. Despite these gains, only Nova Scotia comes close to the national average participation rate. Newfoundland's is the lowest in the country.

Flexibility and Innovation

As noted, the institutions of the Atlantic region have adapted remarkably well to the great increases in enrollment since 1945. They have also shown a willingness to break away from traditional patterns of education by bringing education to many small communities and by opening their doors to many adults who do not meet formal entrance qualifications. In terms of the latter, UPEI led the country in offering tuition-free education to all over sixty-five years old.

The concern with expansion, however, overrode most other interests in the sixties. There were some changes in the traditional lecture pattern, with more accent on individual and small-group learning, although few Atlantic region universities became involved in the major experiments with television. The computer is gradually becoming a learning tool, especially in the sciences.

Memorial University did make extensive external use of television, along with radio, casettes, telephones, and traveling tutors, to carry university education to outlying areas of Newfoundland and Labrador. The work of its extension division was the most innovative, and locally the most important, of any province in Canada. UNB and Saint Mary's have also been actively involved in extension courses and St. Francis Xavier, home of the Antigonish Movement, has been world-famous in this field for decades. Finally, the Faculty of Medicine at Dalhousie University has been providing a very effective continuing education program for members of the medical profession.

Conclusion

At 10:00 A.M. on any Tuesday morning, it is easy to take a supremely negative view of the Atlantic postsecondary system. It was not organized as a system, regionally, and moves by the AAU, MPHEC, and other regional and provincial bodies toward a system have been hesitant. The penury of the forties and fifties, the comparatively heady spending of the sixties, and the relative poverty of the seventies have all tended to reinforce autonomous instincts. Geographically and politically Newfoundland is isolated from the Maritimes and the "Atlantic region" is a somewhat artificial term.

There has been little attempt to formally define the university and nonuniversity sectors, although relations between the two are good in individual cases.

The MPHEC is far and away the most likely agent to coordinate a system approach, but the MPHEC's very existence hangs on its not grossly offending the universities or the governments. Those governments themselves are subject to pressures from, and removal by, their provincial electorates, and major decisions—for example, that regarding the location of a veterinary college—will continue to be made on political rather than on academic grounds.

In contrast to this is the fact that there is an Atlantic region postsecondary community and decisions, formal and informal, are increasingly reached on an Atlantic or Maritime basis. To talk about an Atlantic or Maritime system is to overstate the case. However, a case can be made that PEI, New Brunswick, and Newfoundland have provincial systems. At the regional level, the "system" resembles a tangled seaweed thrown together by storm and current, pushed around by wind and waves, but still floating, even though waterlogged.

Improvements in the system (assuming one is in favor of systems and most postsecondary practitioners in the region are *not*) could occur in four major areas:

— An extension of the MPHEC to cover the Atlantic region (a move which would be bitterly resisted in Newfoundland postsecondary circles, but might have some attraction for the government as part of wider regional cooperation);

— A realization by the AAU that some decisions at the regional level would strengthen all institutions. However, since presidents no longer have real power to commit their institutions, real decisions are always unlikely;

- Preparation of an academic guide for the region, which would recognize the richness and diversity of the individual components and reassure small institutions and the French-Canadian minority that they would not be swallowed by the large institutions;
- And more money *might* help, if used as bait to lure institutions toward closer cooperation. But, as the lady said in the Newfoundland outport: "What we've got plenty of this year is no fish."

FOOTNOTES

1. New Brunswick, *Report of the Royal Commission on Higher Education in New Brunswick*, J. J. Deutsch, chairman (Fredericton: Queen's Printer, 1962); New Brunswick, *Report of the Committee on the Financing of Higher Education in New Brunswick*, J. J. Deutsch, chairman (Fredericton: Queen's Printer, 1967).
2. Association of Atlantic Universities, *Higher Education in the Atlantic Provinces for the 1970's* (Halifax: The Association, 1970).
3. *Ibid.*
4. Association of Universities and Colleges of Canada, Commission on the Financing of Higher Education in Canada, Vincent W. Bladen, chairman, *Report of the Commission* (Toronto: University of Toronto Press, 1965).
5. Association of Atlantic Universities, *op. cit.*
6. Maritime Provinces Higher Education Commission, *A Unique Regional Approach to Coordinating Higher Education* (Fredericton: The Commission, 1975).
7. Prince Edward Island, *Policy Statement on Post-Secondary Education* (Charlottetown: Legislative Assembly, 1968).
8. *Ibid.*
9. I have been strongly criticized in my presentation of this thesis on three grounds: that there is no class structure in Canada; that, if one doesn't look just at dollar signs, many "poor" have a reasonable standard of living; that the children of the poor have been well represented in Atlantic institutions. On the first question, it might be more acceptable to talk about socioeconomic quartiles or deciles but I do not think this alters the facts of the case. On the third, a number of studies of the student population have indicated that the lower half of the socioeconomic population is numerically underrepresented in Canadian universities. I have never seen any studies which indicate the contrary. Only Nova Scotia of the four Atlantic provinces approaches the national average participation rate for all students, which sug-

gests that the imbalance may be even greater in the Atlantic region. The situation for other forms of postsecondary education is better on a national basis but the region trails the rest of Canada in offering these alternative postsecondary opportunities.

10. M. O. Morgan, "Report to Spring Convocation, Afternoon, May 27, 1977," *MUN Gazette*, Vol. 9, No. 20 (June 1977), pp. 1, 13.
11. See Louis Vagianos, "Computerized Networks among Libraries and Universities in the Atlantic Provinces," *EDUCOM Bulletin*, Vol. 12, No. 2 (Summer 1977), pp. 2-7.
12. Nova Scotia, Royal Commission on Education, Public Services and Provincial-Municipal Relations, John F. Graham, chairman, *Report*, Vol. III (Halifax: Queen's Printer, 1974), chapters 61-65.
13. Maritime Provinces Higher Education Commission, *Higher Education in the Maritimes—1976: An Overview* (Fredericton: The Commission, 1976).
14. *Ibid.* See also Maritime Provinces Higher Education Commission. *In Process: Three Year Regional Planning for Higher Education in the Maritime Provinces* (Fredericton: The Commission, 1977).
15. The occasionally incestuous nature of the Maritime postsecondary scene is illustrated by the fact that this trio of commission chairman (Sheffield, O'Sullivan, and Murphy) prepared the report, *Region-wide Policies for Higher Education* (1970), for the Maritime Union Study.
16. Association of Atlantic Universities, *Brief presented by the Association of Atlantic Universities to the Maritime Provinces Higher Education Commission* (Halifax: The Association, 1977).
17. Henry D. Hicks, *A Submission to the Maritime Provinces Higher Education Commission on behalf of Dalhousie University* (Halifax: The University, 1977), p. 12.

POSTSECONDARY EDUCATION SYSTEMS IN QUEBEC

James H. Whitelaw

Like most Canadian provinces, Quebec covers a vast area, but its population is concentrated mainly in the southern and eastern regions, with over one-third in Montreal and its environs. Some 80 percent of this population are French-speaking, most of them descended from the settlers of the pre-1763 French regime. The remaining 20 percent comprise roughly equal proportions of persons of English-language origins and those with other linguistic backgrounds who have joined the English-language community. There is, therefore, a francophone minority within Canada, while the anglophone community is at once a part of the whole North-American English-speaking world and a minority within the province.

The primary and secondary levels of the school system, in accordance with the terms of the British North America Act of 1867, are organized on a denominational basis, Catholic and Protestant, although the latter covers all non-Catholics. At the postsecondary level, there are no longer any formal religious affiliations, except in the case of some private colleges, but French-language institutions, paradoxically, are marked both by the clerical traditions of the past and by revolt against them. There exists a *de facto* division of postsecondary education into French-language and English-language subsystems.

If French-language institutions, originally cast in a European mold, have adopted North-American structures, their ethos remains distinct. While anglophones have gradually come to terms with the French tendency toward abstract thinking and passion for semantic detail, francophones are finding that anglophone pragmatism is less soulless than they thought. The objective observer cannot fail to be fascinated by this manifestation of academic cross-fertilization, but nationalists see such phenomena as a dangerous dilution of French culture. While the media in English Canada are dominated by the powerful neighbor to the south without the protection of a language barrier, Quebec has developed its own voice, particularly in theatre, film, and television.

The miracle of the survival of a vigorous French-language community with deep-rooted cultural traditions has not, however, been accompanied by a full representation of francophones in all elements of Quebec society. Traditionally, French-language postsecondary education emphasized the training of clergy, lawyers, and doctors, with minimal attention paid to preparation for careers in business and industry, which have been largely dominated by anglophones. The Catholic church was a powerful force until about a decade ago, and the vacuum created by the loss of its dominant influence in so short a period of time has been filled by a diversity of ideologies. As for relationships between the two language groups, the "two solitudes" depicted by a well-known Anglo-Quebec novelist thirty years ago[1] have gradually come to know more about each other, even if this knowledge has not always been accompanied by understanding. This process has been particularly evident since 1960, which saw the beginning of a remarkable development in Quebec society, commonly referred to as the "Quiet Revolution," which has seen a renewed and modernized assertion of cultural identity, a determined effort to ensure for francophones a greater voice in the economic life of the community, and a total transformation of French-language education.

As a manifestation of dissatisfaction in November 1976 the Quebec electorate put into office, by a substantial majority, a government dedicated to independence for Quebec. Current debate has crystalized around proposed legislation which, in promoting the use of French in the worlds of business and education, would impose considerable restrictions on the use of English and on admission to English-language schools. It is obviously too early to predict what the effects of this dramatic political change may be on education in general and postsecondary education in particular. What follows therefore is a description of conditions in a state of flux. An attempt has been made to indicate discernable trends as of the end of June 1977.

Acts of the provincial legislature have so far appeared in both languages, and some major reports have been translated into English. Most documentation, however, and most of the literature on education in Quebec are in French. (In this chapter, French terms have been translated for clarity where appropriate.) The term "government" refers to the provincial government, except where there are indications to the contrary.

Design

Institutions

Quebec postsecondary education operates at two separate levels — college and university — constituting two virtually independent systems. Within each of these systems there is a *de facto*, but not *de jure* subdivision according to language — French or English.

Universities

There are four French-language universities — Laval (1852), Montréal (1920), Sherbrooke (1954) and the Université du Québec (1968). Montréal and Sherbrooke bear the names of the cities in which they are located, Laval is in the city of Quebec, and the Université du Québec is a multiunit institution, with constituents in Montreal, Trois-Rivières, Chicoutimi, and Rimouski and services in towns in the west and northwest of the province. Affiliated with the Université de Montréal are the Ecole Polytechnique (1873), the Ecole des Hautes Etudes Commerciales (1915); the Université du Québec system including the Ecole Nationale de l'Administration Publique (1969), the Institut National de la Recherche Scientifique (1969), the Institut Armand Frappier (founded in 1942 and incorporated into the University in 1972), the Téléuniversité (1972), and the Ecole de Technologie Supérieure (1974).

There are three English-language universities — McGill (1821), Bishop's (1853), and Concordia, the latter having been formed by the 1974 merger of Sir George Williams University (1948) and Loyola of Montreal (1899), a four-year liberal arts college in the American sense of the term.[2] Bishop's University is located in the small town of Lennoxville, while the other two are located in Montreal. Mention should also be made of the Thomas More Institute for Adult Education, which offers innovative evening programs for adults, including those leading to degrees formerly awarded by the University of Montreal. The institute is now affiliated with Bishop's University.

Most universities have residential facilities, while those located in the Montreal region have a substantial number of commuting students.

Entry to a university normally requires successful completion of a two-year program in a college of general and vocational education (see later). The first university degree is most commonly granted after three years of study following completion of the college program, and normally corresponds to sixteen years of schooling.

Each university is a corporation under the Civil Code (Quebec civil law), originally either incorporated by royal charter, with subsequent amendments by the government of Quebec, or set up by public or private statutes enacted by that government. Over 80 percent of operating and capital resources come from the provincial government.

Colleges

There are thirty-seven public colleges of general and vocational education commonly referred to by the acronym CEGEP (Collège d'enseignement général et professionnel), four of which are English-language institutions. Some of these colleges have more than one campus. Students enter after completing eleven years of schooling, beginning at age six, and can choose between two-year "general" programs, which constitute the regular route to university, or vocationally-oriented programs leading to employment, which are all, with one or two exceptions, of three years' duration. Graduates of certain of these vocational programs who wish to continue such studies may do so at the Ecole de Technologie Supérieure, recently created at the Université du Québec. They can also enter certain regular undergraduate programs in the universities, provided they have the appropriate prerequisites.

The public colleges have all been created since 1967 and constitute one of the more visible achievements of the Quiet Revolution. Most of the French-language colleges were formed through regrouping or expansion of existing establishments, such as institutes of technology and *collèges classiques*. Most of the latter were originally church-affiliated institutions whose *baccalauréat* degree, involving up to fifteen years of schooling, was awarded by the French-language university to which the college was affiliated. The new colleges are located at different points throughout the province, with a concentration of some 40 percent in the Montreal region and some in quite remote areas. The four English-language institutions were all created from scratch, since in that sector access to the university had traditionally been directly from secondary school, and vocational facilities at the postsecondary level for anglophones had been almost nonexistent.

Residential facilities are available in a number of colleges. Full-time enrollments range from considerably less than 1,000 students up to 7,000. Tuition is free for full-time students, but not for part-time.

Public colleges offer programs from a common official repertoire of programs and courses,[3] and, although each has its own corporation under the Civil Code, funding and control of programs come through the Division of Collegial Education of the ministry, and it is the ministry which awards the Diploma of College Studies (Diplôme d'études collégiales), whereas each university controls its own programs, subject to certain coordinating mechanisms, and awards its own degrees.

Mention should also be made of a small number of highly specialized institutions, including the Ecole de tourisme et d'hôtellerie, the Institut de technologie agricole, and a number of conservatories of art and music which are at the moment under the jurisdiction of other ministries.

At the college level, there are some forty private institutions, ranging in size from less than 200 to over 2,000 students. Some of these offer both preuniversity and vocational programs, normally the same as those offered in the public colleges, while others are specialized institutions, offering programs beyond the secondary level in such areas as secretarial training, music, and art.

Of the private institutions, twenty-five, including one English-language college, are categorized[4] as being "of public interest" and receive financial support from the province—amounting to 80 percent of the previous year's average cost of instruction in a public institution of the same kind, with the right to charge their students no more than 10 percent over and above the balance. Six private institutions are classified as "recognized for granting purposes," and they are funded in the same way, but at 60 percent of the current average cost in public institutions. The remainder have a permit to operate, but receive no funding.

Institutional Governance

Universities

As mentioned earlier, all universities operate under individual acts of incorporation. With the exception of Laval, which has a unicameral structure (Conseil de l'Université), all universities have a bicameral organization, in which the supreme body is a board of governors, with varying titles in French-language institutions, which constitutes the legal authority of the institution. The boards are composed of administrators, faculty, students, and laymen, the latter generally including alumni. Membership ranges in number from nineteen to thirty-seven. The method of appointment varies from one case where all members other than those sitting ex officio are appointed by government order-in-council (Cabinet action) after consultation with the appropriate social and educational organizations, to others where only internal mechanisms are used. Senior administrators are ex officio members of all boards, while elected or appointed members, with the exception of students, normally have a three-year mandate, renewable once. Each constituent of the Université du Québec has its own board, with powers subject to the board of the whole university. Boards of governors, while devoting a large part of their time to financial matters, are commonly required to give formal and final approval to such things as the awarding of degrees, promotions, changes in academic structures, and the operation of student services.

All institutions apart from Laval, with its single legislative body of fifty-one members, but including the various constituents of the Université du Québec, have a supreme academic body, with a varying range of powers delegated or assigned to it by the board of governors in such areas as curriculum, admission requirements, and academic regulations. This body, called a "senate" in the English-language institutions, is known by various titles in the French-language universities *(conseil, assemblée universitaire,* etc.) and normally comprises academic administrators sitting ex officio, and faculty and students elected by their respective constituencies. Proportions vary, but, as an example, the Concordia senate consists of sixty voting members, including twenty-seven faculty members (not counting deans) and nineteen students. In some big universities with a large number of professional faculties, this principle of representation produces bodies with up to one hundred members. Chief officers are appointed by various internal mechanisms — such as search committees and elections — but the president of the Université du Québec is appointed by the government after appropriate consultation.

Faculty and academic department councils have an increasing number of students; in some cases there is parity in the numbers of students and faculty. There has also been some student involvement in faculty hiring, although collective agreements negotiated between the administration and the faculty unions, which now exist in five out of the seven universities, inevitably establish procedures in which students have no official voice. It must be noted, however, that there appears to be a growing disenchantment on the part of both faculty and students with respect to participation in institutional governance. In some instances student bodies have declined to fill the places available to them. In the search for power, participation does not seem to have lived up to original expectations.

Colleges

As far as the public colleges (CEGEPs) are concerned, the mode of institutional governance is laid down in the General and Vocational Colleges Act of 1967. Each college is under the direction of a board (*conseil*), composed of nineteen persons, two of whom, the principal and the academic dean, are ex officio members. Of the balance, five are laymen, selected after consultation with educational and socioeconomic groups of the region; four are faculty members; two are students, and four are parents of students of the college. The remaining two persons are coopted by the other seventeen. All except the ex officio members are appointed by government order-in-council on the basis of recommendations from the groups represented. The chairman of the board is elected each year by the members from among those members who are at least twenty-one years old.

The board has complete responsibility for running the college, but the Act prescribes the creation of an academic council to advise it on matters of curriculum and the hiring of academic administrators. Without specifying membership of this council, the Act requires that at least three members be designated by faculty and that the academic dean be an ex officio member. Recent collective agreements between staff and college contain clauses which do not appear to be compatible with this requirement. Private colleges are free to organize their governing bodies as they see fit. Faculty are unionized in all public colleges and in a few of the private ones.

Relationships of Institutions

The Ministry of Education

The Ministry of Education was created in May 1964 by the provincial legislature, as a consequence of the recommendations of the all-embracing Royal Commission of Inquiry on Education in the Province of Quebec[5] chaired by the late Mgr. Alphonse-Marie Parent of the Université Laval (hereinafter referred to as the Parent Commission Report). The ministry is divided into a number of divisions (*directions générales*) and services, including a Division of Higher Education. Until relatively recently, the director (*directeur général*) of each division reported to the deputy minister (the senior civil servant); this structure was modified in 1974 and immediate responsibility for various levels and functions was shifted to assistant deputy ministers, one of whom is responsible for both college and university levels. For everyday matters, individual institutions deal with the designated assistant deputy minister, or with the Division of Higher Education. Direct contacts with the ministry are most common in the various areas of finance, and in teacher certification and classification; there have also been periodic attempts to set up a systemwide data base. The ministry will normally deal with the rector or the vice-rectors of each institution, unless authorized to do otherwise. Joint committees or working groups made up of representatives of the ministry and of the universities are not uncommon.

The public college system relates directly to the Division of College Education of the ministry. Private colleges receive their funding through the Private Education Service, but otherwise, with the exception of a few highly specialized institutions, they offer the same programs as public colleges, although few vocation-oriented programs are offered. There is no intermediate or advisory body for colleges, although the possibility of creating such a body has been suggested. All academic programs must be approved by the division, as must all budgets in public colleges, so that the ministry in effect controls development in terms of new, renovated, or rented physical facilities, equipment, and so on. Official communication occurs between the ministry and the chairman of the board or the principal, while day-to-day operations are conducted between the Division of College Education and its various departments and the appropriate officers of the college.

The Superior Council
of Education

The Superior Council of Education was created in 1964 to serve in an advisory role to the whole educational system. The minister of education is required to consult the superior council on certain matters. He is, of course, free to consult the council on any topic. One of the council's main duties is to submit an annual report on the state and needs of the educational system. Although it is financed by the ministry and reports directly to the minister, the council is free to organize its activities as it sees fit. In addition to the council itself, the Act which created it provides for a number of standing committees and commissions, including one for higher education and another for college education.[6] Neither universities nor colleges have formal procedural links with the corresponding commission. Members of the council and its commissions are appointed by government order-in-council, after consultation with a wide range of educational and lay groups. As a reflection of the traditional denominational basis of organization of elementary and secondary education, council members are selected with some consideration for denominational representation, and the two associate deputy ministers, one Catholic and the other Protestant, together with the deputy minister himself, are ex officio associate members.

The Council of Universities

This body was set up in December 1968 by provincial legislation. It is an advisory body to the minister of education, and is funded by the ministry. The role and operation of the council will be taken up in greater detail in a later section, but it should be noted at this point that, while it formally reports to the minister, in practice it has regular contact with both the Division of Higher Education and with the universities, either as a body or through its four standing committees on finance, academic programs (a joint committee with ministry membership), research, and planning. Contact is normally made through the rector or appropriate vice-rector of each institution, or persons designated by them.

Purposes and Functions

By far the most complete statement on the purposes and functions of education in Quebec, including all levels of study, is contained in the Parent Commission report, which provided a blueprint for the extensive educational reform carried out in Quebec over the last ten years. Legislation passed since the publication of that report has been almost exclusively concerned with implementation mechanisms, so that the goals of the system are not spelled out in any legislative document.

With particular reference to postsecondary education, we find, recurring throughout the report, the following themes:

— the right of access to studies or training for any qualified individual;
— the responsibility of the education system, from the secondary level on, to provide each individual with a series of points at which he or she may choose either training for immediate entry to a specific vocation, or continuation of studies;
— the need for balance between the practical and the theoretical;
— a balance between governmental authority and institutional autonomy, involving satisfactory participation of all concerned, as part of the "democratization" of education;
— a new "humanism" which would establish a clear and lasting relationship between the academic and the vocational.

Since the publication of the Parent Commission Report, which was formally accepted by the premier of the time, there have been a considerable number of major reports concerned with the postsecondary level which have not generally resulted in specific legislation. Sets of regulations have been promulgated by order-in-council, one of which covers the college level[7] and another establishes certification requirements for teachers.[8]

At the university level, the Council of Universities published a three-part report in 1972-73, entitled *Objectifs généraux de l'enseignement supérieur et grandes orientations des établissements*. The report was based on extensive consultation with the universities and was widely accepted by them.[9] The central theme of the report, was that of lifelong education (*éducation permanente*), both as a means of maintaining and updating professional competence, and as an opportunity for individual self-fulfillment.

At the college level, the purposes and goals are those spelled out in the Parent Commission report—the establishment of a distinct level of instruction, bringing all postsecondary students planning to undertake studies at university together with those seeking a vocational program leading directly to employment. A crisis in the college system in February 1973 prompted the minister of education to request the Superior Council to conduct a study on the "state and needs of college education, that is, on the results obtained thus far, on the problems that have arisen, and on the orientations to be retained for its future administrative and pedagogical development." The council's report,[10] submitted in July 1975 and commonly known as the Nadeau report after its chairman, Jean-Guy Nadeau, has not been officially accepted by the minister—in fact, it has been the object of criticism from most quarters—but it has forced various elements in the system, beginning with the Division of College Education, to react, so that the future of the college system may well be very different, not only in terms of programs and structures, but also in terms of specific objectives. The ministry is working on a white paper on college education, scheduled to appear in the fall of 1977 which, it has been promised, will be sent to a wide range of institutions for review. It is expected to propose modifications of the Colleges Act.

Mention should also be made of the Quebec Professions Board (Office des Professions), created in 1973 by an act of the provincial legislature, which contains a number of articles on the initial and refresher training of professionals in some forty different fields—in particular, health, law, business, and engineering.

Management

Planning

The "Quiet Revolution" in Quebec produced a massive demand for persons trained in areas which previously had not been of major concern to the francophone community, and there has been, in consequence, a truly remarkable expansion in the number of francophones entering postsecondary education institutions. The divisions of the ministry which are concerned with college and university education have been in existence for less than a decade, and have tended to be understaffed, so that the amount of long-range planning at these levels has inevitably been limited.

At the university level the principle of triennial budget strategies has been accepted, but the processes have not yet been worked out and operating budgets are still made up on a year-to-year basis. Capital budgets are worked out in the form of a rolling five-year plan, amended every year in the light of developments. The Division of Higher Education appears to be under considerable pressure from the provincial Treasury Board to provide better enrollment forecasts, but such forecasts as have been made have turned out to be very unreliable, and are further complicated by such imponderables as the effects of immigration and language policies.

The Division of Higher Education, with varying degrees of input from the Council of Universities, has carried out sectoral studies in three high-cost areas — applied sciences, health sciences, and pure sciences[11] — to ensure that programs in these areas are consonant with the needs of Quebec society, both in terms of quantity and quality. The first of these, commonly referred to as OSA (Opération Sciences appliquées), was launched by the Higher Education Division in 1971, following a favorable response from the Council of Universities. Its essential mandate was to make short-term proposals of a corrective nature for the period 1971-73, then to propose an initial five-year plan (1973-78), including budget estimates, and finally to propose the general outlines of a second five-year plan (1978-83). The study would provide the universities with a framework for development, which would also help the ministry, in consultation with the council, to take decisions affecting the development of existing programs, the creation of new programs, or the discontinuation of programs which had outlived their usefulness. The plan proposed would help the system to estimate the human, physical, and financial resources necessary to respond adequately to the needs of the economy, both qualitative and quantitative, with particular reference to the evolution of the labor market and to the preparation of young professionals for new functions.

To carry out the operation, a committee of some fifteen experts was designated, chosen from the academic, professional, and industrial communities. A steering committee of four persons was created under the chairmanship of the director of the Division of Higher Education.

Each university appointed a liaison person, and responsibility for the projects and dossiers was distributed among the universities. Various substantive committees were then formed. The individual reports of the committees were published as they were completed, and the final report, containing a summary of all the recommendations, was published in June 1973. The Joint Programmes Committee of the council and the ministry followed up on the recommendations for academic programs and, of course, a vast amount of useful information was gathered. The follow-up of the operation will depend on the institutions' willingness to comply with the recommendations and the power of the government authority to encourage compliance.

Certification of teachers has always been the responsibility of the Ministry of Education (or the government bodies which preceded its creation). It has consequently maintained close supervision of teacher-training programs, the more so since many of these were conducted by state-operated normal schools prior to incorporation into the universities—a major operation which was all but completed by 1972. At the present time, the future of teacher-training programs is being studied by a joint committee composed of various ministry division heads and the academic vice-rectors of the universities, and chaired by the appropriate assistant deputy minister. Forecasts of teacher needs are notoriously unreliable, and the current unsatisfactory state of labor relations in this area does not help.

The Council of Universities has so far played the most visible role in planning at the university level. As an advisory body, it presents a yearly critique of budget proposals to the minister of education, who is required by the Council of Universities Act to consult it thereon. The 1972-73 report (*Objectifs généraux de l'enseigne-*

ment supérieur et grandes orientations des établissements) was intended to prod individual institutions into defining their respective roles, and into recognizing that they were, whether they liked it or not, part of a system. While there is an increasing amount of contact at the institutional, faculty, and even departmental level, it cannot be said that there is a systemwide approach to planning, even though the council's iterative approach, by requiring a "state-of-the-nation" report from each institution every three or four years,[12] does allow for a substantial amount of institutional input. (So far, quantitative data have not been a particularly important element here, whereas they have been in the ministry's sectoral operations.)

It is, however, important to note that the new provincial government, faced with financial austerity, with faculty unrest,[13] and with widespread concern over the social role of the university in Quebec, has announced a wide-ranging study of the province's universities, with particular reference to quantitative forecasts, the responsiveness of the system to society's needs, management of the system and of individual institutions, and the quality of life in the university. This study is to be carried out under the auspices of the minister of education and the minister of state for cultural development. The Council of Universities has been consulted and its response, while favorable in principle, reflects concern over the vast range of topics proposed for study and the need to make full use of existing mechanisms and studies already completed. The council also stressed the need to tackle specific issues, with the aim of provoking action, and emphasized the importance of conducting the study in as public a fashion as possible. Members of the coordinating committee for the study and the various working groups will be appointed by the government. The government also plans a study on research, involving industry and government as well as the universities.

Administration

Finance

For the public colleges, budgets are determined according to government norms, based on enrollment, for both operating and capital funding. Virtually all funding is provided by the government, so that negotiation which does take place is limited to special cases, such as the provision of new or reconstructed physical facilities.

In the case of the universities, operating grants are supposed to be worked out according to a formula. Up to now, this "formula" has consisted of incremental adjustments—related to such items as enrollment or inflation—to the institutional grants of a base year (1968-69), with further modifications in response to special cases made by individual institutions. The distribution of 1968-69 funds suffered from some inequities.

The process hitherto has been as follows. The ministry determines a total sum for university grants, subject to the approval of the legislature. The proposed distribution is submitted to the Council of Universities, and each institution is advised of the amount proposed for it. This stage is followed by a series of meetings between ministry representatives and each individual university, after which there is a second series of meetings between the Council of Universities and each individual institution. The council then forwards its official reaction (*avis*) to the minister, and the ministry, in due course, makes public its comments, more often than not explaining why it has been unable to accede to all the council's requests. Final adjustments of a technical nature have been made when actual enrollment figures are known. The amount of the operating grant is worked out by establishing the recognized and accepted expenditures (*dépenses considérées*) of each institution, then subtracting from these the revenue from fees and other sources. This has meant that areas of basic operating costs—for which private or institutional donors can support a university without simply subsidizing the government—have been limited to purchases of special equipment, provision of fellowships, funding of special projects, and so on. In September of each year each university has submitted a financial statement for the past year, an estimate for the current year (the university financial year runs from June 1 to May 31), and enrollment forecasts for the next five years to the ministry. It has been understood that the latter are subject to annual revision.

Unlike grants for operating costs—for which the "formula" does not take into account the actual number of students, but only enrollment fluctuations from year to year—capital grants are based on the number of "full-time equivalent" students, worked out on the basis of fees paid, while special projects such as buildings are negotiated separately. The government adopts a very broad definition of capital projects; equipment and the care of the existing plant (beyond routine maintenance) fall into this category. Student services receive a per student grant ($42 for 1977-78) beyond which they must be self-financing.

Attempts to come up with an equitable formula continue, in the context of budgeting by "program" (in the broad sense of the term). At the moment of writing, the ministry plans a series of triennial budget strategies, subject to annual adjustments based on enrollment fluctuation and the evolution of socioeconomic needs and priorities. A system of weighting enrollment by level and academic sector in order to provide a more equitable distribution of funds is being proposed. In times of austerity, it would seem difficult to achieve such a redistribution without reducing support of the "wealthier" institutions in favor of the less fortunate, and the former are hardly likely to favor such a measure. As for the process, the various parties concerned—the ministry, Council of Universities, and the universities themselves—are engaged in consultations over the nature of the triennial budget strategy approach, particularly, the mechanisms for determining the annual grants and providing for official reactions at different points in the process.

A more familiar administrative problem involves the absence of an effective management information system. Some three years were wasted on a costly project[14] which seems to have failed mainly because its sponsors were more interested in the system itself than in the nature and uses of the data to be generated. As things are, the ministry expresses annoyance that the money expended on computer installations in the universities seems to have produced so little in the way of reliable and compatible data—to which certain universities retort that they do not have the funding to provide adequate human resources to make the system productive.

Admission of Students

With the increasing unreliability of grading systems—a continental phenomenon—and the virtual disappearance of standardized examinations sponsored by either the government or other organizations, most students who pass the required number and range of high school examinations can be admitted to a college. A ministerial liaison committee, comprising representatives of the collegial and secondary levels, exists to establish specific requirements for entry to various college programs. Selection of candidates is carried out by individual colleges, in terms of the number of places available in given programs of study.

Another liaison committee, consisting of one representative per university, an equal number of academic administrators from the college, and appropriate ministry personnel, under the chairmanship of the assistant deputy minister associated with postsecondary education, plays a similar role for the transition from college to university. Universities are free to set their own admission policies, subject to a general commitment to accepting college graduates with appropriate prerequisites, and provided, of course, that there is room in the programs. Currently, there is concern over what constitutes a desirable proportion of students from outside the province, and an official policy is expected very shortly, probably taking the form of increased tuition for foreign students. At the moment, no additional fees are charged for non-Quebec students. Policies, in short, are of a general nature, and decisions on individual cases are made at the institutional level. Some institutions involve faculty and/or students in such decisions, and the determination of institutional policies normally incorporates faculty and student recommendations via senates, university councils, and so forth.

Selection of Faculty

Selection of faculty is entirely an institutional matter, subject to such considerations as immigration regulations or college norms. Since funds allocated by the ministry for academic salaries are not transferable to or from salary accounts at either the college or the university level, there are limitations imposed by resource considerations. The extent of faculty and student involvement in decisions on hiring varies, but is greatest at the departmental level. Further, hiring policies are subject to tenure or job-security provisions, or other restrictions built into collective agreements. Negotiation of the latter have tended to be carried out in an atmosphere of confrontation, inspired by industrial models.

Curriculum

At the college level, there is a single curriculum repertoire for the system, both in terms of programs and individual courses. The differences that occur between institutions tend to be those of style and approach rather than content. Provincial committees comprised of college faculty, but acting under the aegis of the Division of College Education, have the primary responsibility for curriculum development.

In the universities, new programs must be submitted to the Joint Programmes Committee of the Council of Universities, to ensure that the sponsoring institution has the capacity or potential to offer the program and that duplication is avoided. Within individual universities, there is substantial faculty and student participation in curriculum development at all levels, from the department up to the final academic decision-making body.

Establishing New Institutions

The postsecondary system in Quebec is virtually complete in terms of the number and distribution of institutions. It is, however, worth noting that the public colleges were each set up following submission of a brief prepared by a local, spontaneously generated, organizing committee of educators and laymen. The brief was submitted to the Ministry of Education, and the minister's decision took into account potential enrollment, geographical location, and the presence of existing institutions or utilizable plant. There seems to be little likelihood that any additional new institutions will be created, and there has been a move toward regional grouping of those already in existence. At the university level, the University of Quebec Act stipulates that new university-level institutions should be established within its framework. Creation of Concordia University in 1974, brought about through the merger of Sir George Williams University and Loyola of Montreal, was carried out under the charter of Sir George Williams.

Research

At the present time, the universities constitute the principal foci of research in the province. The Parent Commission report proposed[15] the creation of a provincial research council, but in so doing stressed the fact that such a body must not draw researchers away from the universities. The Council of Universities Act provided for the creation of a Commission on University Research within the council, and this was promptly carried out. The University of Quebec Act allows for the establishment of research institutes, and in 1969 the Institut National de la Recherche Scientifique was created as a constituent of that university.

The indissoluble relationship between teaching and research has been stressed in several Council of Universities reports, as well as others. The research commission of the council regularly assesses the research aspect of new graduate programs and submits its assessment to the Joint Programmes Committee.

There has been a spectacular increase in research funding over the past ten years: the total for the system has quintupled over that period, while the figure for the French-language universities, which started late, increased almost twelvefold. Although the bulk of research funding comes from federal or nongovernmental sources, in 1968 the Quebec government introduced "catch-up" funding for the French-language universities. These grants were offered in addition to regular and capital grants as part of a general policy to get these institutions on par with other Canadian universities. In 1970 the support program known as Formation des Chercheurs et Action concertée (FCAC) was initiated. As its title implies, the primary aim of the program was to train research personnel and to support team research. For the following year, the Council's Research Commission proposed a joint steering committee, to be composed of representatives of the commission and of the Higher Education Division of the Ministry of Education. The ministry subsequently entrusted the commission with the responsibility for the appointment and functioning of the committee and its area subcommittees.

Coordination

Coordination of the public colleges is in some ways automatic in that this system is totally financed by the provincial government under a set of norms and regulations relating to admissions, student/teacher ratios, support staff, space, curricula, and so on, with systemwide as well as institutional-level collective bargaining. Only in the realm of continuing education are individual institutions free to develop more or less as they see fit. Notwithstanding what would appear to be system-imposed coordination, there seems to be a surprising lack of voluntary coordination in those areas in which the system norms allow for options. The Nadeau report recommended the creation of a council of colleges, modeled on the Council of Universities, but so far there are no signs that this suggestion will be implemented. In the interim, the Federation of Colleges (Fédération des CEGEPs), a voluntary association, has played an effective coordinating role in the interpretation and application of policies and in coping with the many problems arising from scarce resources, labor relations, and so on.

At the university level, the oldest (1963) coordinating body is the Conference of Rectors and Principals of the Universities of Quebec (CREPUQ). The conference is an independent organization; all universities are free to join, and, at the present time, all are in fact members. Like most groups of this nature, it had modest scope and aims when it began. But with the big leap forward of the 1960s, it saw itself as the nucleus of a true "buffer" body, especially when the newly formed Ministry of Education appeared to be interposing itself increasingly in the everyday workings of the universities. The Parent Commission report had already suggested[16] that a commission of higher education be created within the proposed Superior Council of Education to provide the council with expert advice on higher education. The report indicated its approval[17] of the coordinating role of the Conference of Rectors, but also proposed the creation of a bureau for the development of higher education with power to make annual recommendations to the minister of education on, among other things, university grants. When the Council of Universities was created in 1968, its mandate generally followed that proposed for the bureau.

As the system has evolved, the Commission of Higher Education of the Superior Council has not played a particularly visible role, mainly because the Conference of Rectors and the Council of Universities were seen as the only effective bodies, but also, perhaps, because it has been composed almost exclusively of academics. Consequently, its contribution in relaying the views of the provincial population to the Superior Council has not been noteworthy. Now, however, it appears that the Superior Council is attempting to ensure adequate participation of nonacademics on all its commissions and committees.

The Conference of Rectors has gone through a number of phases, from great ambitions with few achievements to its current status—providing the ministry with a convenient and effective means of consulting the universities as a whole. More important, it provides the locus for concerted action, based on analyses prepared by a competent secretariat with full-time research personnel. It has standing committees of academic vice-rectors, administrative vice-rectors, and so forth. Each of these has a limited number of subcommittees, such as that charged with the qualitative evaluation of new program proposals carried out by agreement with the Joint Programmes Committee of the Council of Universities.

The Council of Universities has as its main general function "to give opinions to the minister of education on the needs of higher education and university research and to make recommendations to him on the measures to be taken to meet these needs." The council consists of seventeen persons plus a full-time secretary, all of whom are appointed by the government. The membership includes: nine representatives from universities, including administrators, faculty, and students; four business or labor representatives, a full-time chairman, appointed for a five-year renewable term; the chairman of the University Research Commission of the council (the only standing committee spelled out in the Act); and two civil servants. Appointments of faculty and lay members to the council are made on the basis of wide consultation with educational, professional, industrial, and business organizations.

In addition to the University Research Commission specified in the Act, the council has created three other standing committees. The most visible is the Joint Committee on Programmes, created in May 1970, and composed of six university professors (or academic administrators) and at least one representative of the Ministry of Education. After six years with a part-time chairman, the committee was given a full-time chairman in the summer of 1976. The Finance Committee, with particular responsibilities in the area of government grants, is composed of five university professors or academic administrators, and a representative of the Higher Education Division of the ministry as associate member. The Grandes Orientations (planning) committee, responsible for the iterative planning operation of the council, consists of five members of the council itself. The council is financed as a distinct program of the ministry.

Relationships between Advisory Bodies and Government

The Council of Universities. As has been noted earlier, the council is an advisory body, but the minister of education is required to submit the following items (quoted from Article 4 of the Council of

Universities Act) for review to the council:

i) any program which he intends to implement for the development of higher education and university research at each important phase of its elaboration;

ii) the annual operating and investment budgets of establishments of higher education;

iii) the apportionment among establishments of higher education of the total amount of the annual appropriations made available for higher education and university research;

iv) the steps which he intends to take to ensure coordination between establishments of higher education;

v) rules respecting the standardization of the accounting methods of establishments of higher education.

There have been instances when the minister has not sought an opinion from the council on the preceding items—for example, when the Institut National de la Recherche scientifique was created in 1969, or when the Institut de Microbiologie de Montréal affiliated with the Université du Québec as the Institut Armand Frappier in 1972—but on the whole relations between the two bodies seem to have been remarkably good. If all of one hundred recommendations submitted by the council have not been followed entirely or implemented immediately, only two have actually been ignored by the minister, one of which related to the politically based decision to create Concordia University out of the merger of Sir George Williams University and Loyola of Montreal. The council had recommended that Loyola become a college of general and vocational education (CEGEP), and that its university-level[18] students be distributed between McGill and Sir George Williams.

Contact with the provincial government is ensured by two provincial government representatives on the council, and at least one member of the Division of Higher Education on the Joint Programmes Committee and one on the Finance Committee as an associate member. In terms of government representation, the Joint Programmes Committee poses an interesting case, in that a ministry representative is a party to whatever recommendations may be made on the financing of new programs, and yet this same representative will find himself on the receiving end when the recommendations arrive at the ministry. From the universities' perspective, this situation provides an opportunity for the ministry to participate in formulating the committee's recommendations; at the same time, the ministry representatives find their situation somewhat ambivalent from a decision-making point of view. Presumably the principal advantage of the arrangement is that it provides an additional informational channel between the two bodies. In addition to the formal contact symbolized by the presence of ministry representatives on the council and its committees, there appear to be effective informal contacts between the council and the ministry which contribute significantly to the success of the operation. This success, as so often happens, seems, in large measure, a tribute to the talents of the individuals involved and one is constantly reminded of the fragility of any system in terms of its dependence on the calibre of the principal actors involved.

The Conference of Rectors and Principals. Relations between the Conference of Rectors and the ministry have varied according to the extent to which the ministry viewed the conference as a responsible and representative university voice. There was a time, some years ago, when the director of the Higher Education Division of the ministry more or less refused to have anything to do with the conference. Over the past five years, there has been a growing degree of positive contact between the conference and the ministry as the former has shown itself to be truly representative, with sufficient technical support to produce effective dossiers. It is of particular interest that although the effectiveness of the conference as a university voice was limited from 1973 to 1976 by the fact that the Université du Québec had withdrawn (1973) from the conference—as the result of a dispute over the status of the Institut National de la Recherche scientifique—the conference continued to involve Université du Québec personnel in certain operations, such as qualitative evaluation of new programs, and contacts were maintained at an unofficial level. The ministry recognizes that, officially, it has to deal with institutions individually, but the assistant deputy minister has used the conference as a convenient mechanism for meeting with various academic vice-rectors as a group to discuss a range of items from teacher-training and certification to a liaison between college and university levels.

Relationships between Advisory Bodies and Individual Institutions

The Council of Universities. The council has, as already noted, four standing committees with mandates in the areas of systemwide planning (*comité des orientations*), academic programs, research, and finance. It also sets up ad hoc committees, such as one created to examine the matter of degree nomenclature and program structure. Committee members are appointed by the council, except in the case of the University Research Commission, which is mandated by the Act with members appointed by government order-in-council. Essentially, the membership of the various committees comes from the university world, and the members serve as individuals and not as institutional representatives. Nevertheless, cynics contend that any faculty member accepting nomination to one of these bodies becomes *ipso facto* a member of the indistinct but threatening mass referred to as "the government."

The council is not bound by law to any particular procedures. It has chosen to function with a very wide degree of consultation. For example, the 1972-73 report referred to earlier was based initially upon individual briefs submitted by institutions. A council committee then prepared a first draft from these briefs and requested the individual institutions to respond to it both in writing and during personal visits by the committee. Similarly, the Finance Committee visits each institution before presenting its recommendations to the council for subsequent submission to the minister of education. The council's Joint Programmes Committee, while ultimately responsible both for the quality and appropriateness (*opportunité*) of a program, has entrusted program evaluation to the Conference of Rectors, which sets up an evaluation committee composed of faculty members for this purpose. Universities have to take the initiative in requesting the Conference of Rectors to undertake evaluation.

Inevitably, unpopular decisions have to be made every now and then. Emerging institutions, for example, claim that in the competition for the scarce resources available for new programs, they are at a disadvantage as compared to well-established universities, whose wider range of offerings and more solid financial base make it possible for them to develop new programs through the diversion of existing resources. Again, some of the larger and more well-endowed institutions were initially opposed to the notion of a system. Perhaps a major achievement of the planning activity of the council and the ministry has been to instill awareness of institutional interrelationships and, ultimately, interdependence.

The Conference of Rectors and Principals. While the Council of Universities, as an advisory body to the minister, and a recognized cog in the official machinery, can in a crunch invoke the power of governmental authority, the Conference of Rectors, as a voluntary association, has to proceed by a much more delicate type of consensus. On the other hand, by avoiding becoming a cog in the machinery, it retains greater freedom to maneuver. The conference is presided over by an administrative council consisting of the head of each institution and a varying number of senior colleagues per institution according to size, with an executive committee comprising the institutional heads or their delegates. It operates mainly through groups of persons fulfilling the same or similar functions—committees of vice-rectors, registrars, librarians, and so on—although it also has subcommittees such as the evaluation committee on new programs, reporting to the committee of academic vice-rectors, or the committee on research. At one point it had a frightening panoply of committees organized on the basis of academic discipline—but this was eliminated some years ago in favor of an ad hoc approach to problems in a given discipline area. Thus it was that the conference was primarily responsible for the rationalization of programs in classics at a time when there appeared to be more faculty than students in that area. With the exception of the Evaluation Committee, consisting mainly of faculty members, most of the committees are comprised of academic or other administrators. While this has the advantage of bringing together persons with similar daily preoccupations, faculty and students tend to regard the conference as an administrators' club, and it has recently been accused by the Federation of Quebec University Professors' Associations of conspiring to thwart the federation's interests. It is, nevertheless, a conference of chief officers who associate voluntarily in order to coordinate various activities, which, it must be hoped, are in the interests of the academic community at large.

One of the main problems with any voluntary body is that it is difficult to ensure action. The increasingly complex nature of higher education means that more and more of the senior personnel of which the various committees are composed are subject to increasing pressures in their own institutions—whether these take the form of providing data for governmental agencies, or that of coping with daily personnel problems. Consequently, it frequently takes a long time to get things through the various groups and there have been occasions when subcommittees have become disillusioned by the inability of the senior committees, to which they report, to respond within a reasonable period of time.

Vertical Coordination

Perhaps the weakest point in the system is the vertical coordination between levels. It is only within the last two or so years that the various divisions of the ministry have begun to create internal coordinating structures. For instance, while the training of teachers concerns the university level at which the training takes place, it also concerns the primary and secondary levels, and, to a certain extent, the college level, for which the teachers are trained, not to mention teachers in vocational areas or those engaged in teaching adults. It is true that all levels are represented on the advisory Superior Council of Education and we have mentioned the liaison committees which exist between the secondary and the college levels, and between the college and the university levels, but these liaison committees have so far been primarily concerned with admission requirements. The ministry intends, however, to expand the activities of the university/college committee, and involve higher ranking university representatives. The Nadeau report attempted to sell the idea of postsecondary education as a continuum of "professional" studies (in the broadest sense of the term), but this notion has been dismissed by many as an attempt to abolish the college level in favor of the universities. So, political considerations in this area have tended to obscure the real issues.

Effectiveness

Manpower

Skilled manpower requirements are relatively easy to determine at a given point in time. They can be extrapolated into the future with varying degrees of reliability, but this decreases with the mounting speed of evolution of society's needs and the capacities required to meet them. In highly developed technological societies, one may wonder how accurately a postsecondary system can forecast future needs, either quantitatively or qualitatively and respond accordingly. The longer the time required to produce individuals with particular competences, the more difficult it is to carry out serious planning with any hope of accuracy.

Within these limits, determination of manpower needs presupposes effective contact between educational institutions and potential employers. These may be either of a continuing nature or they may take the form of individual studies. We have previously mentioned the three sectoral studies undertaken in the areas of applied sciences, health sciences, and pure sciences, conducted by the ministry with varying degrees of participation on the part of the Council of Universities and persons representing employers. It has been alleged that one of the weaknesses of the applied sciences' study is that little provision was made for adequate follow-up, which is necessary to make such studies more than a snapshot of a situation at a given point in time. It would seem that studies of this nature should take the iterative approach followed by the Council of Universities in its planning operation.

Reference has also been made to the Quebec Professions Board (Office des Professions), a body set up to offer protection to the public in a variety of professional fields, in particular those relating to health, business, law, engineering, architecture, and allied groups. (The Act which established the board lists some forty different bodies.) One of the main functions of the board is to ensure the regular updating of professional training, particularly through encouraging postsecondary institutions to offer appropriate courses or other activities. But the Act also defines a role for the board and the professional corporation concerned in the design of initial training and mandates joint responsibility on the part of institutions, board, and the corporation for establishing evaluative and licensing mechanisms. In order to ensure such collaboration, joint committees—composed of representatives of the recognized professional body and the universities and colleges concerned, including students—are being set up for each professional area. It is too early to assess the effectiveness of these committees, but the potential for manpower planning in the professional fields is certainly there.

At the college level over thirty provincial committees are concerned with vocational programs. With a few exceptions, these have not been particularly successful, probably because of their provincial scope. More fruitful contacts seem to be taking place at the regional level, where it is hoped that colleges will attract business and industry by ensuring the provision of skilled manpower. In large metropolitan centers such contacts are more difficult to make, largely because the interlocutors are more numerous and diversified.

Given the great interest throughout the postsecondary systems in recurrent education (*éducation permanente*), the possibilities for manpower planning, within the limits mentioned, are good.

The Division of Planning of the Ministry of Education has created an agency (*Groupe éducation et emploi*) with representatives of the Ministry of Labor and Manpower to ensure that at the secondary and, to an increasing degree, the college level appropriate training is offered for the various vocational fields.

Accessibility

A High School Leaving Certificate will normally admit a student to college. Tuition is free for full-time college students, and tuition fees at the university have been frozen for some years in the $450-600[19] range. The Loans and Bursaries Service of the Ministry of Education provides financial support for college and university students, taking into account existing individual and family resources, and normally requiring the students to work in the summer and turn over some of their earnings.

At the university level places are available for most students who receive a Diploma of College Studies (Diplôme d'études collégiales), although not all qualified candidates are guaranteed a place in the program of their choice. In fact, only 10 percent gain admission to medicine, and there are also restrictions in most institutions in such fields as dentistry, law, and psychology. Some universities, in particular Concordia and the Université du Québec, make almost all of their regular programs available to part-time students, most of whom take courses in the evening although there seems to be a growing demand for part-time studies during the daytime. Other institutions offer programs which are open only to adult learners. All universities accept as degree candidates persons who have been out of school for a few years even if they have not completed college or other prior studies. The acceptable minimum age for entering a university varies from twenty-one to twenty-three years old. In some cases make-up courses are available for those who did not acquire the necessary courses at lower levels. In the colleges, shortened programs which involve technical courses but eliminate general education courses are available to vocation-oriented students over twenty-one years old. The Université du Québec recently opened an Ecole de Technologie supérieure, which provides a three-year Bachelor of Technology program to those persons who have completed certain three-year programs in the colleges. The Université du Québec also serves the more remote regions of the province through its Télé-université, modeled to some extent on the British Open University.

Both the colleges and the universities offer a substantial range of noncredit courses to meet a wide variety of community needs. At the moment, there is a lack of coordination between the secondary, college, and university levels in this area, and, consequently, duplication occurs. On the other hand, a more restrictive policy—designed to eliminate unnecessary duplication—might run the risk of reducing flexibility and killing initiative. The notion of *éducation permanente*, in the sense of lifelong learning, is, however, much present at the postsecondary level, and it is anticipated that much future development will occur in this area. As we mentioned earlier, the Quebec Professions Board is already applying itself to ensuring the regular updating of professionals in a number of vital areas.

Research

There has been significant cooperation at the provincial level between the Council of Universities and the Ministry of Education in the FCAC (Formation des Chercheurs et Action concertée) operation, and universities have participated through six subcommittees set up to evaluate project proposals; the subcommittees have essentially been composed of faculty members. It has recently been suggested that the evaluation committees should include more nonuniversity members. Initially, the FCAC program stressed team projects, especially those likely to train young researchers, to which was subsequently added support for research centers. The latter part of the program is now being phased out in favor of broader-based "major research programs" within certain priority fields. These priorities have been set by the Ministry of Education without prior consultation with the council or the universities and, although there has not been much objection so far, there is great concern, both in the council and in the universities, that the ministry might act in an increasingly unilateral fashion, and, in the end, more or less dictate the directions which research is to take. There has also been increased emphasis on applied research, with an understandable concentration on the socioeconomic and cultural needs of Quebec society. There is concern that the emphasis on applied research will create problems for young scholars engaged in basic research who are not yet in a position to obtain federal support, and are less likely to do so with the leveling-off of federal funding.

Relationships between the council's Research Commission and the ministry have, therefore, been productive, but the recent swing to what appears to be a more directive role on the part of the ministry must presumably be interpreted as another example of the increasing role of the Treasury Board or other government agencies in the field of higher education. Apprehension has also been created by the fact that the major lines of development approved by the Council of Universities for each institution—and originally conceived by that body as not much more than a means of encouraging individual institutions to identify themselves within the system—appear to be used more and more as major criteria. In fact, some research proposals have recently been declared ineligible for funding on the grounds that they are not in keeping with these recognized lines of development. At the time of writing, the government has submitted a Green Paper on research to the Council of Universities. The paper explores university, governmental, and industrial aspects of research.

The Conference of Rectors maintains a Committee on Research, which, after a period of reduced effectiveness during the absence of the University of Quebec, has been collaborating well with the Research Commission of the Council of Universities, and played an active role in modifying restrictive legislation affecting research personnel.

Flexibility and Innovation

With the remarkable transformation of Quebec society over the past fifteen years, a number of major innovations have been possible—for example, introduction of the self-contained college level, providing the regular entry route to university as well as a range of terminal vocational programs. The innovative Université du Québec system was created. Over a hundred normal schools, many of them small church-related institutions, were integrated into the universities. The Parent Commission's recommendations on "democratization" were incorporated in the legislation setting up the public colleges and the Université du Québec. This principle, in relation both to accessibility and internal governance, has been introduced at various speeds and in varying forms in the other institutions. The potential exists for a reasonably high level of participation of faculty and students in the elaboration and evolution of curricula. Innovation tends to come from below rather than from above, and the system now seems to be going through the experience, common on the North-American continent at least, of trying to find a desirable equilibrium between overenthusiastic innovation and reinstatement of some of the traditional virtues that have been prematurely discarded. The desire for innovation has been most visible in the colleges, which as completely new institutions are not hidebound by traditions of the past.

The Council of Universities has shown considerable receptivity to innovation. For example, it accepted a proposal from one university for an interdisciplinary doctorate in humanities, in spite of fears that this might turn out to be simple carte blanche to offer *de facto* undisciplinary programs in areas where these do not exist. In another case, prompted perhaps more by pragmatism and a fine sense of political expediency rather than zeal for innovation, the council directed the creation of a doctoral program in business, to be given jointly by the four Montreal-based universities. In its reports on the evolution of the university system, the council has invited each institution to identify an area (*secteur modèle*) in which it would like to experiment. As so often happens, scarcity of resources constitutes an obstacle to innovation, but the ministry has hitherto been prepared to consider special cases in this area.

The Université du Québec was created with the view that it would be innovative. It was to stress serving part-time students and to take on a major role in all aspects of teacher training. In an attempt to get away from "disciplinism" it was structured so that faculty would still be organized by department, but students would be grouped in theme-oriented "modules," using departmental services, but involving both faculty and students in their planning and general operation. Such a structure was made possible by the fact that the university with its constituents, though they were in some cases largely a reorganization of existing institutions, was conceived by a group of young and dynamic planners, working essentially from outside the system. As it has turned out, the modular structure is still far from being generally accepted, one of the problems being that of harmonizing vertical and horizontal components. An evaluation is due shortly.

One of the constituent elements of the Université du Québec is the Télé-université, which was identified by the Council of Universities in 1973 as one of the main experimental operations of that institution. Its title is etymological — education at a distance — and television plays a small part in its activities, less than 8 percent in 1975. It has so far aimed mainly at adults and has been used primarily in refresher courses for teachers of mathematics and of French. It is expected to use existing resources as much as possible and to make the results of its experimentation available to other elements in the system.

Another experiment, this time at the college level, which does not as yet appear to have left much of a mark, is the public Collège Montmorency, designed to make extensive use of library and audiovisual materials. Its local sponsors were successful in catching the imagination of the associate deputy minister responsible for college education and of the deputy minister himself. As a result, resources were provided by the ministry to appoint senior administrators for the college some two years ahead of construction, so that they could conduct a detailed survey of similar types of institutions elsewhere. It remains to be seen whether this institution will act as a stimulus for the system.

At a less spectacular level, the Division of College Education, taking the view that research at the college level is most important in the area of pedagogy, regularly provides funds for experimentation. For example, one college received $100,000 for a project designed to improve reading skills, and $60,000 for another in the field of computer-assisted instruction.

Efficiency

Planning

If planning involves making the optimum use of available resources, then the main problem, apart from the specter of shrinking resources, is the fact that the budgeting periods are so short. So far, it can be said that the universities have never had anything but the foggiest notion of the resources likely to be available to them even three or four years ahead, and, as has been noted, operating grants are still worked out from year to year. Furthermore, almost everything is either in, or coming out of, a state of transition. The French-language sector is still catching up in terms of participation rates, while the English-language universities are adjusting to the obligatory college level. Political and social ferment makes forecasts of student populations much more than a simple demographic exercise. The provincial government, however, has not yet succumbed to the temptation to dictate, and the consultative process, proceeding largely by consensus rather than by formal edict, has been less inefficient than might be expected. Each year, however, the shadow of the Treasury Board looms larger. Even while ministers talk about decentralization, and the Council of Universities stresses diversity, austerity leads toward uniformization.

Administration

The postsecondary systems are recent phenomena, even if some of the institutions which compose them have a long and distinguished history. They have not yet had the time to build up a large anonymous bureaucracy, despite claims to the contrary on the part of some self-appointed liberators. Deputy ministers, and even ministers, have tended to be from the educational world, and efficiency of administration is often facilitated by relationships at the personal level. Clear and timely decisions on funding, however, have not been forthcoming from the higher levels of government, so that the ministry's hands have often been tied. Delayed decisions on budgeting result in last-minute scrambles at the institutional level; administrators frequently have to go out on a limb financially. It all comes down to the fact that it is difficult to staff a new program for implementation in September of a given year when funds are not authorized until late spring of that same year.

In view of the fact that the capacity of a certain number of programs at both levels cannot meet the demand, there is a tendency for students to make multiple applications to postsecondary institutions. Clearing-houses exist in the Montreal and Quebec regions to coordinate admissions to the colleges within the respective areas. The possibility of setting up a central admissions office for the universities has been raised unofficially in some quarters. However, such a step seems unlikely at the moment, partly because the universities are afraid of losing control over their own admissions, and because the central computerized operations have not been too successful, but mostly because the small number of institutions, especially where two language-based subsystems exist, does not seem to warrant the time, effort, and expense.

The procedures involved in the Council of Universities' approval of new programs are seen by many to be unnecessarily time-consuming. In the past, given the time required for internal institutional evaluation, the process has usually taken about three years, from the first gleam of inspiration in a faculty member's eye to the admission of the first students. The Council of Universities is aware of the delays and attempts are being made to reduce the time involved, but the fact that the ministry acts on the financing of new programs only once a year creates inevitable delays.

One of the more frustrating delays occurs in the area of nominations. A genuine attempt to conduct wide consultation has been maintained in the selection of members of the Superior Council and its commissions, the Council of Universities, and governing boards of colleges and certain universities, and here one can certainly fault those consulted for not always being prompt in responding; but the principal delays appear to occur in the processing of nominations by government order-in-council. As an example, student members of college boards are nominated for a one-year term, and frequently half of their term is over before the appointment comes through.

Coordinating Bodies

The coordinating bodies suffer from the fact that, apart from a handful of full-time personnel, the participants are persons who already carry heavy responsibilities in their respective institutions. Given the current restlessness in the system, persons with line responsibilities—in the area of personnel, for example—are particularly hard-pressed to attend meetings. Similarly, the pressure of internal concerns upon decision-making bodies within individual institutions makes it difficult to obtain prompt reactions to proposals presented by the coordinating bodies. Perhaps it would be fairest to say that it is remarkable how much is achieved under the circumstances, and to underline the very significant contributions made so far by a small number of individuals in leading positions. One of the most difficult accomplishments at the institutional level is to instill an awareness of the difference between legislative and coordinating bodies among academic personnel, and to modify the all-too-common perception that everybody outside the institution, including its own representatives on external bodies, constitutes a grey, insensitive, and menacing "they."

In closing, it must be stated that Quebec is also subject to those problems which are widespread in North America — for example, the age-profile of tenured faculty which will make it difficult to bring in younger people. Those universities which have expanded very rapidly in the past ten or fifteen years are particularly vulnerable to this phenomenon. Overshadowing all considerations, however, is the political and economic uncertainty brought about by the recent change of government. It remains to be seen how much the relatively stable situation in the Ministry of Education will respond to a new minister, how much the Minister of State for Cultural Development will influence the educational world, and whether the advisory and coordinating bodies will be able to maintain a satisfactory degree of autonomy. Quebec is indeed a province *"pas comme les autres."*

FOOTNOTES

1. Hugh MacLennan, *Two Solitudes* (Toronto: Collins, 1945).
2. The government had refused Loyola's application for a university charter on the grounds that this would create a disproportionate number of university institutions for the English-language minority. Loyola was therefore urged to investigate the possibilities of merger with an existing university.
3. These are contained in an annual publication of the Ministry of Education, entitled *Cahiers de l'enseignement collégial.*
4. Under the terms of the Private General or Handicapped Children Education Act of 1968.
5. *Report of the Royal Commission of Inquiry on Education in the Province of Quebec* (Quebec: Government of Quebec, 1963-1966) (Original French).
6. Originally proposed in the Act as a Commission of Technical and Vocational Education.
7. No. 3 (1966).

8. No. 4 (1966).
9. The report was published in three volumes: the first a description of the status quo; the second an essay on the future of university education which was later incorporated, together with a certain number of specific studies, in René Hurtubise et al., *L'Université québécoise du proche avenir*, (Montreal: HMH, 1973). The third contains an outline of the character and strengths of each institution, and proposes major lines of development for the future.
10. *The College: Report on the State and Needs of College Education* (Quebec: The Superior Council of Education, 1976) (Original French version, 1975).
11. A brief description of this operation by its director is to be found in Serge Lapointe, "La planification sectorielle: L'Opération sciences fondamentales," *Canadian Journal of Higher Education*, Vol. 6, No. 3 (1976), pp. 43-49.
12. The first of these appeared in March 1976 as volume 4 of the 1972-73 report, under the title *Perspective 1976 des orientations de l'enseignement supérieur*.
13. Both Laval and the Montréal constituent of the Université du Québec were closed down for four months during the 1976-77 academic year.
14. Carried out under the aegis of the Comité d'élaboration d'un système informatique de gestion universitaire, which functioned between 1969 and 1973.
15. Vol. II, recommendation 133.
16. Vol. I, paragraph 199.
17. Vol. II, paragraph 367.
18. From 1969 to 1974 the English-language universities operated two-year college programs, while public and private colleges were being set up. Although, at the time of merger, Loyola was technically a classical college affiliated with the Université de Montréal, which granted its degrees, it was in every way an undergraduate liberal arts institution.
19. The figure quoted is for the "regular" September to May session.

ONTARIO
B. B. Kymlicka

Ontario is the most populous and the most developed province of Canada. Its eight million inhabitants constitute 36 percent of the total Canadian population. It also contains the most industrialized and urbanized areas of the country. Ontario is the nerve center for the financial and cultural activities of English-speaking Canada. Its importance was accentuated after World War II when it experienced rapid population growth—both as a result of the baby boom and because it was the recipient of the heaviest immigration, from other provinces and other countries.

Inevitably, such a rich and varied society developed a highly complex and extensive postsecondary educational system.[1] Both the extent and variety of this system increased during the 1960s. For example, in 1961 only 27,000, about 6 percent, of the eighteen- to twenty-four-year-old age group was enrolled full-time in some kind of postsecondary institution; in 1976-77, Statistics Canada estimates a total full-time enrollment of 228,440—21 percent of the age group.[2] During the same period, the number and types of institutions offering postsecondary education increased dramatically. The number of universities increased from eleven to eighteen (including the Ryerson Polytechnical Institute, the Ontario Institute for Studies in Education, and the Ontario College of Art). Based in part on existing technical institutes and adult training centers, the provincial government created a whole new system of community colleges—called Colleges of Applied Arts and Technology (CAATs)—that comprises twenty-two separate institutions, some with a number of campuses.[3] There are also four colleges specializing in agriculture.

But the proliferation of institutions, startling as it was, does not indicate the complexity of the system. New professional schools—

law, medicine, engineering, and colleges of education—were created within the universities and there was a remarkable increase in graduate programs. Within the CAATs, nearly 2,000 programs are now being offered.[4]

For the most part, this growth was accomplished by public funds. A 1972 Commission on Post-Secondary Education report estimated that in 1951-52 the universities of Ontario received a total of some $16 million in public funds and the remaining postsecondary institutions received an additional $2 million for a grand total of $18 million;[5] the comparable sum in 1976-77 is estimated by Statistics Canada to be $1.5 billion.[6] As a consequence, the government of Ontario plays a dominant, and increasingly bureaucratic, role in the policy making and administration of postsecondary education in the province.

Indeed, it is possible to view the development of higher education in Ontario over the last ten or fifteen years as being dominated by one characteristic: the governmental takeover of all aspects of postsecondary education either through the creation of new, public institutions or through increased (both absolute and relative) financial support to the existing public and/or private institutions. Interwoven with that trend are the institutional responses to governmental takeover: alternate demands for greater funds and insistence on autonomy; the changing economic and social conditions within the province and the corresponding ideological changes as reflected in the rhetoric and in the articulated aims and objectives of government; and the internal changes the institutions themselves have undergone as they tried to accommodate themselves to government pressures and to faculty and student insistence on greater participation in the governance of the institutions.

Nor is there any indication that a long-lasting solution—procedural, substantive, or jurisdictional—is in sight. On the contrary, the government's shifting of priorities away from postsecondary education, the greater and greater centralization of decision making in government bureaucracies, the trend toward unionization of faculty and support staff and, potentially most important, the demographic trends are all likely to generate increased uncertainty with respect to the aims and responsibility of postsecondary education.

It is, in fact, possible to argue that in spite of the extent of government influence, the government—considering the power available to it—has exercised remarkable restraint. Compared with other jurisdictions, direct control of individual institutions by the Ministry of Colleges and Universities has been limited and filtered through its advisory committees and the collective organizations of the universities and their faculties.

Institutional Framework of Education in Ontario

Figure 1 provides an outline of the formal structure of postsecondary education in Ontario. It is worth noting that since 1973, CAATs have gradually taken over institutions that are responsible for training nurses—a transfer of some 9,500 students from fifty-six nursing schools formerly associated with hospitals.[7] Note also that Grade 13 is part of the secondary school system, though under the fiscal arrangements with the provinces to 1977 the federal government counted the senior matriculation year (Grade 13 in Ontario) as part of postsecondary education. In 1974, Ontario received $41,551,388 from Ottawa to support the 51,074 students enrolled in Grade 13 in public schools.[8]

The administration of the whole system is varied and bears traces of the historical origins of the various component parts. The major elements—community colleges (CAATs) and especially universities—are marked by jurisdictional uncertainties. In the smaller subsystems—such as the colleges of agricultural technology, offering mostly diploma courses and under the direct jurisdiction of the Ministry of Agriculture and Food—the relation is clearer and more traditional. In the professional fields, especially in the health-related professions, administration is complicated by the role played by the Ministry of Health and various professional organizations. More recently, all postsecondary educational institutions became subject to detailed scrutiny by the federal Department of Manpower and Immigration. The department declared that "the occupational demand factor for teachers at postsecondary level has been permanently reduced to zero thereby making manpower validation a mandatory requirement for the selection of academics as immigrants."[9] In implementing this directive, the federal Department of Manpower and Immigration works in close cooperation with the provincial Ministry of Colleges and Universities. The result has been that a new, and far more stringent, procedure for obtaining an immigration visa for non-Canadian faculty members has been imposed. Thus, the scrutiny the government had been applying to immigrant doctors was extended to all prospective faculty members in postsecondary education. In the universities, of course, this limits one of the traditional — and oft-proclaimed — tenets of institutional autonomy in the area of determining who shall teach.

The two main components of postsecondary education in Ontario, the twenty-two colleges of applied arts and technology and the eighteen universities, report to the same provincial department — the Ministry of Colleges and Universities (MCU). Associated with the MCU are two bodies that, while they have a similar name, have different powers. One, the Council of Regents for Colleges of Applied Arts and Technology, is in effect the provincial governing board of the colleges; the other, the Ontario Council on University Affairs (OCUA), is strictly an advisor to the minister of colleges and universities. Unlike the Council of Regents, the OCUA possesses no executive powers. Originally, both councils were served by staff of the Ministry of Colleges and Universities. Recently, however, the OCUA has developed its own, though very small, secretariat. The minister, of course, is also advised by the staff of his own ministry — a feature that, in the area of university affairs, is more apparent than in the case of the CAATs.

The individual universities (with the sole exception of the University of Toronto which has a unicameral form of government) and the CAATs are managed by boards of governors. Their composition varies, but most of them have some members appointed by the Council of Regents, some by local governments, and some selected by the boards themselves. In the case of universities, some have elected members from the academic community, both students and faculty as well as representatives of the support staff. No college has faculty or student representatives on its board. In the case of universities, the power of the boards of governors is shared by academic senates or their counterparts; faculties in the CAATs have little power with respect to academic self-government. The university senates are dominated by elected faculty members. Some senates have also a substantial student representation. Both types of institutions have presidents as chief executive officers and they use similar nomenclature for their middle management —

deans, directors, chairmen of departments, and so on. All CAATs have unionized faculty and staff and negotiate their conditions of employment on a provincewide basis with the Council of Regents. A few of the universities have unionized faculty members (fewer still have unionized nonacademic staff, with the exception of some tradesmen), though there seems to be a movement toward some kind of collective bargaining in most of them.

The universities, as institutions, and their faculty associations have formed and developed provincial associations. The organization that expresses the institutional interest is the Council of Ontario Universities with headquarters in Toronto. The council grew out of the earlier Committee of Presidents and now plays a vital role in the administration of the provincial university system. It has considerable professional and other staff that serve as liaisons among the OCUA, the MCU, and the individual institutions. The Ontario Confederation of University Faculty Associations (OCUFA) also has a central office in Toronto; its strength, however, seems to lie more in its potential political influence than in any formal meshing of its activities with the government and its bodies. The nonacademic staffs have only recently developed provincewide links by forming the Confederation of Ontario University Staff Associations (COUSA). The students are the least organized, though there are perennial attempts to forge a provincewide student organization. Since the late 1960s, however, these attempts have not been very successful, although there is a fluctuating affiliation of student councils from individual institutions within the Ontario Federation of Students, a provincial body.

Although the boards of governors and presidents of the colleges of applied arts and technology have a provincial association, it has no central office or professional staff. It is possible that the colleges either feel no need to organize or that the Council of Regents looks disfavorably upon such a development. As we have mentioned, both the faculties and the support staff of colleges are unionized and engage in collective bargaining with the Council of Regents through the Ontario Public Service Employees Union. College students, as those of the universities, have a spotty record of forming provincial ties.

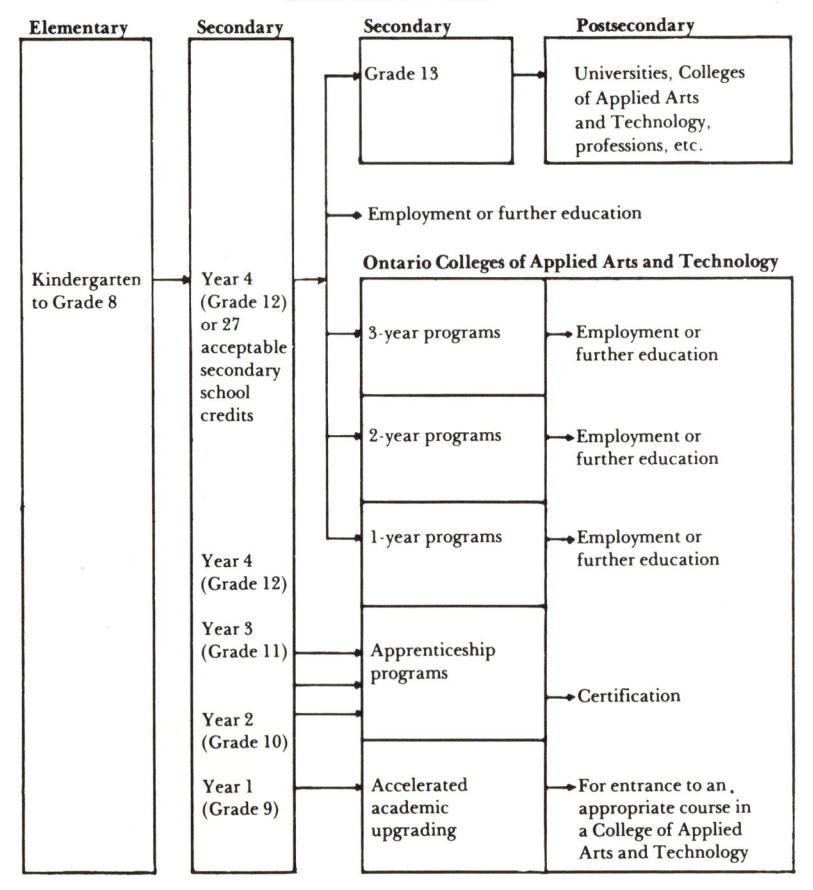

FIGURE 1
Educational Flow-Chart

Elementary	Secondary	Secondary	Postsecondary
Kindergarten to Grade 8	Year 4 (Grade 12) or 27 acceptable secondary school credits	Grade 13	Universities, Colleges of Applied Arts and Technology, professions, etc.

→ Employment or further education

Ontario Colleges of Applied Arts and Technology

- 3-year programs → Employment or further education
- 2-year programs → Employment or further education
- 1-year programs → Employment or further education

Year 4 (Grade 12)
Year 3 (Grade 11)
Year 2 (Grade 10)

- Apprenticeship programs → Certification

Year 1 (Grade 9)

- Accelerated academic upgrading → For entrance to an appropriate course in a College of Applied Arts and Technology

Source: *Horizons,* June 1976.

1. Honor graduates of the four-year programs may be accepted for enrollment in a three-year college program.
2. Grade 13 graduates may be accepted with advanced credits to certain programs.
3. An applicant who does not have a clear admission may be given the opportunity to write qualifying examinations.
4. After assessment, deserving applicants may be eligible for advanced standings and/or for accelerated programs.
5. Refer to the official college publications for specific admission requirements, and detailed information on programs, including starting dates.

Universities

Coordination

Until the 1950s there was no formal government office dealing with universities in Ontario. In 1951, the provincial government appointed a part-time consultant on university affairs. The order-in-council stated: "It is expedient to establish a close liaison between the government and universities of Ontario with a view to greater coordination of the universities' work and to provide for the advising of the government upon the manner of distribution of provincial and federal grants."[10]

Characteristically, the first advisor was a retired university principal, R. C. Wallace. When this advisor was found to be "too gentle to crack the whip,"[11] the government appointed a succession of educational bureaucrats and former politicians. With increased direct governmental expenditure on universities—from $8 million in 1951 to $20 million in 1958—the government created a University Committee, consisting exclusively of senior civil servants. Because this committee began to ask questions and collect information on what was then considered internal university affairs (salaries, teaching loads, and so on), the university community and its supporters complained about the composition of the committee and, in 1961, were successful in persuading the government to change its membership to include representatives of the public. Thus, the search for an impartial "buffer" that would give the government good and acceptable advice and also protect the universities from direct governmental intervention began.

The quest, of course, was for a mythical beast, though the myth that sustains it is a useful one and provides the necessary rhetorical justification for the institutions' reluctance to surrender whatever remains of their independence. By the same token, it allows the government to direct policies without being formally responsible for the consequences. In 1964, as a result of urging by the Committee of Presidents, the membership of what was then called the Committee on University Affairs was again changed—this time to include five academic representatives. But the new members comprised only a minority on the committee. In 1967, an academic, Douglas T. Wright, was appointed full-time chairman.[12] He was succeeded in that position by another academic, J. Gordon Parr, who went on to become the deputy minister in the Ministry of Colleges and Universities. Following a brief period during which a psychologist and prominent member of many governmental advisory bodies in education, Reva Gerstein, served as chairman, J. Stefan Dupré, a university professor, then became chairman, and the committee was renamed the Ontario Council on University Affairs (OCUA). Dupré was succeeded in turn by William C. Winegard, a former Ontario university president.

There are two additional and important aspects to the development of the OCUA: one is that its jurisdiction has expanded and its activities have been intensified; the other lies in its relation to the other body created by the government to deal with the universities—the Department of University Affairs and its successor, the Ministry of Colleges and Universities.

In many ways, the seeds of the OCUA's present authority can be seen in the 1951 order-in-council which provided for a part-time consultant. Broad in scope, it foreshadowed the equally far-reaching powers given to the succeeding committees. For example, in 1964 the restructured Committee on University Affairs (CUA) was given the following mandate (which had also been given to its predecessor, the "Advisory Committee on University Affairs"): "to study matters concerning the establishment, development, operation, expansion, and financing of universities in Ontario and to make recommendations thereon to the minister of university affairs for the information and advice of the government." Moreover, because it was merely advisory, it was, and is, possible for the CUA, and now the OCUA, to venture into areas that a formal government ministry might find more politically difficult to enter.

Financial Support

The earliest, and the most obvious area in which the government exhibited interest in postsecondary education was in financial support. The primary task of the first, part-time, consultants was to advise the government "upon the manner of distribution of provincial and federal grants." By 1960, the University Committee was charged with receiving requests from universities with respect to their financial needs, both capital and operating, to gather the information needed for making decisions concerning grants for these purposes, and to advise the minister of education on the amounts of annual grants.[13]

Slowly, but surely, the informal system—in which the premier of the province, following a luncheon or meeting with the president of a university, decided how much money the provincial government would contribute to that institution—was replaced by a more formal, but still bilateral, relation between the advisory committee and the institution. As the amount distributed became larger, the government found it necessary to establish a mechanism for distributing the funds in a demonstrably equitable manner—that is, it began to look upon the institutions as one system. Happily, this desire coincided with the wishes of the newly created Committee of Presidents of the Provincially Assisted Universities and Colleges of Ontario (later called the Committee of Presidents of Universities of Ontario and now flourishing under the name of the Council of Ontario Universities). A number of committees, most of them joint committees of the CUA with the Committee of Presidents, were established to deal with financial issues and from them the policy that was to dominate financial support of universities from 1967 to the present evolved: formula financing.

The formula was devised more through negotiations than fact-finding, and it was based upon a basic income unit (BIU), estimated to be equivalent to the annual cost of instruction of a first-year undergraduate student in the arts and pure sciences. Students who were enrolled in more expensive programs were assigned an additional "weight," depending on the agreed and estimated cost of their programs. The highest weight was six, for the support of Ph.D. students. To determine the amount of a university's grant, the value of the BIU—determined by the government—was multiplied by the weighted number of students enrolled. From this the total of tuition fees, figured according to a standard scale, was subtracted. The grant was then equal to the difference.[14]

It was claimed that the purpose of the formula was "to provide an objective mechanism for determining the share of the total provincial operating grant to be allocated to each university."[15] Its advantages were to be that it would provide: equitable treatment, preservation of university autonomy,[16] government control of the magnitude of university grants, facilitation of long-range planning on the part of universities, and an incentive to efficient management. By not considering private donations, the formula also reassured both the donors and the institutions that any acts of generosity would not result in deductions from government grants.

Needless to say, the very simplicity of the policy, and hence its chief virtue, was soon compromised by equally simple vices. Increased enrollment and the concomitant proliferation of programs (especially at the graduate level), quickly demonstrated that additional policies were needed to coordinate the system as a whole. The result was a multiplication of interpretive rules and modifications of the policy itself. Table 1 provides a brief summary of major changes in the formula since 1967-68.

TABLE 1
Summary of Major Changes in the Formúla Since 1967–68

Year	BIU Value	Formula Weights	Counting of Students
1967-68	$1,320		
1968-69	$1,450 + $24 computer grant		
1969-70	$1,530 + $26 computer grant	(i) undergraduate medicine 3.0 to 5.0 (ii) undergraduate dentistry 3.0 to 5.0 (iii) undergraduate veterinary med. 3.0 to 5.0 (iv) interns and residents 1.5 to 2.5 (v) thesis only category (wt 1.0) discontinued students to be claimed either as full or part-time	(i) definition of graduate students for category 5 requires only general not honors degree plus other new conditions. (ii) FTE part-time graduates including graduate summer school changed from a division of course registrations by 5 to a multiplication of part-time numbers by .30 reported and weighted on a trimester basis.
1970-71	$1,650 computer grant incorporated in BIU value	(i) optometry from 2.0 to 3.0	(i) graduate summer school conversion factor changed from .30 to .50
1971-72	$1,730		(i) 10-month fiscal year. (ii) graduate formula fee increased from $133 per term to $242.50 per term, free third term introduced
1972-73	$1,765		(i) conversion factor for part-time undergraduates changed from course registrations divided by 6.0 to division by 5.5 for institutions with integrated full- and part-time programs. (ii) $100 increase in formula fee for two terms (iii) free third term ended; graduate bursary introduced
1973-74	$1,825		(i) slip year introduced (ii) part-time undergraduate conversion factor to 5.0
1974-75	$1,955	(i) upper years undergraduate social work from 1.0 to 1.5 (ii) masters social work 3.0 to 4.0 (iii) forestry technology 1.0 to 1.2 (iv) engineering technology 1.0 to 1.2	
1975-76	$2,111		(i) graduate bursary terminated
1976-77	$2,312 undergraduate $2,555 graduate		(i) undergraduate enrollment based on 1/3 1974-75 and 2/3 1975-76, graduate based on 1975-76 actual with 2 year freeze. (ii) foreign student fee of $750 term based on current enrollment. (iii) fractional unit counting introduced. (iv) three-term undergraduate reporting.

Source: Ontario Operating Formula Manual, Ministry of Colleges and Universities (June, 1976), p. 27.

As can be seen from Table 1, the formula was suspended for two (now three) years with respect to graduate studies. The various committees of all concerned organizations are now attempting to devise a new policy to replace the formula both for graduate and undergraduate studies. It is also necessary to point out that, from the very beginning, formula financing was not the only instrument used in the distribution of operating grants to universities. Recently established institutions received extra-formula grants ranging up to twice the amounts calculated by the formula. Originally called "emergent university grants," the title of these funds was changed to "compensatory grants"[17] and later simply "supplementary grants."[18] In addition, and in line with the announced government policy to provide special help for education in northern Ontario, institutions located in that sparsely populated region receive supplementary funds. To accommodate the financial burden imposed on the bilingual institutions, the government also provides special funds to six institutions to ease that cost. All in all about 80 percent of the universities' operating revenue comes from the government, 15 percent from students, and 5 percent from private sources. The formula provides for the distribution of 95 percent of the government share.

Important as the distribution of the operating grants was, it soon became apparent that other funding areas also needed revision. A joint committee, similar to the one responsible for operating grants, was established to deal with capital grants. More complex, and less obviously impinging upon the autonomy of the university, the matter of building or renovating costs was from the very beginning almost wholly in the hands of the provincial government. Thus the committee dealt not only with enrollment projections and inventories of space and its utilization,[19] but also with the "organization of building" and with "design criteria:" ". . . there are increasing indications that some radical rethinking of design criteria is required to provide more effectively for flexibility of future use and occupancy, to acknowledge the likely probability that the economic life for nonmonumental building is not more than forty or fifty years. . . ."[20] From its beginning in 1964, the Department of University Affairs had an architectural services branch that assessed capital project requests from the provincially assisted universities. Final approval, however, had to be obtained from the Ontario Universities' Capital Aid Corporation, chaired by the deputy provincial treasurer.

For a brief period, the government allowed the universities to engage in building expansion and, provided they stayed within the cost limits imposed by the Architectural Services Branch of the ministry, the institutions could calculate their "entitlement" to capital grants with relative ease. This policy, as the OCUA complained in its Second Annual Report, "was temporarily suspended by the imposition of the near-moratorium in 1972. But the intervening years have exceeded the bounds of the temporary, and generated what council deems to be a policy vacuum."[21] As in the case of operating grants, the system is now attempting to define a new policy to govern capital grants.

Although financial issues led to the establishment of the governmental bodies in the area of postsecondary education—and attracted their earliest attention—it soon became apparent that financial considerations cannot be easily separated from other, including academic, matters. It was natural that the early part-time consultants, coming as they did mostly from the Department of Education, should express interest in the salaries of professors, their teaching loads, and other activities. With the restructuring of the CUA in 1964, and especially after 1967, the attention shifted to other areas: graduate studies, research, computing facilities, libraries, and medical education, to name a few, became the subject of special inquiries—at times sponsored by joint committees of the OCUA, MCU, and COU. The inquiries showed the gradually expanding administrative curiosity, if not always claimed jurisdiction, of the governmental bodies. More revealing, and probably indicative of things to come, is the MCU, OCUA, and COU participation in the Tripartite Committee on Macro-Indicators. According to the committee's first report (issued in March 1977), its origins lie in a meeting of COU, MCU, and CUA officials in February 1974: "At that meeting, MCU officials sought detailed information that would enable the minister to make the universities' case for adequate provincial support to the cabinet and before the legislature."[22] The Council of Ontario Universities demurred, but offered to provide "macro-indicators." About one year later, the chairman of the CUA wrote to each of the Ontario universities asking for the promised "macro-indicators" and it responded by offering a faculty/student ratio. On June 2, 1975, Dr. Dupré, chairman of the newly appointed OCUA, sought and obtained the agreement of the MCU and COU to establish the Tripartite Committee. The activities of the committee revealed the most common battleground upon which the universities meet the government and its advisory bodies: the collection and interpretation of information dealing with the essential activities of the universities—notably the teaching of students. Considering the origins of the committee and its composition, it was not surprising that "it became evident that neither the Statistics Canada nor MCU's . . . forms provided fully satisfactory information on numbers of faculty in Ontario's Universities."[23] Nor is it surprising to read that the COU objected to a new system of data gathering and consequently the committee decided "to confine its activities to analyzing and refining, where possible, existing sources of student and faculty data."

The reason why the information sought by the Tripartite Committee is important lies in the increased complexity of considerations that go into determining the increase in the BIU for operating grants. Ever since one former minister of colleges and universities proclaimed the need to get "more scholar for the dollar," government has been insistent on holding the unit cost of postsecondary education down. As a result, both the OCUA and the MCU now consider the following factors before deciding on an increase in the BIU: prospective increases in wages and salaries; fringe benefits; inflationary pressures on nonsalary items; maintenance of services; something the OCUA calls the "efficiency factor" (one suspects an arbitrarily arrived at judgment of how much the universities can be squeezed—it was 1.5 percent of the 1976-77 calculations and 1 percent is proposed for 1977-78); excess capacity factor (i.e., a differential of marginal costs between institutions with capacity enrollments and those below it); and consideration of revenue other than fees obtained by the universities. This is a far cry from the simplicity that marked the beginning of formula financing; it is still, however, a fair distance from the tight control the government has over the CAATs, as we shall see later.

Ministry of Colleges
and Universities

The government's interest in the affairs of universities has been strengthened, particularly by the creation, in 1964, of the Department of University Affairs. Prior to that, governmental functions in relation to universities were undertaken by the Department of

Education. The university community, by and large, supported the creation of a new government department devoted exclusively to the affairs of universities. It was certainly preferable to remaining under the auspices of the Department of Education, with its long history of a highly centralized administration, especially since at that time, it was in the primary stages of creating a new subsystem of postsecondary education — the colleges of applied arts and technology. The Act establishing the Department of University Affairs was brief but broad, and successive Acts have retained that basic characteristic in so far as universities are concerned. After seven years, the department was enlarged by the transfer from the Department of Education of its applied arts and technology branch and the Council of Regents — both responsible for the administration of CAATs — to the renamed Department of Colleges and Universities.

Following the recommendations for reorganization of the government made by the Committee on Government Productivity in 1972-73,[24] the departments were renamed ministries and the Ministry of Colleges and Universities was given some additional responsibilities (in particular, those dealing with apprenticeship training and certification, transferred to it from the Department of Labour). Some of these newly acquired responsibilities were later transferred again to other ministries. By 1975 there were 675 employees in the Ministry of Colleges and Universities.[25] Although the minister claimed that in 1975 there were only twenty people employed in the University Affairs Division of the MCU,[26] this was an understatement. The ministry also includes a number of branches that supply common services to both the universities and colleges divisions. The department's student awards section alone, even before amalgamation, had around one hundred employees.

By any measurement, the Ministry of Colleges and Universities has grown into a major organization. Unlike the early Department of University Affairs, which was located on one floor of an office building and shared quarters with the advisory Committee on University Affairs, there is both physical and, one is led to believe, administrative separation between the MCU and the OCUA. The ministry's interests are becoming increasingly distinct from those of the OCUA, as can be seen in the composition of the Tripartite Committee. Obviously, the ministry, being the sole possessor of executive powers, generates attitudes and demands different from those of the advisory OCUA. It was for this reason, and in order to protect the collective independence of the Ontario universities, that the Commission on Post-Secondary Education recommended in 1972 that the government transfer some of the executive functions (especially those dealing with the distribution of grants and with coordination) to the OCUA—a proposition that, perhaps understandably, was not accepted by the government.

But the thorny issue of responsibility has not been tackled and provincewide planning and coordination is taking place through a complex process of negotiations between all those involved. It is a matter for speculation whether such a system can cope with the upcoming problems and whether MCU will resist the temptation to display the awesome powers available to it through financial control and through the broad delegation of jurisdiction, still dormant, in the Act that created it.

Voluntary Cooperation

Given increased government intervention in postsecondary education, it was only a matter of time before the individual institutions realized they could be better served if they spoke to the government with a single voice. Indeed, this was even the wish of the government and, especially, of the Advisory Committee on University Affairs, which called the first meeting of the presidents of the Ontario universities in March 1962.[27] Here, the presidents were told that university enrollment projections, made for the government by R. W. B. Jackson, far exceeded the current capacities of the institutions, and the committee asked the universities for advice.[28] Although the presidents perceived the urgency and saw the need to participate, they were also aware of the ambiguous status of their group and thus questioned the validity and duration of any proposals they might make to the government. As presidents, they could not commit their institutions to expansion without the concurrence of their boards of governors. They also felt they should discuss the issues with their senates, and, frankly, they did not fully trust each other since there had been occasions when chairmen of boards and/or presidents had approached the government directly. There was also the newly created Ontario Council of University Faculty Associations that claimed the right to participate in the development of any policies.[29]

Still, from 1962 on there developed a system of voluntary cooperation among the institutions on a provincewide basis. Over the years, the Council of Ontario Universities (COU)—as the Committee of Presidents was renamed in 1971, reflecting an earlier decision to include an "academic colleague" in each university's representation—thrived though it never completely succeeded in overcoming the inherent problems we have mentioned earlier. The scope and complexity of its activities have been described by its recent chief executive officer, John B. Macdonald, as comprising the largest higher education consortium in North America.[30] In addition to the expected committees devoted to nominations, information, operating and capital financing, student aid, and so on, the COU also has a great number of affiliates ranging from councils of various deans (law, engineering, arts and science, and so forth) to associations of computer services directors, registrars, and sundry service personnel.

The COU exhibits all the characteristics of a federated—or even confederated—system: it can move and act only if practically all members agree to do so. Inevitably, it takes considerable time for all individual members to agree on anything, and time often overtakes it. As all voluntary associations, it finds it easier to oppose a common enemy than to initiate any binding policies that would tie its members. It has no powers other than those allocated to it by its institutional members—and they can take these back at will. If it is to present a common front to the government, it must reconcile the interests of a diverse membership which ranges from a small, basically undergraduate, college to a large multiversity.

Looked at from this perspective, it is remarkable how successful the COU has been. No doubt, much of the credit for the success of the COU must go to the professional staff it has engaged—from Edward F. Sheffield (1966-68) to John B. Macdonald (1968-76), who served as the chief executive officers. It is also possible that the government and its advisory bodies find the COU a useful intermediary, that it assures the necessary cooperation of the institutions in compliance with the wishes of the government. As with most pressure groups, the COU has developed a symbiotic relationship with the OCUA and MCU.

There is, perhaps, no better way in which to illustrate the universities' COU-OCUA-MCU linkage than to describe the development of controls imposed on graduate studies. The Advisory Committee on Graduate Studies, established in 1964, soon became an affiliate of the Committee of Presidents in 1966, and was renamed the Ontario Council on Graduate Studies (OCGS). Because it was generally agreed that not all universities should have Ph.D. programs in all fields, the OCGS proposed a system of appraisal prior to approval of any new Ph.D. programs. However, because the OCGS was an offshoot of the voluntary Committee of Presidents, participation by individual institutions could not be enforced. The teeth were supplied by the government: it proclaimed that it would not fund any new Ph.D. (or, for that matter, master's) programs if they did not successfully pass the appraisal procedure. Subsequently, an Advisory Committee on Academic Planning (ACAP)[31] was formed "to guide the development of provincial discipline groups and to coordinate the work of rationalizing graduate studies in the province."[32] Thus, a "planning assessment" procedure, concerned with need, was added to the appraisal procedure concerned with quality.

In 1971 the Ministry of Colleges and Universities placed a general embargo on the funding of all new graduate programs — a drastic measure somewhat modified by later developments. As the COU *Review 1972-73 to 1974-75* put it:[33]

Modifications to the embargo list occur in two ways.

1. ACAP was given the task of conducting, for each embargoed discipline, a provincewide "planning assessment" which would serve as the basis for the preparation by COU of a provincial plan for the particular discipline. Acceptance of such a plan by the ministry was adopted as the key to the lifting of of the embargo for that discipline.

2. Also, proposed revisions to the universities' individual plans are reviewed each year by ACAP and must be approved by COU and the ministry. Their collective impact on each discipline is assessed and serves as the basis for an annual review of the embargo list.

Graduate program planning arrangements are summarized by the COU *Review* as follows:[34]

The operations of appraisal of individual university programs (for quality) and assessment of a discipline across the province (for planning) are performed separately and independently, although frequently decisions about one may bear on the

other. The funding of a new program, for example, requires that:
1. it fall into a category that is free of embargo;
2. it form part of the approved plan of the proposing university; and that
3. it receive a favorable appraisal.

The near moratorium is likely to continue until the MCU, OCUA, and COU arrive at a new and satisfactory policy on the funding of graduate studies. It is a sign of the strength of the COU, and its OCGS and ACAP affiliates, that government bodies feel the need not only to consult but preferably to obtain the agreement of the universities' association before a new policy can be proclaimed.

As was mentioned earlier, the COU covers practically the whole gamut of the universities' activities. Basically, however, it tries to accomplish four goals. First, it attempts to actively participate in the decision-making process that determines policies for the system as a whole. In particular, this allows it to exercise influence upon governmental bodies in the areas of planning and funding. Second, it attempts to coordinate the activities of its members. In part, its effectiveness here is derived from its first function: in other words, the principle is "if we do not do it ourselves, the government will do it for us." Third, it engages in research, much of which is directed to the support of its first two missions and for the public at large. Institutional representatives are always predisposed to view problems and answers from the point of view of their individual institutions. However, the COU provides for the mutual sharing of information and encourages a broader and more objective view of provincial educational matters. Again playing a role common to pressure groups, it can provide the public with the universities' interpretation of relevant public issues concerning postsecondary education.

Faculty Associations

The Ontario Confederation of University Faculty Associations (OCUFA), as the name implies, is also a voluntary association. Unlike the COU, however, OCUFA has a limited range of interests as well as resources. Since the trend toward unionization of faculties began, it has focused much of its attention on various aspects of collective bargaining, the issues subject to that process, and the more tangible items that affect the hiring of university faculty. Moreover, because local faculty associations are also affiliated with a national organization of faculty associations, the Canadian Association of University Teachers (CAUT), OCUFA has been freed from the onerous task of dealing with problems that arise when individual faculty members charge that academic freedom or tenure has been infringed upon. These cases are investigated and reported on by the academic freedom and tenure committee of CAUT. Not that OCUFA ignores broader issues concerning the universities: like the COU, it prepares briefs to the government, informs the public of the collective faculty views, and facilitates the exchange of the necessary information among its own members.

Colleges of Applied Arts and Technology

The creation of colleges of applied arts and technology was a sudden and bold maneuver.[35] Faced with Sheffield's and Jackson's projections, the government of Ontario had to decide how it would accommodate such dramatic increases in enrollment. At the same time, Ontario was experiencing a drastic shortage of skilled manpower, especially in the technological and semiprofessional fields.[36] Simultaneously, the federal government offered generous support for the building of vocational and technical schools as one of its shared-cost programs.

The Ontario government sought and obtained advice on the problem from a great number of sources, and on May 21, 1965 the minister of education, William G. Davis, informed the provincial legislature that colleges of applied arts and technology were to be created. The speech which he gave on that occasion is still the best—though rather lengthy—explanation of the reasons for and purposes of community colleges.[37] Basically, the new institutions were to serve three purposes:[38] to provide courses of types and levels beyond, or not suited to, the secondary school setting; to meet the needs of graduates from any secondary school program, apart from those wishing to attend university; and to meet the educational needs of adults and out-of-school youth whether or not they are secondary school graduates. The colleges were not to have any residences—hence their common designation as community colleges—and "at the present time at least," were to offer no courses for transfer to university.

Coordination

Under the relevant legislation and the regulations issued under it, individual colleges were left with what seemed to be considerable autonomy.[39]

> Nevertheless, the minister is responsible for providing a provincewide *system* of educational opportunities through the twenty-two individual colleges. Consequently, the legislation provides for policy coordination within the CAAT system through the Council of Regents. The Council of Regents is the communication link between the government and the board of governors. Queries concerning various board matters are normally directed to the chairman of the Council of Regents.

Thus, while there is considerable initiative left to local boards of governors, their "requests reach the ministry via the Council of Regents which assesses the merit of the requests in terms of provincial requirements as well as local community needs."[40]

In 1975, after a prolonged struggle fought within the colleges as to who should represent the faculty and within the system as to recognition, the legislature gave the Council of Regents "the exclusive responsibility for all negotiations on behalf of employers conducted under this Act."[41] In addition, the council has authority in the following areas: appointments of members to local boards of governors (it appoints eight and provides the formula for municipal appointments of the remaining four); the approval, disapproval or modification of master plans proposed by individual colleges (subject to final approval by the minister); and control over the general planning conducted by the individual institutions. The *First Annual Report* also cites the following under "Delegated Authority:"[42]

> The approval of new and modified educational programs has always been delegated to the Council of Regents because of the multiplicity of detail involved. The Council consults with the minister before approval is given to any program involving a change of government policy.

One of the main functions of the council, of course, is to advise the minister on the allocation of operating grants. The brief history of the CAATs is rich in this experience. During the early years, the ministry used line-item budget control and, in the view of many, appropriately so. Subsequently, the subsystem changed to a form of financing similar in many ways to that used by the Ministry of Colleges and Universities to distribute funds to the universities. In 1974, the minister "asked the council to advise him on new methods of financing of the colleges of applied arts and technology, in view of the demise of the open-ended operating grants formula."[43] The minister accepted the council's recommendation and a new funding system was employed for the 1976-77 academic year.

The new system has three component parts—plant and property grant, activities grant, and adult occupational training grant—and aims obviously at a greater control of costs through a more detailed accounting system and by employing various "indices" and categorization of "activities."[44] In spite of the disclaimer that the council wished "to avoid the return to line budget reviews," it is difficult to imagine how else the new system can work.

Voluntary Associations

As we mentioned earlier, the CAATs do not have a strong collective organization that can deal with the Council of Regents and the ministry on their behalf. One reason for this absence is the attitude of the Council of Regents: it prefers to view itself as the proper body to speak for the colleges:[45]

> The council frequently serves as the bridge between the boards of governors and the minister, providing a forum where issues of general concern can be discussed, clarified, and if necessary, brought to the attention of the minister. At the same time, the chairman and the executive secretary of the council attend meetings of the Committee of Presidents to inform the presidents of the interests and actions of the council, and to acquire an appreciation of the issues and concerns of the presidents and the colleges.

As indicated in the committee lists, the council has taken steps to involve both governors and college presidents on a number of its committees. In this way, college input is made directly, and the collective wisdom of all levels of responsibility can be brought together in an efficient and effective manner in the development of policies for the college system.

Another, and perhaps consequent, reason for the lack of independent corrective action on the part of CAATs seems to be the inability and/or unwillingness on the part of the presidents of the colleges to organize. As one of them observed: "We have no research staff. We have no backing. We have no budget. Once a month we do our job, whatever it is. We have not been—I am not saying that we want to be—a lobby."[46]

There is an umbrella organization of the colleges: the Association of Colleges of Applied Arts and Technology of Ontario (ACAATO). Originally, ACAATO was made up of three members from each college, the chairman and vice-chairman of the board of governors, and the president. A reorganization made it into an "association with an executive and, as components, a Council of Governors and the Committee of Presidents."[47] Faculty members have been invited from time to time to attend meetings of the association, as have students, but neither teachers nor students are members.

It is difficult to tell whether the foreseen decline in the independence of the colleges and the full impact of provincewide collective bargaining will cause the presidents of the colleges to increase or lessen their cooperative efforts.[48] Given the attitude of the Council of Regents and the usual reluctance of institutional leaders to surrender voluntarily even a small part of what remains of their institutional independence, the prospects are not too promising.

The affiliation of local faculty associations, with the union representing the provincial civil servants, resolved a prolonged, and at times bitter, struggle to establish an independent provincewide organization of faculty associations. Although there are signs that not every local faculty association is happy with the present affiliation and arrangements, the heterogeneous character of college faculties almost guarantees that a viable alternative organization is not likely to develop.

Students in CAATs make sporadic efforts to establish a provincewide association but with the exception of the late 1960s—

when they belonged, together with the university students, to the Ontario Federation of Students — they have not been very successful.

Financial Assistance to Students

Ontario's postsecondary students may receive federal loans provided by the Canada Student Loans Program and, depending on need, a provincial grant. The two schemes are integrated and administered by the province through the Ontario Student Assistance Program (OSAP). The loans are bank loans, guaranteed by the federal government, and are interest free for as long as the recipient remains a full-time student and for six months thereafter. The interest rates applicable following that period vary with the rise and fall of commercial rates. The maximum time for repayment is nine and one-half years. Loans are available for study in other provinces or other countries; grants are tenable in Canada only. The provincial grant is administered as a supplement to the federal loan scheme and, as a rule, the first $1,000 is a federal loan and whatever may be awarded over that — on the average about an equal amount — is a provincial grant that, in the vast majority of cases, need not be repaid. (Plans for modification of these arrangements were under consideration in mid-1977.)

Because the awards are based on financial need, there are the usual problems and bureaucracy accompanying such a scheme: the determination of the independence of the student from his/her parents or his/her spouse, the calculation of the financial resources available to the applicant (e.g., the income of his/her parents), and the estimation of education costs (e.g., fees, books and equipment, trips home, local transportation, baby-sitting, and so on). The responsibility for the administration of the program rests, in the first instance, with student awards officers employed by all publicly supported colleges and universities; in other words, the great administrative cost of the program is borne by the institutions.

The OSAP program, including the loan scheme, is the largest student assistance program in Ontario. In addition, there are two smaller scale programs for needy students: the Ontario Special Bursary Program (up to a maximum of $1,000 awarded to students in particularly distressing situations); and the Ontario Student Loans Plan for those who do not qualify under OSAP (up to $900 per semester available mainly to part-time students and those engaged in programs not requiring Grade 12 for admission). There are also a number of programs designated to support bilingualism. These are joint federal-provincial schemes administered by the province.

Apart from loans and bursaries, there are also a number of scholarship and fellowship programs. Among these, the most important is the Ontario Graduate Fellowship Program, which during 1976-77 provided 945 graduate students with an award of $1,450 per semester. Although the rationale of this program is different, it is basically a scaled-down version of the one which originated in the late 1960s and which was one of the main incentives for the development of graduate studies in Ontario.

Purposes and Effectiveness

Because one can discern "effectiveness" only if "purposes" are clearly defined, it is convenient to discuss the two aspects together. It is also advisable to discuss first the traditional academic goals — the search for and dissemination of truth and new knowledge.

Ontario has at least one institution with the tradition and some of the attributes of a major international university — the University of Toronto. Individual faculties and/or departments that can rightfully claim similar status can be found in other Ontario universities. Not surprisingly, it can also be said that Ontario provides its citizens with the most varied and frequently even the best university faculties and facilities in Canada.

One of the crucial aspects of the purely academic purposes of postsecondary education, if one may describe them as such, lies in research. This is an area that is of interest to both the federal and provincial governments. Essentially, the issue here is twofold and no different from the pedagogical services of the universities. First, there is the perennial problem of who should assume support for research. Because the support for all levels of postsecondary education is shared by the federal and provincial governments, both maintain that they support research through the support of graduate education. As long as postsecondary education was popular and had both public and government support, this division of responsibility obscured the underlying absence of planning and a firm, long-term commitment to research. But, now that public expenditure has declined, problems have surfaced. The fact that recently graduated Ph.D.s are facing diminishing prospects for employment has exacerbated matters. Since the funding of research is associated with support of graduate students, the stabilization, and in some cases decline, in graduate enrollment has restricted the funds available for research.

To meet the challenge, new approaches to funding research are being discussed. One involves separating funding for research from the funding of graduate studies. Although advantageous in many ways, such a separation is objected to by many academic researchers as undesirable or impossible or both. Those who argue against separation consider research and graduate studies to be "joint products," in the jargon of the economist, like the wool and mutton of sheep. Furthermore, any scheme to separate the two is certain to be resisted if it is to be based on a survey of faculty allocation of time between "research and teaching." Nevertheless, if the question of adequate support for research is not resolved soon, one of the main purposes of higher education, the search for new knowledge, is bound to suffer.

Much the same problem faces the other main service of postsecondary education: teaching. Again, because both the universities and colleges have been funded on the basis of enrolled students (the recent change of funding policy for CAATs is too new to appraise), the projected decline in enrollment will, most likely, lead to increased demands for teaching by faculty members and possibly even some firing. Indeed, given the age distribution of most university faculties—predominantly in the thirty to fifty-five year old age bracket—there is little hope that attrition would help the situation.

There is some dispute whether such a development would lead to a marked decline in the quality of university and college instruction. What is less disputable, however, is that it would lead to developments that would change the current character of the internal governance of universities (for example, by the unionization of faculties) and of univeristy-government relations.

Current Issues

Because the accomplishment of the major purposes of universities depends on governmental policies and because universities can be affected in many ways (at times in intangible ways that determine attitudes and habits), it seems appropriate to attempt to identify the main issues underlying the current uncertainties in postsecondary education in Ontario. Practically all governmental policies *vis à vis* the universities have been developed during a period of "dizzying enrollment increase."[49] The policies were, in fact, aimed at accommodating and encouraging that increase and they successfully accomplished their goal. But they also created two other sets of circumstances. One was the creation of unrealistic attitudes among university personnel—faculty, staff, and the administration—that the generous funding of the past would continue. Moreover, these attitudes have been often translated into articulated policies and procedures within the institutions and may be difficult to change—for example, faculty participation in management, policies on promotion and tenure, and so on. Secondly, many young teachers were brought into the universities during the expansive period of growth. These young faculty members now comprise the majority in their institutions, and their frame of reference is somewhat distorted by their early experience in the "good old days."

Another consequence of the good old days of generous financial support was that jurisdictional ambiguities were often overlooked. In times of restraint, however, the question of who is responsible for what—and to whom—becomes much more urgent. For example, it is clear that effective planning can be accomplished only if there is an effective executive authority to carry out, or enforce, the plans. It is also rather clear that voluntary cooperation during periods of stress such as declining enrollments may bring will help to produce an effective authority. It thus seems more than likely that some centralization of authority in the hands of the government will take place.[50]

The needs of effective planning may provide one incentive for greater centralization; financial difficulties may provide another. It also seems more than likely that the government will have to cushion the full impact of declining enrollments even more than it has thus far. At the same time, it is hard to envisage any alternative to the current formula financing that would be acceptable to the government but would not lead to increased participation of the MCU in the management policies of the institutions.

There may, indeed, be two developments that would justify, if not make inevitable, such centralization. One is the possibility of provincewide negotiations with university faculty associations. There have already been suggestions to this effect (the so-called "two-tier" negotiations) and, of course, there is the example of CAATs. Secondly, if the decline in enrollment is as stark as it is predicted to be, it is possible that interinstitutional transfers of programs and/or faculties may be necessary. The only agency that could accomplish this would be the government.[51]

Innovation

While research and teaching are the two predominant tasks of postsecondary education, society also expects postsecondary institutions to be flexible, responsive to changing needs, and sufficiently innovative to increase the accessibility of postsecondary education for students other than those in the traditional age categories. Ontario, and its government in particular, can be justifiably proud that it created not only a vastly expanded subsystem of universities, but also an entirely new kind of institution: CAATs. True, the colleges were created in a financial heyday of postsecondary education and under a generous federal cost-sharing program, but this does not detract from the bold conception of the colleges nor from the determined effort to root them in local communities (few of them have student residences). Noteworthy also is the fact that the colleges have not become junior colleges that would serve simply as feeder institutions to universities. Nor have they lost the flexibility that allows for change in programs. As a result, CAATs' responsiveness to changing market demands and student preferences is far superior to that of other postsecondary educational institutions.

One of the most promising instruments for innovation — television — has had a checkered career throughout Europe and North America. In Ontario, the gradual development of educational television has resulted in better articulation of its goals and better understanding of its limitations. The Ontario Educational Communications Authority grew out of a television service provided by the Metro Toronto Education Association (META) and is now a provincially appointed, autonomous agency. Although it has recording facilities in only one location, the TVO as the network is called, has relay stations in major cities of populous southern Ontario and has recently added two new stations in northern Ontario. Almost one-fifth of its programs are in French and it offers a mixture of high-quality entertainment and public affairs programs. So far, it has ventured into offering direct instructional service only twice — each time in close cooperation with a number of universities which were willing to provide supplementary programs and university credit upon successful completion of the course.

The main thrust of TVO, then, is not to compete with other postsecondary educational institutions, but to supplement their services and to offer the public programs that would broaden its general education. The former is pursued through providing video tapes and films to educational institutions and, to the extent possible, through planning programs that can be used as supplementary aids with courses offered by the institutions. The latter is a balancing act: the need to make the program lively and appealing to the public must be balanced by the awareness that both the privately owned television stations and the federally supported Canadian Broadcasting Corporation are sensitive to any direct competition. So far, the TVO, with minor exceptions, has not only managed to accomplish that difficult task, but has also gained increased acceptance by the public at large.

An interesting but still underdeveloped aspect of TVO is its infrastructure of regional councils. These have been established in order to tie programming closer to regional needs. Perhaps because of a paucity of resources at the regional level, these councils have not been very active so far.

Accessibility

Accessibility to postsecondary education, of course, means more than the availability of educational services; it also means that all of the population must be able to take advantage of these services. In particular, accessibility depends on the financial resources of prospective students. In a previous section we described the main programs of financial assistance provided to students by the federal and provincial governments. It is a subject of perennial discussion whether the structure of these loans and grants help, deter, or are irrelevant in increasing accessibility to postsecondary education for children from lower income families. There can be no question, however, that the 1960s and early 1970s saw a dramatic increase in the participation rates of high school graduates in postsecondary education. But it is less clear whether this was accomplished through direct financial assistance offered to students, the indirect support which kept tuition down, or the creation of new institutions, especially the CAATs. In any case, the question of accessibility is now being modified by changes in the economic situation of the province (and hence in the demands for skilled manpower) and by the increased diversity of those whom postsecondary institutions now seek to serve. It is, in fact, this diversity that is seen by many as the partial answer to the anticipated decline in the number of high school graduates and as the inevitable concomitant of lifelong education. Retraining, updating of obsolete skills, increased demand for recertification, and increased competition for jobs based on educational qualifications are foreseen as forming the next reservoir of potential students. To meet these demands, however, the system requires not only the modification of financial assistance which Ontario has begun, but also an increase in flexibility and innovation on the part of institutions to provide new methods for delivery of their programs.

FOOTNOTES

1. There are a number of good histories of postsecondary education in Ontario. The most exhaustive is in Volume IV of a seven-volume *magnum opus:* W.G. Fleming, *Ontario's Educative Society* (Toronto: University of Toronto Press, 1971); and the writings of Robin S. Harris are indispensable, e.g. *A History of Higher Education in Canada, 1663-1960* (Toronto: University of Toronto Press, 1976), and "The Evolution of a Provincial System of Higher Education in Ontario," in D.F. Dadson, ed., *Five Lectures on Higher Education* (Toronto: University of Toronto Press, 1966).
2. Canada, Statistics Canada, Education, Science and Culture Division, *Advance statistics of education, 1977-78,* (Ottawa: Statistics Canada, 1977), Table 3.
3. Ontario, Ministry of Colleges and Universities, *Horizons: A guide to educational opportunities in Ontario beyond the secondary school level* (Toronto: The Ministry, 1976).
4. *Ibid.,* p. 12.
5. Ontario, Commission on Post-Secondary Education in Ontario, *The Learning Society: Report of the Commission,* chairman Douglas T. Wright, succeeded by D.O. Davis (Toronto: Ministry of Government Services, 1972), p. 158.
6. Canada, Statistics Canada, *op. cit.,* Table 12.
7. The Honorable J. McNie, minister of colleges and universities, *Legislature of Ontario Debates* (April 13, 1973), p. 923.

8. Ontario Ministry of Education, written reply to a question, *Legislature of Ontario Debates* (October 28, 1976) p. 4, 222.
9. From a directive issued by Manpower and Immigration to universities, April 27, 1977.
10. The order-in-council is an administrative directive issued by the Cabinet and is comparable to the executive order of the President of the United States.
11. Fleming, *op. cit.*, Vol. IV, p. 22, citing the Premier, Leslie Frost.
12. Subsequently, when the Commission on Post-Secondary Education in Ontario was established to review all postsecondary education in the province, Dr. Wright also became chairman of that body. Later still, in 1971, he became the deputy provincial secretary for social development, the senior civil servant of a newly created ministry within the Ontario government, charged with the coordination of policies for the social services, health, and education, including postsecondary education.
13. Ontario Department of Education, *Report of the Minister 1960* (Toronto: Queen's Printer, 1960), p. iv.
14. There are a number of sources describing the system as it was originally envisaged, the most accessible being that published in the *Report of the Minister of University Affairs of Ontario 1967* (Toronto: Department of University Affairs, 1967), pp. 98-105.
15. *Ibid*, p. 98.
16. "University autonomy is clearly preserved," said the Committee on University Affairs in its 1967 report (p. 12), though according to the minister's report of the same year the minister knew better. After repeating the claimed advantages of the formula, the report added: "Regulations about the acceptable purposes for which grant income may be used are a separate matter for possible exploration by the Committee on University Affairs," *op. cit.*, p. 98.
17. "Because these universities told us they were sick of being called emerging universities," [J.G. Parr, *Legislature of Ontario Debates* (June 4, 1973), p. S-917.]
18. See Ontario Council on University Affairs, *Second Annual Report, 1975-76* (Toronto: Ministry of Colleges and Universities, 1976). p. 65.
19. The result of this effort was a technical but intriguing publication called *Buildings, Space/Cost Data* published by the Capital Support Branch of the Ministry of Colleges and Universities, 1972.
20. Ontario, Committee on University Affairs, *Report 1967* (Toronto: Department of University Affairs, 1967), p. 33.
21. Ontario Council on University Affairs, *op. cit.*, p. 49.
22. Ontario, Tripartite Committee on Macro-Indicators, Preliminary Report, *Trends in Student-Faculty Ratios in Ontario Universities 1971-72 to 1975-76* (Toronto: Ontario Council on University Affairs, 1977), p. 1.
23. *Ibid.*, p. 2.
24. Ontario, Committee on Government Productivity, J.B. Cronyn, chairman, *Report Number Nine* (Toronto: The Committee, 1973).
25. *Legislature of Ontario Debates* (May 26, 1975), p. X-458.
26. *Ibid.*, p. S-452.
27. For a good history of the origins of the Committee of Presidents, see: *From the Sixties to the Seventies: An Appraisal of Higher Education in Ontario* (Toronto: University of Toronto Press, 1966), pp. 39-55.

28. The presidents responded quickly, and by May 1962 a report was submitted to the government. The report was revised in January 1963 and finally published in the spring of that year: Committee of Presidents of Provincially Assisted Universities [and Colleges of Ontario], *Post-Secondary Education in Ontario, 1962-1970* (Toronto: The Committee, 1963).
29. *From the Sixties to the Seventies*, pp. 39-40.
30. John B. Macdonald, "Council of Ontario Universities," in *Agencies for Higher Education in Ontario,* edited by Edward F. Sheffield (Toronto: Ontario Institute for Studies in Education, 1974), p. 33.
31. An ambiguously placed committee insofar as it reports directly to both the COU and the OCGS.
32. Council of Ontario Universities, *Review 1972-73 to 1974-75* (Toronto: The Council, 1976), p. 15.
33. *Ibid.* "Costs of the planning assessment program, originally shared equally between the universities and the government, have now been shifted entirely to the universities." (p. 17).
34. *Ibid.,* pp. 15-16.
35. There are a number of good historical surveys of the CAAT system. D. McCormack Smyth's M. Phil, thesis for the University of Toronto, 1970, was on "Some Aspects of the Development of Ontario Colleges of Applied Arts and Technology." Cicely Watson prepared a report on *New College Systems in Canada* for the Organization for Economic Cooperation and Development (Paris: OECD, 1973). W.G. Fleming, in his study, devotes Chapters 15-17 of Volume IV to CAATS. There is also a good survey of the colleges in *The Ontario Colleges of Applied Arts and Technology*, prepared for the Commission on Post-Secondary Education (Toronto: Queen's Printer, 1972).
36. In 1965 the total enrollment in existing technical and business administration courses offered by the institutes of technology was only 2,536 students. Fleming, *op. cit.,* Vol. IV, p. 452.
37. It is reproduced *in toto* in: Ontario Council of Regents for Colleges of Applied Arts & Technology, *Guidelines for Governors* (Toronto: Ministry of Colleges and Universities, 1975), Appendix A.
38. *Ibid.,* p. 25.
39. Ontario Council of Regents for Colleges of Applied Arts and Technology, *First Annual Report, 1975-76* (Toronto: Ministry of Colleges and Universities, 1976), p. 8. This is the first such report coming from the Council of Regents. It appeared ten years after the establishment of the system.
40. *Ibid.*
41. The College Collective Bargaining Act, 1975, Section 2 (3).
42. Ontario Council of Regents, *First Annual Report,* p. 9.
43. *Ibid.,* p. 20.
44. "Although there has been considerable advance during the past year in the development of uniform reporting procedures, the committee notes that several colleges have made little headway toward standardization of financial procedures." *Ibid.,* pp. 21-22.
45. *Ibid.,* pp. 10-11.
46. J.M. Porter, "Committee of Presidents of Colleges of Applied Arts and Technology," in Edward F. Sheffield, *op. cit.,* p. 50.

47. *Ibid.*, p. 51.
48. "There is no doubt that autonomy is going to be reduced. Really the only question is 'How much will it be reduced, and how fast, and how soon, and when will they kill it?'" *Ibid.*, p. 47.
49. As J. Gordon Parr, then chairman of the Committee on University Affairs, described it in Edward F. Sheffield, *op. cit.*, p. 17.
50. For a more dramatic expression of this view, see the citation from President Porter above.
51. The harbinger of this trend may be seen in the required cutbacks in admissions to teachers' colleges still under the jurisdiction of the Ministry of Education. Some university faculties of education have cut back voluntarily.

WESTERN CANADA
Duncan D. Campbell

Sweeping down the slopes of Western Canada's Rockies is a wind locally called the *chinook*. Like the *foehn* in Switzerland, the *zonda* of the Argentine, and the *Nor'Wester* of New Zealand, it can translate the landscape of winter to a promise of spring overnight. With just such suddenness the climate of higher education in Western Canada has been transformed. In each of the four provinces that comprise this westerly half of Canada—British Columbia, Alberta, Saskatchewan, and Manitoba—the initial core institution, a university, and a disparate group of colleges, technical schools, and similar institutions added in only a decade are now being woven into higher education networks, each with distinct component elements and mechanisms of coordination.

Because they have emerged so recently, the character of these networks remains largely unexamined. Their problems and the issues they raise are largely unidentified. What is clear, however, is that the center of gravity in higher education is shifting, suddenly, from the single institution to a network—and there it seems likely to stay.

Environment and Social Influences

Striking environmental features characterize and clearly influence the four western provinces of Canada. Certainly the most obvious of these is that of sheer mass. The four western provinces range in size from 247,000 to 359,000 square miles, each nearly large enough to accommodate the whole of the United Kingdom thrice over. Yet a population density of about four persons per square mile stands in vivid contrast to the 589 persons per square mile in Britain. Nor does the population size within each province remain stable. While the number of inhabitants in British Columbia swells rapidly and population in Alberta grows at a more moderate rate, Manitoba's population is increasing marginally and Saskatchewan remains stable or in slight decline. In all the provinces, the emigration of the population from rural areas to urban centers is pronounced. In 1921 nearly 70 percent of Albertans lived in rural areas; by 1971 the proportions were almost exactly reversed.

Furthermore, the population is concentrated in relatively few metropolitanlike centers. The effect is sharply evident, for example, in British Columbia, the most westerly province. There, of 35,000 students enrolled in postsecondary academic programs, fewer than 7 percent receive instruction in the nonmetropolitan areas, while participation rates for academic postsecondary education in metropolitan areas are two to three times greater than elsewhere in the province.[1] While "British Columbians live in narrow valleys and on islands and river deltas that are scanty footholds in a 'sea of mountains,'"[2] Manitoba, in a categorically different geographical context with its flat terrain, faces a similar problem. Only one of its cities approaches the status of a metropolis, but it accommodates more than half of the provincial population while the remainder is widely scattered. The population of its university cities comprises 56 percent of the total population of the province, compared with 65 percent in British Columbia, and 52 percent in Alberta. In sharp contrast, the figure for the flat Saskatchewan plains is 26 percent. As a University of Saskatchewan committee reported in a study aimed at discovering what the Saskatchewan public wanted from that institution, "We were continuously reminded of the remoteness of the university from the bulk of the community."[3]

While physical characteristics exert an immediate and obvious influence on the organization of higher education within each of the four provinces, economic, political, and social cross-currents shape it as well. In British Columbia, for example, a polarized political climate exists; the pendulum swings from conservatism to socialism and there are perennially thorny relationships between management and labor. The influx of a large immigrant population, job seasonality, and regional economic disparities produce additional problems. In Alberta, other factors affect higher education, among them open terrain and easily identifiable regions, good transportation networks, and clearly definable demographic areas and resource areas. In Saskatchewan and Manitoba, cooperative enterprise is widely accepted—as illustrated by the mammoth wheat pool organizations—but there is no real industrial base, and there are pressing demands to accommodate higher education to the social needs of native people. There are sharp disparities in wealth among the four provinces. Although the economic base is different in each, the principal emphasis is on agriculture and the exploitation of nonrenewable natural resources. Religious and ethnic affiliation exert little influence on the organization of higher education in the western provinces.

A variety of changes in western Canadian society are exerting strong pressures on higher education. There is growing awareness of the importance of education and the need to develop special skills. At the same time, the supply of skilled immigrants has been tapering off, and postsecondary education has been obliged to produce skilled manpower for the nation. Radio and television, through national networks, link the most remote regions of the country. Women are a large and permanent part of the labor force. The average age of the population is rising and the eighteen to twenty-four year old population is expected to diminish sharply in the mid-1980s. Patterns of participation in postsecondary education are in transition; the bulk of credit and noncredit university students attend on a part-time basis, and a broader range of students is now seeking higher education.

A new array of student groups, each with a legitimate claim on existing postsecondary institutions, presents itself: women, in other than the traditionally sex-oriented roles such as nursing and teaching; the elderly; the unskilled and semiskilled workers wishing to enlarge their personal satisfaction or employment potential; the semiemployed, including seasonal workers; paraprofessionals, for example, those in the health, social services, and education fields; business and professional people; residents in small towns and more remote areas; emigrants from rural to urban communities; native people and the so-called disadvantaged who see higher education as an alternative to the discouraging pattern of their lives; and high school, college, and university graduates, who may earlier have assumed that their education came to an end when they last left the classroom, diploma in hand.[4] Crowning all of these changes is the rapidly escalating cost of education, the diminished public esteem for higher education, and the intense competition it now faces for a share of provincial revenues.

The Development of Higher Education Networks

British Columbia

Chronic delay, a quarter century in a moribund state, and then feverish growth in the last decade have marked higher education in British Columbia over the century of its development. In the nineteenth century, the response to the need for some initiative in higher education was to pass the Act to Establish and Incorporate a University for the Province of British Columbia in 1890. A decade elapsed before high schools in the two principal cities, Vancouver and Victoria, provided the first year of a bachelor of arts program in affiliation with McGill University of Montreal, three thousand miles to the east. Delayed yet again by World War I and indecisiveness, the University of British Columbia took over the classes of McGill University College in Vancouver in 1915 and, after a hiatus of five years, Victoria College resumed its work under the new university. Chartered as a college in 1950, Notre Dame University of Nelson, a small denominational institution, achieved university status in 1963 (it ceased to operate in 1977).

The Universities Act of 1974 provides for a board of governors to deal with finances, properties, and salaries for each university. Two faculty members (elected by their peers), two students (elected from the student association), and one person (elected by and from the full-time employees of the university who do not hold faculty status) are members of the board of governors. The academic governance of each university is vested in its senate; at the University of British Columbia, the senate includes fifteen nonfaculty persons, eleven of whom are elected by and from the convocation.

The intermediary body established in 1974 to effect coordination of and linkage between the then four university institutions—British Columbia, Notre Dame, Simon Fraser, and Victoria—is the Universities Council, clearly described in the Act as "for all purposes, an agent of the Crown in right of the province." Its membership (which excludes, among others, employees and students of the universities) numbers eleven under a chairman appointed by the lieutenant-governor in council (the government of the province). Its powers, clearly delineated in the Act, include those of: development, research, short- and long-term academic planning; providing advice to the government with respect to the establishment of new university institutions; the approval of new faculties and new degree programs; the coordination of institutional budgeting and the allocation of funds provided by government; the power to require universities to consult with each other to minimize duplication of effort; to coordinate the solicitation of funds for research; and to establish evaluation procedures for departments, faculties, programs, and institutes. It is explicitly required not to interfere in three matters: the formulation and adoption of academic policies and standards; the establishment of standards for admission and graduation; and the selection and appointment of staff. Interestingly, it is enjoined to hold its meetings in public at locations throughout the province, and the public is encouraged to participate.

Certainly, the most influential document in the extremely rapid expansion of alternative institutions of higher education, one which indeed changed the entire character of higher education in the fifteen years following 1962, was that prepared by John B. Macdonald, then newly appointed president of the University of British Columbia.[5] At that time, the majority of the student population of the University of British Columbia and its subsidiary college at Victoria was drawn from the densely populated lower mainland area. There was pronounced tension between the scattered hinterland and the southwestern corner of the province, which was served by the universities. Then, as today, "it would be unwise to underestimate the feeling of the nonmetropolitan residents of the province that most opportunities are only available at the coast despite the significance of the hinterland's contribution to the province's wealth."[6]

Reduced to its essence, the problem facing Macdonald was how — in the face of the tidal wave of students then predicted, the almost total concentration of higher education facilities in the provinces major city (Vancouver), the rising indignation of the remainder of the widely dispersed population at the lack of access to higher education and the need for different kinds of learning opportunities — he might effect a radically different and much expanded structure for the provision of higher education and at the same time protect the university from an inundation of students that would swamp its resources. The major recommendation of his report was that postsecondary education in British Columbia should be decentralized by establishing two-year colleges and additional four-year institutions throughout the province.

The government accepted the proposal almost immediately. Clearly it sat well with both public and educational authorities in the enormous hinterland outside of metropolitan Vancouver. Consequently, the University of British Columbia's college in Victoria became a full-fledged university institution in its own right in 1963 and Simon Fraser University was created with astonishing speed—a mere eighteen months—in 1965 at Burnaby. Even more remarkable, within a dozen years sixteen alternative institutions were developed in rapid order. Today these alternative institutions comprise fourteen community colleges widely scattered throughout the province, two art schools, an institute of technology (which functions under separate status), and three nursing schools.

Typically, the colleges offer programs in vocational and technical fields and two years of transferable academic credit, the latter is considered equivalent to the first two years of the general arts and science programs of the universities. The universities offer credit on a course-by-course basis; inevitable disputes in the process of awarding credit are resolved by a government-appointed Post-Secondary Coordinating Committee which also functions to maintain good communication between the colleges and the universities in various subject areas.

But while the Macdonald report offered an essential stimulus, it was not the only factor which produced the present network of community colleges. Rather, it was a case of an idea whose time had come. The school districts themselves have played the critical role in the development of community colleges in British Columbia. Indeed, the school boards which cooperate to initiate a college are designated as "parent agencies" in the 1974 Public Schools Act. A college council, which comprises elected school-board trustees, government-appointed members, and others "representative of nonsectarian and nonpolitical community interests" conducts the affairs of the institution. Financial support comes jointly from participating school boards through local taxes and from the provincial government. The provincial Department of Education coordinates expenditures and college programs. In 1971, the vocational schools of the province, previously detached from the system, were merged with adjacent community colleges to improve coordination and economic conditions and to facilitate comprehensiveness. British Columbia is the only province in Canada in which community colleges have been integrated into school systems and supported in part by local taxes. With respect to their structure and mode of operation, they are unique in Canada and, though similar to some U.S. models, retain essential differences.[7]

Dennison's study of the impact of community colleges[8] suggests that, of all Canadian provincial college systems, British Columbia has developed a model which is most community-oriented in virtually every respect—finance, governance, curriculum, and administrative policy. Dennison's characterization of the community colleges was confirmed and amplified by a 1974 Task Force, which stated:[9]

- A fundamental purpose of a community college...is to provide learning opportunities and encourage learning throughout the wider community as well as within college walls....
- [They ought to] be designed to meet an increasing demand for recurrent education for part-time as well as full-time students....
- Each type of educational institution should provide different and distinct learning experiences, with none viewed as better or worse, higher or lower, than the other. Each type of institution should be a true alternative....
- [What the immediate future requires of the college is that it] offer educational opportunities in the community through the use of mobile facilities, existing buildings, media resources, and visiting and resident instructors....
- Educational programs should be developed...not primarily to perpetuate the use of buildings nor to satisfy the special interest of educators....
- Community colleges should encourage and foster a wide variety of learning styles and instructional methods....
- The governance and operation of every college should reflect the concerns of all elements within the college and its wider community....
- Community colleges must be highly responsive to community needs for learning....
- Future college development [as a matter of priority should

attempt to meet] the educational needs of those who are geographically, socioeconomically, or physically disadvantaged.

The colleges provide a wide range of services: career, vocational, and technical programs; university and technological institute transfer programs; adult basic education programs; continuing education programs; community educational development services (in which communities are assisted in identifying, assessing, and meeting their educational needs); media communications; program evaluation; and educational advisory services. Currently a Post-Secondary Program Division of the provincial Department of Education advises and regulates colleges.[10] A Committee of College Principals facilitates the exchange of information among these institutions.

The next stage of development may well be that forecast by a 1976 commission. According to the commission's report, the remedy for current inequity in higher education must satisfy three basic tests:[11]

— It must substantially increase the opportunities for people resident in the interior to complete a degree program.
— It must be consistent with the maintenance of traditional university standards of academic excellence.
— It must achieve the first two goals with reasonable economic efficiency.

The major recommendation of the commission was its proposal to create a new multicampus university, requiring the establishment of four university centers which would, in turn, coordinate with other universities and would emphasize directed study. Similarly, the commission predicted an expanded outreach role for the British Columbia Institute of Technology and for each of the community colleges.

Alberta

British Columbia had been firmly established as a Canadian settlement for well over half a century before Alberta was carved out of the Northwest Territories in 1905. Essentially a rolling, agricultural parkland or prairie, the bulk of its population was widely scattered and only two towns, Edmonton and Calgary, had populations of any size. Almost immediately, at its first session in 1906, the legislature created the University of Alberta in Edmonton.

Henry Marshall Tory, fresh from the established universities of the east, became its first president. A vigorous man with strongly held opinions, he brought with him the most sophisticated notions of higher education of that day. He was, it should be mentioned, strongly influenced by the radically different approach being taken in Wisconsin—"Our campus the state"—derived from the 1862 United States' Morrill Act, which provided funds for land-grant university institutions dedicated to technological improvement of agriculture through adult education. With the aid of the Department of Extension, which has since been remarkably successful in its role of "taking the university to the people," Tory proceeded to establish a provincial institution, firmly planted in this predominantly rural community.

In the period immediately prior to and succeeding World War I, the Research Council of Alberta, an agency connected to both government and the university, was established as were two church colleges, St. Joseph's and St. Stephen's, each linked with the new university. The initial stages of university level work in Calgary were greatly affected by affiliation with a denominational institution, Mount Royal College. The Banff School of Fine Arts, created by the Department of Extension, with only enthusiasm and popular support as its assets, was established during the depression years and has since become the most notable institution of its kind in Canada. Following World War II, a most significant development took place: the university assumed complete responsibility for the training of teachers, through a newly established faculty of education—a step which paved the way toward the professionalization of teachers in Canada.

The sixties constituted the period of greatest growth and tumultuous change in Alberta.[12] Full-time enrollment at the university jumped from 4,600 in 1958 to 18,600 in 1968. The budget during the same period climbed from $5 million to $51 million. As elsewhere in Canada, the university faced a seller's market in its efforts to recruit staff. The changes in federal funding for postsecondary education which occurred in 1967 set the stage for greater provincial control and systematization of higher education. The Duff-Berdahl report[13] fueled the fires of faculty demand for greater decision-making power in the affairs of the institution and, in retrospect, the Universities Act of 1966 confirmed a radical shift in power from president and board to faculty councils and departments. By ensuring the autonomy of the Calgary branch of the university, the Act resolved the smoldering resentment which existed not only between the University of Alberta and Calgary but also between the citizens of each of these highly competitive cities. It also anticipated the emergence of other provincial universities — the first of which was the University of Lethbridge, established in 1967. Athabasca University, created in 1970 as a conventional institution, has since redefined its mission to provide instruction to students throughout the province, many of them adults, by correspondence courses supplemented by telephone consultation with an instructor.

For each university, the 1966 Act provides for a board of governors with responsibility for finances, physical plant, and business affairs. Membership of the board initially included a chairman appointed by government, the university chancellor, its president, and others (two of them members of the academic staff of the university); subsequently three students were added. Comprehensive responsibility for academic affairs is assigned to the general faculties council of each university. Its membership, drawn from across the campus, currently includes nearly fifty students. In addition, each university has a dean's council and each faculty of the university has a council which, subject to the control of the general faculties council, is empowered to conduct its academic affairs.

More significantly, with the passage of the 1966 Act, a system of higher education, its implications only dimly seen then, was inaugurated. The Alberta Universities Commission was the original agency designated to coordinate the universities. It was composed of nine members and a full-time chairman, and had a small staff. The deputy minister of education and the deputy provincial treasurer were ex officio members, while the remaining six citizen representatives were appointed by government. The commission advised the government on the annual levels of support required for university operation across the province, including capital needs, and on the distribution of funds provided. Among its supplementary responsibilities, which were defined somewhat nebulously, was the regulation of new programs offered by the universities.

The Universities Coordinating Council, consisting of the principal officers of each university and other academics, was also created by the 1966 Act. Its responsibilities were to advise the general faculties councils and the Universities Commission, either voluntarily or on request, on any matter affecting the universities as a whole, to determine affiliation agreements with other institutions, principally colleges, and to exercise control over the evaluation of the qualifications of graduates who seek to be admitted to the professions.

The Universities Commission was short-lived. Although it had been created to avoid the accusation of favoritism in the allocation of funds to institutions and to relieve the government's burden in this area, its membership included no university personnel. The commission's role was essentially passive: that of reacting to initiatives from the universities, directly and through the Universities Coordinating Council. However, recommendations were developed and presented by commission staff—who were immersed in the day-to-day operations of the university, in contrast to the lay members of the commission—and these recommendations had considerable influence. This buffer agency was concerned almost exclusively with finance. On the matter of institutional program development both the statute and the commission were circumspect, perhaps because the Act implicitly cautioned the commission against intruding into the affairs of the universities.

The commission is not solely to blame for its failure. Government views and policies with respect to university education and, for that matter, the role of the commission itself appear never to have been clearly defined. According to one assessment:[14]

> ...the Alberta Universities Commission, in the context of university coordination, emerges as a body constrained by government to operating within a relatively narrow field, discouraged from taking an active part in several important areas of planning and coordination, and apparently unwilling to exercise more than a reactive role in its dealings with the universities.

The Universities Coordinating Council, the other coordinating instrument established simultaneously with the commission, was scarcely more successful. Its role was not clearly specified in the 1966 Act, nor did its membership succeed in identifying its purpose; thus, its ability to contribute to the deliberations of the Universities Commission was severely limited. Virtually the only point of contact between the two bodies was the occasion on which the council approached the commission for its annual operating grant. Preoccupied with housekeeping, and the debate of admission requirements or professional certification, the council appeared unable to resolve substantive issues or to undertake sustained planning.

As in British Columbia, the most extraordinary extension of the higher education network occurred with colleges; they developed in four stages.[15] The first began with the emergence of private, church-related junior colleges in the early part of the century and culminated with the establishment of the first public community college at Lethbridge in 1957. This phase, as is readily apparent from the records, was characterized by the domination of the University of Alberta (the province's sole university at that time) through its Committee on Junior Colleges, which supervised affiliation regulations and the conduct of the transfer program. The primary concern of that committee was to protect the university's own interests through rigorous screening of college instructors and monitoring of their academic standards. The consequence of this arrangement, which became increasingly less tolerable to colleges as these new institutions emerged, was the concentration on academic work, essentially duplicative of university studies. But the prestige of the university was such that the leaders of the junior colleges were obliged to accept this one-sided relationship, though they were discontented with it.

The second stage was sparked by the passage of the Public Junior Colleges Act of 1958 and was characterized by rapid expansion of the public college system (itself a reflection of the economic buoyancy of the period), substantial public confidence in higher education, and popular demand for alternatives to university education. Following the established pattern, emerging colleges operated in the main under affiliation agreements with the university, but these were subject to rapidly accumulating friction which, in turn, generated political concern over the control of this increasingly costly segment of public education. The fact that the influence of the University of Alberta's Committee on Junior Colleges — initially under the direct control of the university's senior officers — was subsequently delegated throughout that institution to faculties and departments was a circumstance which further complicated and exacerbated relationships. Within this superior-inferior relationship, it is not surprising that little attention was paid to public need in higher education, to the integration of a system of existing college institutions, or the establishment of new colleges. To resolve growing public concern, the government established a Provincial Board of Post-Secondary Education in 1967, a powerful central agency whose express function was to advise government.

The third phase of development involved the replacement of that board, in 1969, by a specific agency for coordinating the effort of colleges—the Alberta Colleges Commission. Though it exerted a constructive influence, it was not totally successful since it did not have jurisdiction over the province's two institutes of technology and its three agricultural colleges.

Gordon Campbell[16] has provided a useful outline of stage four—the present state of affairs. Since 1969, the midstream of college development, the Alberta Colleges Commission has played the major coordinating role. However, the commission was established at the same time the Universities Commission was still in operation and the consequence of "the establishment of a twin-commission system of coordination [was to perpetuate] the cleavages between the university, the community colleges, and a variety of other institutions managed directly by the province's Department of Education."[17] Yet this "combined development" model provided for continued differentiation among and within varieties of institutions, improved linkage among them, and stabilized, temporarily, what might otherwise have been a discordant, ad hoc proliferation of agricultural schools, colleges, institutes, and universities.

Currently, the network includes four universities (the University of Alberta, the University of Calgary, the University of Lethbridge, and Athabasca University), six community colleges, the Banff School of Fine Arts, two institutes of technology, three agricultural colleges, five vocational centers, and three private colleges.

As in British Columbia, one key document—a commission study directed by Walter H. Worth, *A Choice of Futures*[18]—precipitated a pattern of organization that marks much of the coordination of higher education in Alberta today. It is extremely difficult to summarize the Worth report, since its many proposals are scattered throughout the text of the entire volume. Suffice it to say that no element of Alberta's postsecondary network has not been modified by the philosophy of the report and the policies flowing out of it devised by the Department of Advanced Education, of which Worth soon became the deputy minister.

The most significant change arose from a determination to bring about a coordination of services, administratively and educationally, within the variety of levels in the system. More recently, priority has been given to rationalizing the role, mandates, and growth patterns of all institutions. The underlying belief, clearly, is that comprehensiveness as a goal ought to be achieved not merely within the institutions and subsystems, but within the whole of the postsecondary network. The establishment of a Department of Advanced Education (to which, subsequently, the manpower function was added), created the potential for systemwide planning and coordination; the disbandment of the two commissions was supportive of this potential. Recently, the creation of a Council on Admissions and Transfer has stimulated interinstitutional cooperation and facilitated student movement within the system (an achievement which evaded the Universities Coordinating Council).[19] The recent implementation of a policy on adult education is aimed at extending noncredit educational opportunities throughout the province. One institution, Athabasca University, has been assigned the role of providing nonconventional educational opportunities to the other-than-conventional student.

Thus, from *de jure* control of the narrowly based framework of higher education in the mid-1960s, and after considerable experiment, the government now exercises rigorous control of the whole postsecondary network.

Saskatchewan

Though they were created during the same decade and their geographic, demographic, and social characteristics were similar, Alberta and Saskatchewan have pursued quite different courses in the development of higher education. However, Alberta's newfound wealth from oil resources in the 1950s, while not the only factor, must certainly be labeled a fundamental factor behind the quite different approaches taken by these two adjoining provinces.

As was the case in British Columbia and Alberta, the initial and key institution was a university, the University of Saskatchewan in Saskatoon, created by statute in 1907. As in Alberta, the quality of its original leadership has clearly influenced present developments in higher education. The new institution was remarkably fortunate in its first president, Walter Charles Murray, whose report to the university senate in 1908 set out these goals:[20]

> The university's watchword must be service to the state in the things that make for happiness and virtue as well as in the things that make for wealth. *No form of service is too mean or too exalted.* It is fitting for the university to place within the reach of the solitary student, the distant townsman, the farmer in his hours of leisure, or the mothers and daughters in the home, the opportunities for adding to their stores of knowledge and enjoyment.... Whether the work be conducted within the boundaries of the campus or throughout the length and breadth of the province, there should be ever present the consciousness that this is the university of the people, established by the people, and devoted by the people to the advancement of learning and the promotion of happiness and virtue.

Nor was this merely rhetoric of the kind which flows so generously at convocation, but a clear statement of belief. Murray immediately established an extension department of which it is recorded, "it would be difficult to exaggerate that department's effectiveness, through its agricultural service and its women's work service, in making the farmers of the province conscious that the University of Saskatchewan was indeed *their* university."[21] The view that it is the obligation of the institution to serve the public directly is as strongly held today as it was half a century ago and is vividly and, indeed, pungently reiterated by the citizens to the University of Saskatchewan. Predictably, this emphasis on institutional outreach subsequently shaped the course of community colleges.

With its sister institutions in the western provinces, the university continued to develop at a modest pace until 1945, when the influx of veterans in the succeeding five years and the enormous surge of students of the sixties flooded the campus. From a small, liberal arts beginning, the institution has become one of Canada's major universities, providing an extensive array of professional education and a solid base for scientific research, while preserving its status as a center for scholarship in the liberal arts.

In the capital city, Regina College—which had been established by the Methodist church to provide a wider variety of educational opportunities than had hitherto been available—was accepted in 1925 as an affiliated college of the University of Saskatchewan and offered first-year arts and science classes. In 1959, a decision was taken by the university's board of governors to raise its southern branch to full degree-granting status as a second, but not autonomous, provincial campus. Each of the campuses situated in cities other than Regina was headed by a principal.

Some of the rationale for this decision was set out by the first president of the two-campus institution, J. W. T. Spinks.[22] The general principle was that a modern university should be large enough to justify a faculty for all the major fields — which implies a staff of the order of 700 and a student body of about 10,000. Since that critical size had been reached, the view was that the province would be better served by creating a second campus (to be followed, perhaps, by a third) rather than allowing the original campus to expand indefinitely. Acceptance of the concept of two "autonomous academic groups" brought in its train a practical problem: how, given the political tensions existing between the province's two rival cities and the aspirations of the faculty in each, could the available funding be distributed equitably? The problem was resolved by establishing a state university in which all existing and all future publicly supported institutions of higher education would be constituent members. While it was acknowledged that any form of coordination would involve a certain loss of autonomy, an important consideration implicit in the arrangement was that the opportunity to negotiate directly with provincial government would be maintained.

In essence, the new structure reflected in the 1968 Universities Act comprised a board of governors, a senate (a body composed jointly of academics and lay persons), and a general university council representing faculty opinion; the whole was supported by numerous advisory bodies and an extension department which served as a sensitive monitor of the community. Each campus was presided over by a principal functioning as the academic and administrative head of the campus, and each had an academic council supported by committees on finance and personnel responsible for academic programs.

This arrangement did not survive long. A few years after the adoption of this structure a bill to reorganize the framework of university education in Saskatchewan was introduced into the legislature. The proposal, as one observer described it in wry understatement, provoked much public discussion. The legislation was withdrawn and a Royal Commission on University Organization was established, which encountered the same hostility as that which had existed earlier in Alberta; conflict of interests on the part of municipal and business bodies of the two communities, bitter rivalry between the citizens of the two principal cities of the province, and suspicion and distrust among the academics of the senior and junior institutions. Nevertheless, the commission findings were immediately incorporated into legislation.[23] Two distinctly separate universities were created from the two campuses of the University of Saskatchewan and an intermediary, a Universities Commission, was established.

The Universities Commission, designated "for all its purposes an agent of the Crown in right of Saskatchewan," comprises nine members appointed by the provincial government. Its duties, set out in considerable detail in the 1974 Act, center around the rationalization of institutional budgets, the distribution of capital and operating funds allocated to it by government, the gathering and publication of information relevant to university education, and the coordination of university programs. Particular emphasis is placed on joint planning and cooperative ventures with other elements of postsecondary education in the province. In deference to principles of institutional autonomy, the commission is expressly enjoined in the Act "...not to interfere in the exercise of powers conferred on an institution in relation to...the formulation and adoption of academic policies and standards...the establishment of standards for admission and graduation...the selection, appointment, suspension, and removal of staff."

We should mention here the linkage of church colleges with the universities. Campion College and Luther College, both church institutions, had been affiliated earlier with the University of Saskatchewan. In the last decade both of these became federated colleges of the University of Regina while St. Thomas More College is federated with the University of Saskatchewan. In Saskatchewan, federated colleges are those physically on the university campus which provide courses approved by the University for the university's own degrees and which receive government financial support on a level comparable to the university. Colleges affiliated with the universities, but which are not physically on the campus, may offer certain courses which are acceptable to the universities for transfer credit.

Earlier, in 1972 a new Department of Continuing Education had been created to give direction to postsecondary education, a responsibility previously held by the Department of Education.

According to the legislation that created it, the Department of Continuing Education was granted broad powers:

> All that part of the administration of the Government of Saskatchewan that relates to the University of Saskatchewan and to education and that is not by law assigned to any other department or agency of the Government of Saskatchewan shall be under the control of the department and the department may make such arrangements as are deemed necessary for the education of nurses and for the education and training of ancillary nursing personnel.

Its task, in short, through the medium of adult education, was to fill the interstices of the educational framework of the province. Its first requisitioned report, from an Advisory Committee on Community Colleges, elaborated on the concept of "middle-range education," a peculiarly Saskatchewan term, earlier set out by Harvey:[24]

> Middle range education is mainly for adults. It can take place in any institutional or non-institutional setting, with any degree of formality or informality, but the definition excludes the regular day program of the public school systems and the regular degree programs of the universities.

The kind of education characterized here is, of course, adult education which had been the focus of vigorous effort by the University of Saskatchewan since 1910.[25]

> As an individual, a person plays many roles in life. These roles change, often with great speed. To meet these changes a person needs access to new learnings throughout life. Individuals must be able to recognize new learning requirements and assume greater responsibility for setting and pursuing their own goals. Self-assessment should be encouraged at an early age and when it has not been previously acquired should be emphasized in adult learning situations.
>
> The adult learner has special characteristics. For an adult, the traditional student-teacher relationship is often both ineffective and inappropriate and greater recognition must be given to both an adult's ability to learn for himself and the real life experience he brings to bear. His membership in the group is important. Learning takes on a social dimension. The teacher is a resource, and the experiences become meaningful through group interaction, rather than teacher directives. The student role of an adult is but one of many major

roles he assumes, and must be played as part of his total responsibility to his occupation, family and nation.

Man is affected by personal and social factors. The influence of an individual on his community depends, in part, upon his knowledge, attitudes and skills. The interaction of individuals who share similar concerns produces a social dimension known as a community. This community, in turn, influences the people within it.

The force and direction of the report[26] is aptly sketched in its flyleaf summary: priority to rural regions; existing facilities used; minimum permanent staff; local people as staff; existing resources used; extensive use of media; programs based on need assessment; formal programs contracted; informal community-based programs; and provincial libraries as resource centers.

Submitted to the minister of continuing education in 1972, the report was acted on immediately. The Community Colleges Act of 1973 led to the creation of fourteen community districts; in each a board was charged with the responsibility of determining educational needs and facilitating their provision through contract with existing technical institutes and the two universities. Here was a unique solution to the delivery of higher education—colleges without walls—one entirely consistent with Saskatchewan's reputation in social development and the thrifty deployment of resources.

Gordon Campbell summarizes the thrust of colleges in Saskatchewan thus:[27]

> In Saskatchewan, the community college unit of the ternary system resembles none other in Canada. High priority is given, not to buildings and campuses but, rather, to extending through community organization the services of the universities, institutes of technology, the provincial library and other government agencies. Saskatchewan is creating a new structure that emphasizes learning arrangements, rather than a physical plant; the structure is concerned more with its relation to other agencies than with the colleges as an institution per se.... An educational communications network (video, audio, film, print) is being incorporated within the college system to permit maximal accessibility to learning programs in a province with a substantial rural population.... The Saskatchewan system demands that a college have a large degree of freedom in working out ways to serve the many different rural communities.

While Saskatchewan is not large in terms of population, it is vast in terms of land area, agricultural, and mineral resources. Moreover, it is a province in which the impact of mechanization on agriculture, combined with the general trend toward urbanization, has a potentially disastrous effect on rural communities and complicates the delivery of higher education. In a demonstration of resourcefulness typical of the province, adult education, as in the past, has been harnessed to the preservation of the rural lifestyle through decentralized educational services.

Thus, the purpose of the Community Colleges Act was twofold: first, to present educational programs not provided in the established school systems, some at the college level, aimed at meeting the particular needs of persons in the communities; and second, to provide the local machinery through which educational programs provided in conventional institutions might be extended to the whole of the province. In each of the fourteen regions, a college board, comprising the principal and four to seven residents, of whom one might be a student and another a member of the instructional staff of the college, functions as a grassroots link with government to monitor local needs, to formulate appropriate policies, and to provide programs of instruction, and other educational activities of the college.

Staff establishments are small and a minimum investment is made in capital resources. Operational funding is by a formula-based grant intended to cover approximately 80 percent of the cost of noncredit programs, each based on short-term contracts with the providers—principally but not exclusively universities and technical institutes. Appropriately, the community itself is involved in the identification of both the programs required and available resources.

Three technical institutes today provide additional types of postsecondary education. A Saskatchewan Technical Institute functions in Moose Jaw (the third largest city of the province). A second, the Kelsey Institute of Applied Arts and Sciences, was established in Saskatoon, followed by the Wascana Institute of Applied Arts and Sciences in Regina (which incorporated the former Regina Vocational Centre). All provide two-year, one-year, and shorter duration courses in technical and vocational subjects.

The design of the college subsystem links local and government efforts. The Department of Continuing Education's field staff, enjoined to develop a close working relationship with the regional community colleges have, as their principal objective, the development of community and human resources, a task to be accomplished primarily through the brokerage function.

In the year ending June 30, 1976, the third year of operation, there were 73,000 registrations in 5,500 college classes in 582 centers. One of the results of this innovation (of which President Walter Charles Murray would have approved) is that it has stimulated within the established educational agencies of the province— particularly the universities and technical institutes, regional libraries, and government departments—a willingness to consider and examine how they might meet the day-to-day requirements for service to the community colleges.

Manitoba

When immense herds of buffalo still darkened the broad plains of Alberta and Saskatchewan and a tiny settlement in British Columbia represented merely an out of the way port in a developing empire, southern Manitoba was a well-established crossroads of North America.

The University of Manitoba was founded in 1877, seven years after the creation of the province of Manitoba. It was established not as a conventional institution but as a kind of umbrella organization functioning as an examining and degree-granting body (on the model of the University of London) for the three existing church colleges: St. Boniface College, a Roman Catholic French-language institution which traced its beginnings to 1818; St. John's Anglican College which had been created by a mission in 1820; and the Presbyterians' Manitoba College, established in 1851. From its inception, colleges were affiliated with the University of Manitoba. Before the turn of the century, the Manitoba Medical College and a fourth academic college, the Methodists' Wesley College, were also affiliated with the university. It was not until 1900, however, that the University of Manitoba was first empowered to instruct students; by 1904, six professorships had been established.

In 1899, a Baptist college was founded in the city of Brandon. Although a special relationship developed between the university and Brandon College, the latter did not affiliate until 1912 and then not with the University of Manitoba but with McMaster University in Ontario, an arrangement which continued until 1938 when, having relinquished its church relationship, Brandon College entered into affiliation with the University of Manitoba.

Between 1902 and 1916, the Manitoba College of Pharmacy and the Manitoba College of Agriculture came under the university's auspices. In 1914, the university and the Manitoba Law Society established, under their joint auspices, the Manitoba Law School. A fifth private arts college, St. Paul's, connected to the Roman Catholic church, was affiliated with the university in 1931.

Only in 1914 did the University of Manitoba offer students a bachelor of arts and bachelor of science degree taught entirely by its own staff, a situation not altogether surprising because, until 1917, it lacked the organization, physical plant, and assured government financing to enable it to function as a teaching and research institution.

Following the merger of three of the major Protestant denominations in Canada in 1924, Manitoba College and Wesley College coalesced to become United College. On July 1, 1967 United College and Brandon College became the University of Winnipeg and Brandon University respectively. Subsequently, St. John's College and St. Paul's College entered into a "community of colleges" structure within the University of Manitoba, and St. Boniface College retained its affiliation in modified form.[28]

Thus in random fashion a variety of college institutions was spawned and, over time, either designated as universities or incorporated within the University of Manitoba—which had to wait nearly four decades before it undertook the teaching functions of a conventional university and could claim customary support from government.

These aside, there are five, nonpublic, postsecondary institutions today in Manitoba: the Canadian Mennonite Bible College, the Canadian Nazarene College, the Mennonite Brethren Bible College, the Winnipeg Bible College, and St. Andrew's College. All of these institutions offer programs culminating in degrees which are not academic, as, for example, Bachelor of Christian Education, Bachelor of Sacred Music, and Bachelor of Divinity. None receives financial assistance from the provincial government for operating purposes; each has a limited, distinctive working relationship with either the University of Manitoba or the University of Winnipeg.

A current observation in the literature of higher education is that there has been a tendency of universities in recent decades to become ever more alike, to lose their distinguishing characteristics, and, in so doing, rob the students of real choice in their higher education. Nevertheless, the three universities in Manitoba—the University of Manitoba, the University of Winnipeg, and Brandon University—differ not only in size but in character of their approach to higher education and, to some extent, in the constituencies they serve.

The University of Manitoba, the senior institution, comprises eighteen professional faculties and schools in addition to its faculties of arts and science. It is the only institution offering a spectrum of graduate studies, which alone account for about 10 percent of the total registration, currently of the order of 14,000. The University of Winnipeg, functioning in the same city, is considerably smaller, with a full-time enrollment of about 2,900. It offers undergraduate instruction in arts, science, and education, and a few masters' programs jointly with the University of Manitoba. It attracts something less than half of its students from outside metropolitan Winnipeg. Brandon University, the smallest of the three, has a full-time enrollment of about 1,200—of whom half are drawn from the Brandon area.

Rather curiously, a circumstance which does not apply in the other three western provinces, the universities in Manitoba operate under two different provincial Acts. The University of Manitoba Act, 1968, set out in customary detail the functions and powers of the various bodies within the institution. Central decision making rests in the hands of two bodies: a board of governors and a senate. The powers of the former lie primarily in the area of finance and physical plant, while those of the senate, the institution's senior academic body, relate to academic matters. A University and Community Council, its purpose to "foster mutual understanding between the university and the general public," has a potential membership of a hundred citizens, students, and staff. But without power, resources, or a clearly defined role, it is prohibited from playing a significant role and in fact is moribund.

The other two, however, the University of Winnipeg and Brandon University, operate by order-in-council enabled by a Universities Establishment Act, a statute which provides for the establishment of new universities and assigns to the lieutenant-governor-in-council the right to specify the structure and powers of these institutions and others as they might be developed in the future. Both the University of Winnipeg and Brandon University are now drafting a bill to be submitted to the legislature.

A Universities Grants Commission, established in 1967, is mandated to advise government on the financial needs of institutions, to distribute the annual grants authorized by the legislature, and to adjudicate proposals from the universities for the establishment of new services or programs. Government's expectation was that unnecessary duplication of expensive programs would be avoided and the institutions' dissatisfaction over the proportions of the grants would be minimized. In fact, the commission was given the authority to require universities to drop services or programs which they could no longer justify;[29] approval is required prior to the creation of new programs or services.

The University Grants Commission consists of nine persons, appointed by government, one of whom the government designates as chairman. Provision is made for the necessary administrative staff, and the Act declares an intention that the commission "should restrict its activities to the fiscal arrangements of universities" and not interfere with the basic right of a university to formulate academic policies and standards, standards of admission and graduation, and the appointment of staff. In carrying out its duties, the Act directs the commission to, on the one hand, study the needs of higher education at the university level and, on the other, to:

> ...give advice and assistance to the universities and colleges in the preparation and implementation of plans for the provision and development of physical and academic facilities in the universities and colleges to assure that adequate postsecondary educational resources of the type normally provided by universities and colleges are available to the citizens of the province without waste or unnecessary duplication.

In framing its procedures, the commission established these guidelines: to carry on direct, frequent discussion with the institutions it services; to stimulate interinstitutional consultation and encouragement to universities to develop their own institutional research and planning facilities; to attempt to underwrite the cost of professional services needed by the universities in dealing with the commission.

Statutory sources do not reveal the principles applicable or the goals sought in higher education. These are suggested by the Oliver report,[30] which emphasizes: equality in the access to university and college education by citizens; openness and public participation in decision making; institutional accountability; the achievement of greater coherence of the existing components of the system; clarification of the institutional mission; enhanced flexibility within institutions to enable them to respond more quickly to a variety of demands; and careful planning within the universities, coordinated by the intermediary. One speculates that what is forecast here is something which has already taken place in Alberta: the evolution of the controlling agency from resource-allocator to resource-allocator-coordinator to resource-allocator-coordinator-planner.

Across North America, the variety of institutions labeled "colleges" is large indeed, each an expression of a particular kind of need for a postsecondary educational alternative to the university. While those in British Columbia, particularly, and to a lesser extent those in Alberta, appear to be modeled after the United States' junior colleges, Saskatchewan's colleges are unique institutions rooted in the provision of adult education. Manitoba's three colleges, in contrast, had their beginnings in the 1942 Vocational Training Act of the federal government. Indeed, until recently, the name of each made clear that it was a technical institute. Though now termed community colleges, the change in name has been more decorative than substantive; their principal emphasis, as the Oliver report noted, remains on the technical.[31]

> The community colleges in Manitoba are very much trade or vocational schools. They are not really "community" colleges since they respond only partly to specific local needs. They offer a relatively narrow range of choices and they all rely heavily on the demands made by Canada Manpower in determining what courses they will offer and to how many students.

The report frankly deplores the overwhelming influence of a federal agency, Canada Manpower, on the colleges and claims that the excessive influence of this agency has caused other educational needs of the province to be ignored. Each of the three colleges serves a different kind of constituency. Red River College, with a student population of about 5,000, is the most sophisticated and offers a wide range of programs catering to the needs of the province as a whole, but largely serving urban Winnipeg, the single major center of population in the province. It remains the province's central agency for training in technology simply because the other two areas do not have the population base to warrant major development. The Keewatin Community College, located in the sparsely inhabited northernly half of the province, offers only one technology course—in mining. However, it plays a special role in that a substantial portion of its students are native peoples. Thus, one of its chief responsibilities "is to help open options in lifestyle to native people and other northern people who might not seek further training if they had to leave the region to do so."[32] A third, Assiniboine College, located at the province's second center of population, Brandon, serves the southwesterly portion of the province.

While in British Columbia and Alberta, varying degrees of authority are exercised by local college boards, in Manitoba the institutions are managed directly by a Department of Continuing Education and Manpower advised by a council (but in fact, the council has been moribund for five years). If one accepts the sharp criticism of college organization made by the Oliver report,[33] rigidity has been a principal characteristic of all aspects of the community college, the consequence of extreme centralization of decision making in the government. The staff within the college institutions have lacked autonomy to such a degree that decisions affecting even the minutiae of day-to-day operations are affected—a degree of centralization which, perhaps, reflects government distrust of the university model. More involvement of faculty and students in the decision-making process and a more productive linkage with the community are needed. Moreover, "One of the great problems in the community colleges now, in addition to who should make decisions, is the fact that very few long-range decisions of any sort have been made by anybody....There seem to be no goals for the colleges, no guidelines, no plans for the future."[34]

One speculates that, were the colleges more free of government control, they might well be more productive and more flexible. Given that greater degree of freedom, they might serve even more students and reach those not now reached by higher education.

The Application of Coordination

Goals and Outputs

Particular social, economic, political, historical, and geographical factors have shaped higher education development in each of the four western provinces. In each, over the span of less than one-hundred years, marked by spurts of expansion and innovation, a unique, highly individual framework has evolved. A dozen years ago, a mere handful of institutions comprised the network of post-secondary education. These existed in virtual isolation from one another and negotiated whatever support they might from government, quite independently of one another. Today, the networks comprise a substantial array of universities, colleges, technical institutes, vocational centers, and similar institutions.

The contemporary term describing this array—"system"—may be misleading. In precise usage, system connotes an assembly of specialized parts or functions acting cooperatively for a common purpose[35] and implies criteria such as: the elements of the system are collectively aimed at mutually understood and clearly defined ends; principal direction to the elements of the system emanates from a single source; and there is evident and effective articulation between and among the elements of the group toward the achievement of the defined end. One concludes that the networks of higher education institutions in western Canada are more aptly described as agglomerations of institutions, some closer to an eventual emergence as systems than others.[36]

Goals

Implicit in, and fundamental to, the concept of system in higher education is the notion of goals. What we observe in the higher education networks of the western provinces is that goals are nowhere articulated in official terms. Certainly, intimations of general purpose are found in statutes. Alberta's Universities Act, 1966, for example, directs that "It is a duty and function of each university to contribute to the educational and cultural advancement of the people of Alberta at large," while the 1974 Act, creating the Saskatchewan Universities Commission, outlines the powers of that body and implies its goals:

— Inquire into the financial requirements of the institutions and advise the minister;
— Gather and make available...information relevant to university education in Saskatchewan;
— Plan and coordinate...the university sector of postsecondary education in the province.

Similar statements are to be found in the records of debates in legislatures, in the public speeches of elected officials, and in the platforms of political parties—all rhetorical in character and removed from the higher education network or its institutional components. Similarly, goals are implicit in the recommendations of major commissioned reports and in a variety of position papers prepared by bureaucrats.

Nowhere in the western provinces have the goals of higher education been made explicit, either within the network or within its individual institutional components—with good reason. Defining goals is clearly a task of extraordinary difficulty, particularly for the universities whose task is infinitely subtle and complex. Until this decade, a buoyant economy and relatively dependable flow of students have made the need to articulate goals less urgent. The possibility of gaining consensus on a statement of goals has seemed remote within institutions that have increasingly reflected "democratization." Nor can one ignore the not uncommon academic view that the very existence of a published goal statement might be a hostage to fortune.[37] Yet as P.J. Gordon puts it, uncertainties in universities with regard to goals, technologies, and the locus of decision may result in a "garbage can" choice. At the point when decisions must be taken—when the can is opened—problems spill out.[38]

The impediment to the formulation of goals does not lie wholly within the network components. While the life of an institution is not in doubt, the political lifespan of the government may be. The articulation of goals for the system of higher education in hard and fast fashion or, indeed, speculation of what they may be in the future, is inhibited by the prospect of the next election.

One might, however, distinguish between goals and that looser concept, role, defined as a proper or customary function. In postsecondary education in western Canada there is considerable agreement as to the role of the elements in the system. That of the university has been shaped throughout the duration of the institution. One observes in each of the provinces that, on an ad hoc basis, institutional roles, though crudely defined, are emerging. For example, the University of British Columbia, the senior institution in that province, is perceived as placing principal emphasis on building a research professoriate of international repute; that of its sister institution, Simon Fraser, is viewed as outreach-oriented, the nature of its organization approaches *avant garde* (as illustrated by its use of the trimester system), while the image of the University of Victoria appears to be that of a sound, liberal arts institution bent on forwarding the creative arts rather than developing either the extent or level of its graduate work. Similarly, in Saskatchewan there can be no confusion as to the roles of the three subsystems that comprise the network—the universities, the technical institutes, and the colleges, the latter unique in Canada in their structure and exclusive orientation to adult education.

Nor is there evidence as to the extent to which the directions of the higher education networks are linked to and supportive of those of society—and again for good reason. The western Canadian provinces are, in social and economic and political terms, highly variegated. Canadian society itself is in a state of flux. Generally, the purposes of the community colleges, vocational centers, and technical institutes are more likely to reflect those of society, because of their vocational orientation, their emphasis on public service, and their identification with a particular region or community. With respect to the purposes of the universities, the public appears less content. The ideals of self-individualization, of research and scholarship, of the duty to criticize, of the bent of the institution toward conservative values are notions but dimly divined in the public mind. Nor among academics themselves is there clear understanding—or for that matter, ready acceptance—of the politicians' role in mediating the expressed wishes of the electorate with respect to higher education.

Except perhaps in Alberta, there is little evidence of government pressure on institutions to clarify their respective missions. In that province, government has invited each postsecondary institution to submit a definition of its respective role ("role" here defined as parameters within which each will operate). Subsequently, these are to be translated into sets of short-term objectives with the goal of producing "growth development plans."

Public or institutional leaders, of course, do have goals whether or not these have been articulated. Within the university sector the goal is currently to achieve institutional consolidation at existing budget and facilities levels. The public's orientation toward vocational training and meeting job market demand would appear to be stronger than in the past. The provision of broader opportunities for self-development clearly has general public endorsement and is reflected in the creation of such institutions as Athabasca University in Alberta and the group of community colleges in Saskatchewan. The operating policies of western Canadian colleges generally emphasize "open door" admission, broad choice in program, varieties in types of instruction, flexibility in schedule, counseling, and ready reaccess. Within government, the terms "cost efficiency" and "institutional productivity," however they may be defined, seem much in vogue as does the theme of greater cooperation among institutions and sectors. A determination to expand offerings, particularly those off the campus, and to seek broader recognition of informal learning for career purposes is apparent among the community colleges. The theme of access to higher education—the means of facilitating the entry of students into institutions through the development of new programs, the reworking of existing programs, the reconsideration of the goals of each program, the extension of the geographic availability of programs—is shared by college and technical institutions, government and public alike. And, finally, the extension of education to native peoples, improvement in the quality of teaching, expanded public service output, and improvement of professional education are frequently stated goals.

Nonetheless, nowhere in the network is there clear evidence of concerted and sustained reflection as to what goals will fit both present and future needs. The reforms which have been attempted seem to have been framed not in reflection of thoughtfully chosen criteria but rather have been determined on a purely pragmatic basis, despite Montaigne's counsel that "No wind blows in favor of the ship that has no port of destination."

Outputs

The outputs of the network of higher education are, generally: the provision of manpower trained to the appropriate level in the appropriate volume; research; public service; and "self-actualization," that awkward term reflecting the assumed influence of liberal studies.[39]

Manpower. Though, in each of the provinces, a government bureau exists to reconcile manpower needs with training capacities, none of these conducts the task on that sophisticated level suggested by the French term *planification.* In British Columbia, the responsibility is jointly shared by the Department of Education and the Department of Labour and, to a lesser extent, by the institutions themselves. Within government in British Columbia, the outline of a more specific planning structure is beginning to emerge, which may require the consolidation of the current responsibilities in the area of both departments. In Alberta, the function is consolidated within the Department of Advanced Education and Manpower and specifically in a planning secretariat. The manpower function in Saskatchewan was recently transferred from the government's executive council jointly to the Department of Continuing Education and to the Department of Labour, while in Manitoba an associate deputy minister in the Department of Continuing Education and Manpower is responsible.

There appear to be two central objectives with respect to manpower: the projection of future manpower needs; and response to federal government requests for "training places" in provincial institutions. It should be noted that in Manitoba, of the $27 million currently expended on community colleges, $20 million comes from the federal government for "places" purchased and with respect for other work performed by the colleges in Manitoba. But there is little consensus that the manpower planning function in any of the western provinces is performed effectively or that the data gathered can be interpreted other than at a very high level of generality, or, indeed, that in anything other than a dictatorship, the task can be performed at all.

Clearly, some elements of the network—the vocational centers and the technical institutes, for example—are much more immediately related to national manpower requirements than are others and, as has been observed, can "turn training programs off and on like a tap." There is considerable evidence, particularly in elements of the higher education network other than the university, of response to changing public demand for new kinds of training and education through programs which tend to be informal and subjective. In the universities, the task of providing appropriately synchronized supplies of manpower is inhibited by the turn-around time of relatively long-lasting programs, though institutions may exercise some influence in their control of admission to the professional programs such as law and medicine. The fact remains that the task is difficult and perhaps impossible in a society which places a premium on freedom of choice and which is characterized by rapidly shifting technology and extreme population mobility.

It might be noted in passing that, while in the last two decades enrollment in higher education has expanded, there is little objective evidence of policies consciously and specifically designed to increase the proportion of students from the lower levels of society, even in the adult education area which is typically the most responsive and flexible.

Research. Of equal interest is the means by which the research needs of the several provinces are discovered and matched to the capacities of the respective networks of higher education. On the face of it, the desirability of rationalizing provincial research requirements with research capacities seems obvious. Yet the path is not easy and the obvious, if difficult, question is this: what research is how important and to whom? A principal difficulty is that both federal and provincial governments are jointly, though not equally, engaged in the provision of financial support to research, though in neither jurisdiction is the policy on research clear. The bulk of research support comes from the federal government.

There are, of course, informal ways in which research needs are related to research capacities. Departments of agriculture and health in the provincial governments have long-standing advisory relationships with university faculties of agriculture, medicine, and science in research provision and in each of the provinces. Provincially established research councils focus some attention on required research in engineering and the sciences.

Some recent developments are of interest. In Manitoba, discussions have been initiated with a view to establishing some mechanism for rationalization of research. The province of Saskatchewan has recently established a Science Council with a Policy Secretariat (funded through a subvote of the Department of Continuing Education) which is expected to influence research development in that province. In Alberta, a Cabinet Committee on Science and Research Policy, guided by an advisory committee, has a similar role to play with respect to research.

Public Service. The third output of the higher education network, public service, has not been defined at all. Typically, in terms of ascending order of sophistication, it may include noncredit and informal adult education offerings, the provision of credit courses extramurally, the establishment of museums for public use, art galleries and theatres, consulting assignments undertaken by individual institution members in the community and, at the topmost level, the specifically focused attention of the institution (or network) to the solution of high-priority social problems.

In none of the provinces are there provincewide mechanisms to match public service need to the public service capacity of the higher education network. There do exist, however, mechanisms in two of the provinces which play an important related role. Saskatchewan's newly organized group of community colleges is clearly and obviously intended as a mechanism for discovering and serving the needs of the adult citizens in the respective communities. It is the task of the community colleges to assess local needs in adult education and, on a contract basis, negotiate such instruction as is necessary from the three technical institutes and the two universities. Alberta's eighty "further education councils" are unique in Canada and serve to relate public needs in adult education with institutional capacities for public service. The councils are so situated across the province that no community is without one. They receive in excess of $2 million annually from the government and use these funds to subsidize and thus to encourage community contributions to adult education from local and external agencies. Other informal mechanisms exist which perform a similar function. In Manitoba, Inter-Universities North, a cooperative venture of the three university institutions in that province, facilitates the provision of credit courses in northern Manitoba.

There is clear evidence that each of the western provinces has attempted to provide opportunities in adult education to all of the citizens of the province, however remote they may be from institutional centers. Earlier, we referred to the adult education thrust of the Saskatchewan community colleges. In Manitoba, the Department of Continuing Education is giving increased attention to government-organized, noninstitutional adult education. In Alberta, Athabasca University, exclusively an outreach institution, has been assigned responsibility for meeting adult education needs through independent study. In all the western provinces, university extension agencies are firmly established and supported by a long tradition of effective service. Not only the universities but the community colleges, technical institutes, and a host of agencies outside the public sector are expanding their adult education offerings, and their work is increasingly supported by training and research.[40]

There are those who express concern at what, to them, smacks of social planning—in the suggestion that the matching of public service to public service capacities of institutions within the higher education network should be centralized. Their argument, in part justified, is that the provinces are better served by the laissez faire approach, particularly given the well-documented entrepreneurial skills of adult education practitioners in western Canada.

The Future. With respect to the future, one factor in particular seems likely to affect both the quantity and quality of the output of the higher education network. Reliable population projections, among them that reported by Zsigmond, suggest a pronounced decrease in the eighteen to twenty-four-year old population after 1982.[41] In some provinces, especially Saskatchewan and Manitoba, the impact on institutions will be more pronounced because of emigration. Precisely how this (and related trends) will affect institutional output is a current conjecture embracing speculations such as: fewer full-time students will permit more careful attention to part-time students; should unemployment rates remain high, more young people will be encouraged to undertake study, particularly on a part-time basis; the higher standards predicted will attract more students; there will be a greater interest in credentials; the demand for continuing education will remain high; since part-time students are tied to the locality of their employment and since that locality is largely the metropolitan centers, the institutions situated in these centers will experience the greatest growth.[42]

Structures and Power

As few as a dozen years ago, federal or provincial government involvement in higher education in western Canada, other than in funding, was minimal. Indeed, few of the colleges and institutes which now comprise the network were in existence. University concerns were discreetly handled by the president and board in decorous negotiation with the minister. The economy was buoyant and higher education ranked high in public esteem. Today, regulation and control of the network are the dominant themes in a remarkably changed environment of higher education.

Observation suggests that the degree of acceptance of government intervention in the higher education network appears to vary with the province. In Saskatchewan, for example, two university institutions, a very new Universities Commission, and an embryonic community college sector exhibit relations which seem relatively serene. In British Columbia, in contrast, the impression is that of a continuing rearguard action against government intrusion, fought by three highly independent university institutions and a community college system. Recently, in Alberta, the government withdrew a draft for legislation intended to deal with higher education, following acrimonious protest from the universities and, as well, from professional associations. The senior university institution, the University of Alberta, is currently in dispute with the government over the latter's intention to alter the existing fee structure.

Nonetheless, in the public mind across the four western provinces there would appear to be considerable consensus on the obligation of government to oversee the operation of higher education—a reflection of the severe competition for public revenues, coupled to the fact that 80 to 85 percent of the universities' revenues come from government, and virtually 100 percent in the case of colleges and institutes. Indeed, the fact that the postsecondary system now absorbs such a large part of the gross national product appears to the public as ample reason for the government to scrutinize its operation.

The emotion-charged rhetoric of the academic administrator aside, there is little evidence that the government has damaged institutional integrity—the core elements of which are who shall be taught, who shall teach, and what shall be taught. Nonetheless, wariness and suspicion remain. The crux of the debate is the view, on the one hand, that the government should exercise the same control over institutions of higher education that it exercises with respect to other concerns, and the contrary argument is that the effectiveness of the university in particular, as a unique, social institution, will be permanently damaged by insensitive intervention.[43]

Excepting Manitoba, in each of the four western provinces

government's control of the community colleges is shared with college boards, though the balance of authority and responsibility and the respective role of each board is not always clear or stable. The sharpness of government's profile in the power structure varies with the province; in Alberta and British Columbia it appears rather more clearly defined than in Saskatchewan. In general, the relative newcomers to the higher education network—the community colleges, technical institutes, and vocational centers—tend to be more susceptible to the wishes of government and more malleable than the universities. Major changes within the network are most frequently precipitated by bodies external to it, such as commissions of inquiry or quasijudicial investigating groups established to resolve disputes or simply to respond to public demand.

It might be noted that, throughout the network and within the institutions that comprise it, the distribution of power has become ever more diffuse. By way of illustration, the readily identifiable layers of power in the Alberta university, which has a roughly vertical hierarchy, number no fewer than eleven.[44] The consequence, to adapt Gilbert and Sullivan's homely truth, is that "when everybody's somebody, nobody's anybody." Such an extraordinary dispersion of power transforms the university president from a leader to a middle-level manager, for whom power is elusively elsewhere. Presidential direction of universities in recent years has been less sustained than in the past. (One western Canadian institution has had five different presidents in ten years, with one interregnum, a circumstance scarcely compatible with effective leadership.) Moreover, in the play of power, the fragmented leadership of the institutions must confront a single authority in the government, in the person of the minister.

The university itself is the object of criticism from within and without. It is characterized as prone to ritualism, impervious to change, calcified, outdated in its decision-making processes, monopolistic in spirit, tending toward privilege and self-service, and devoting greater energy to rights than to responsibility. Its intransigence is used to explain the impossibility of voluntary coordination and institutional self-reform. The university department itself must be recognized as a power base to be reckoned with (though, noting the reluctance with which it prepares for the future, Grambsch quips "...if the Edsel were a department, it would still be in production"[45]). Yet its critics concede that, to preserve itself, the university or college must not compromise its integrity nor lose its unique identity, not let itself be used or become beholden and uncritical, not seek political power or deny its accountability.[46]

A variety of external agencies exert informal influence on the network. Among them are government departments of agriculture, organizations such as the Saskatchewan Federation of Indians, professional associations, and accrediting agencies. The federal government research-granting bureaus are also a significant power base external to the network. Inevitably, there is an old boys' network in each province though these are diminishing in influence.

For the moment at least, it would appear that the power bases in each of the provinces are in equilibrium, though new players will undoubtedly make their entrance. In the main, the present participants perceive the network not as centrally propelled but as functioning through a series of self-generated interactions.

Interestingly, in three of the four western provinces that have university intermediaries it is apparent that the universities would rather have direct contact with the political element of government. But this desire is a potential source of trouble. In all of the provinces, whether an intermediary functions or whether responsibility for the universities is centralized in a government bureau, attempts are made to circumvent conventional authority through "end runs." To the extent that institutional representatives, some more politically astute than others, are, in this way, able to penetrate government, intermediary control of its programs is made difficult or impossible, since certain decisions will be assumed to have been based on political considerations rather than on the rationally determined needs of the network of higher education. The seemingly inevitable consequence will be to render the intermediary helpless; the Cabinet will become a board of higher education.[47]

Predictably, in western Canada the regard in which the intermediary is held by the institutions and the government is mixed. The latter regards it as a shrewd, conservative body with a cost-accounting bent, intent only on the unimaginative, if meticulous, allocation of funds. The former see it as a threatening element, the willing tool of government, aimed at a radical reshaping of the university institution by whatever the means. Nevertheless, the likelihood of a return to the days when universities bargained directly with government is doubtful; equally doubtful is whether the universities would fare better in achieving their ends.

The intermediary in western Canada is the object of frank suspicion and spiteful criticism. Restated in positive terms, these criticisms suggest the working policies it must adopt if it is to gain the confidence of institutions and government. Its statutory authority should be strong and unequivocal. It should be scrupulous in ensuring that relevant information is disseminated. It should ensure regular discussion among the principals in both institutions and government through what has been termed an "organized system of informal contact." It should take pains faithfully to report the sentiments of government concerning higher education, particularly when the financial requests of the institution have been only partially met. It should carefully consider the volume of information it ought reasonably to request from university institutions, the cost of assembling it, and the purpose for which it is to be used. It should recognize the role of continuing education and the significance of its underlying philosophy for higher education. With respect to the decisions and choices it must make, the applicable criteria should be specified and agreement on them sought. Its staff, incorporating a strong research capacity, should be of such quality as to engender the confidence of the universities, but not so large as to excite the usual criticism leveled at bureaucracy. As an operating tactic, it may lean heavily on the institutions themselves and on strong academic advisory committees in the course of studies preceding an articulation of policy. It should not permit itself to be dominated by a single, powerful institution. The citizen membership of its council should be neutral in terms of political affiliation, not representative of a single class or profession, but genuinely representative of the social fabric of the province as a whole. Finally, there is reason to believe that the intermediary as an agency is more likely to be able to function satisfactorily if it is dealing with three or more institutions. Despite their shortcomings, one would conclude that the institutions in western Canada get better decisions in matters of substance through their intermediary than they might otherwise get through the political processes of direct negotiation with government.[48]

Given Alberta's experience in the demise of both of its former intermediaries, the Universities Commission and the Colleges Commission, there is speculation that the functions of similar intermediaries will inevitably be assumed by government. Whether or not this will occur seems to depend in part on the government's willingness to deflect direct appeals to it from the institutions or their supporters and upon the value the government places on the advantage afforded by the existence of the intermediary—of dealing at arm's length with institutions—particularly in periods of financial crisis or controversy. What is unclear is whether, in a dynamic society, the intermediary is merely a step in a cycle—and, perhaps, a recurring cycle. Another interesting speculation is this: at what point does increasing centralization of control of higher education by government become dysfunctional?

Apart from their thus far unrewarding search for parity of esteem with the universities, the community colleges face additional problems, including: the stabilization of a mutually acceptable balance in decision making between government and local authorities; rigidity or diffusion of purpose within the college board; the achievement of diversity in educational choice for the student; the strengthening of program offerings; the balancing of community manpower needs with training opportunity; the upgrading of teacher qualifications; and providing for coordination with other institutions, particularly the universities within or across provincial boundaries. Not unexpectedly, given the short span of their existence, there has been little research on these and a host of related problems.

The university and college staffs' decision to adopt union status will most certainly change the power structure of the higher education network, though nowhere in the western provinces are the consequences of it wholly clear. In Manitoba, the Faculty Association of the University of Manitoba is certified under a provincial statute; in each of the other provinces, nonacademic staff members are certified by a variety of unions (as many as fourteen in one institution). Similarly, in Saskatchewan, the faculty associations of the two universities are now certified though the first collective agreements have still to be negotiated. In Alberta and British Columbia, university interest in unions is not especially strong, a fact ascribed to the already dominant influence that faculty associations exercise on the affairs of the universities. In none of the provinces except British Columbia are college staffs certified under a labor act as unions. In British Columbia, the government is concerned over whether the currently independent staff associations will strengthen the force of their demands by bargaining as a provincewide group.

The stakes, among them these, are high: that the strong collegial relationships which at present characterize the universities may be severely diminished; that the formalities of operating the institution will increase and the apparatus of institutional government will be codified; and that the roles of deans and department heads, in particular, will be redefined. Perhaps the most important factor is the potential impact of salary demands, the upward limits of which are ultimately set by available provincial revenues which are highly vulnerable in resource-based economies. Finally, this concern remains: that, at the point at which all university staff members in a province are unionized with government paying a projected 85 to 90 percent of all university costs, the tendency of government might well be to regard faculty members not as academics but as civil servants — and to treat them accordingly.

To summarize, the current tendency in western Canada among both systems and component institutions is toward coordination and consolidation. The balance struck in each province between institutional autonomy and government domination varies, as do the instruments employed. Each represents a delicate compromise between government's requirement that the institution remain sensitive to social purpose and the promotion of change, and the institution's need for freedom and the protection of its flexibility. Though the provincial governments' impact on the network of higher education in each of the western provinces is much more obvious than it was a decade earlier, there is little in the way of solid evidence to indicate the benefit thus accruing to higher education in terms of the cost of this intervention. That is, no such cost-benefit analysis indisputably confirms (or contradicts) the outcomes of coordination in terms of greater economy, the absence of proliferation, the encouragement of innovation or the suppression of change, or the introduction of conformity.[49]

The prospect of continuing change in the organization of higher education here as elsewhere seems beyond dispute.[50]

> In short, the organizational geography of superindustrial society can be expected to become increasingly kinetic, filled with turbulence and change. The more rapidly the environment changes, the shorter the life span of organization forms.

In administrative structure, just as in architectural structure, we are moving from long-enduring to temporary forms, from permanence to transience. We are moving from bureaucracy to ad-hocracy.

Though the provincial governments will continue to be involved in higher education, nothing suggests that the present mechanisms will remain. The most pervasive barriers to productive change "are not limitations in money or staff time, as often suggested. The real barriers are subtle limitations in vision, attitudes, and expectations, conditioned as they are by present-day practices."[51]

Planning and Budgeting

The hallmark of the well-integrated and rationally ordered "system" of higher education is planning.

Among the four western provinces, considerable variation marks the degree of sophistication with which the task is approached. In British Columbia, for example, no planning division expressly concerned with higher education operates within the Department of Education, while in Alberta a large array of bureaus in the substantial bureaucracy of the Department of Advanced Education and Manpower oversee every aspect of higher education development.

With respect to colleges and technical institutes in each of the provinces, the central responsibility for planning — in the areas of finance, program, physical plant, and communications — rests with the government departments which annually review funding proposals. These proposals are the product of discussions by the college boards (Manitoba colleges, which do not have boards of governors, are assisted by advisory committees and advisory boards) and the principal, aided by his administrative staff. Of the four western provinces, Alberta is most apt at producing, for the guidance of the whole network, policy documents intended to assist the framing of institutional development.[52]

With respect to universities, annual proposals are generated from, at the University of Alberta, the Academic Development Plan developed by its staff and administration and subsequently approved by the General Faculties Council. It should be stated here again that, by their very nature, universities are at odds with planning. Elaborate planning, particularly in today's campus climate of participatory democracy, is a process of extraordinary complexity, not to say cost in terms of staff time. An implicit danger in the process is that universities will fall increasingly under the direction of professional administrators and an adversary relationship with academics will develop which will corrode the university's purposes. Yet, given the order of funds involved, the responsibility to avoid waste and duplication, and the urgent pressures of government, universities are compelled to plan.

Planning by definition is a rational, sequential process. Yet, given the length of the planning chain in the network of higher education — from institutional department to institutional administrators to board to intermediary to government department — it is inevitable that planning is viewed as, at best, an act of faith and, at worst, irrelevant. A former university president puts the point this way:[53]

> Politicians allocate funds within the political realities of a given year or situation. If the universities seem to be an area of activity with a high political quotient, they will get preferred treatment. However, if grants to universities are not a matter of life and death as far as a government being elected or defeated and if the public is not concerned that universities stand near the front of the queue, then I would be very surprised if they end up in that position.

The view within institutions is that much of planning represents merely a conventional dressing up of figures, an activity of little real value since the ultimate decision is made in terms of political considerations and with little regard to the conclusions of the planners. It is this grey area, the point at which the inevitable political decision is made, that is confusing to the institutions. The reality is that, whatever the final political decision, it will invariably be based on a combination of factors of which one, certainly, will be how much confidence the ministry has in the institution — based on evidence of careful planning and the discipline it imposes on the institution. Within institutions, an investment in planning, even if it is not expert, creates at least an awareness of problems. Within government, sustained master planning appears to be more honored in word than in deed, although periodically, special-purpose commissions identify major problems, set out long-term goals, and establish basic philosophic positions.

The process of budgeting in any complex, multiagency organization is difficult enough. But in the network of higher education there are particular problems which pose new levels of complexity. Among them are: predicting the likely student intake, a figure directly affected by, among other factors, the state of the economy; predicting the likely rate of inflation, the single most significant variable in budgeting; the negotiation of staff salaries which may take place out of phase with, and in isolation from, the budget process; the fixed liabilities of institutions in terms of plant, services, and tenured staff; and the inability of the institution to generate significant revenue to supplement grant support. The inflation factor, particularly, and the reluctance of politicians to involve themselves in planning based on more than one-year cycles inhibits effective triennial or quinquennial planning. Nevertheless, it is clear that universities need a longer horizon for financial planning, to avoid the potential damage of successive short-term decisions in response to immediate pressures.[54]

The use of rationing devices, such as the number of full-time equivalent students (FTE), is not used as the sole basis for budget planning in any of the western provinces. Enrollment-based grant formulas are considered an unsatisfactory approach; indeed, in Manitoba, two of the three university institutions could not exist on revenues derived from conventional formula grants. An alternative approach, zero-base budgeting, involves estimating what it would actually cost in any year for individual institutions to perform their functions—an exercise which annually involves thorough-going task analysis. Typically in western Canada, the approach used is incremental (or historical or additive) budgeting: a percentage increase established by government in the light of changed teaching loads, research costs, changes in fixed costs (such as utilities), and special projects is applied to the budget base of the preceeding year. An interesting new approach is that undertaken by the University of Manitoba, "challenge budgeting," in which individual faculties and departments are advised at the beginning of the budget process of proposed decreases in their budget from the previous year and are invited to justify why they feel these funds should not be decreased.

To summarize, budgetary planning within the postsecondary networks is based on incremental funding (though formulas may be applied as a check). Operational funds provided to universities are applied at the discretion of the latter, while those provided to the nonuniversity elements of the network are rather more closely tied to specific instructional plans. Capital funds provided to each are invariably designated for specific projects. The processes employed within the planning-budgeting chain—from institutional department to faculty to administration to board of governors to ministry—seem to be well understood by those affected. But, as we have mentioned, there is less clear understanding or appreciation of the significance of the final, and necessarily political, decision taken by government, a circumstance which breeds doubt and even cynicism within institutions about the usefulness of the planning process.

What seems increasingly evident is that the days of financial security are all but gone. The future, shaped by radical renegotiation of federal-provincial fiscal arrangements, would seem to lead inevitably to further provincialization of postsecondary education and to an environment in which the provinces may be largely thrown back on their own financial resources.

Working Relationships

The extraordinary growth of the higher education network in each of the western provinces has given rise to new sets of relationships. Where, a decade ago, there may have been only one university, today there are two or more. Working relationships among the universities can be characterized as generally cool and distant, frequently competitive and occasionally antagonistic. It was interinstitutional friction, combined with vigorous partisan feeling of citizens in competitive cities, which led the University of Alberta to grant autonomy to its Calgary branch in 1966, and the University of Saskatchewan to establish two separate institutions. In British Columbia, tensions among the three institutions are never far from the surface. James Perkins' plea remains largely unaccepted: that universities "must surrender a great deal of their individual autonomy with respect to other education institutions in order to secure the more important objective—an appropriate independence of the whole system of higher education from government and the state."[55]

It might be supposed that the creation of an intermediary agency in British Columbia, Saskatchewan, and Manitoba would have knitted the universities together in a common front, but this is not yet apparent. In Alberta, the Universities Coordinating Council was established by statute in 1966 for the express purpose of providing the institutions with a focus for cooperative effort; the council has not been successful in its role. It is evident to one western Canadian president "that no scheme will work well—even if it is illegal not to cooperate in making it work—if the people affected don't want it to work or don't trust one another."[56] The reverse is true as well; given good interpersonal relationships, even the most apparently awkward system can be made to function effectively.

The consequences of a lack of mutual regard and of indifference toward cooperative effort are indisputably negative. The government, faced with fragmentation among the institutions, is the more readily enabled to achieve its ends. At the same time, the student is faced with stumbling blocks, since the universities are unwilling to articulate their programs so as to facilitate ready transfer of credit from one institution to another. Obviously, public support for the universities is not enhanced by clear evidence of interinstitutional bickering.

In contrast, in each of the provinces the colleges and institutes, closely tied to government as they are, appear to be somewhat more cohesive. No doubt, this in part reflects the fact that the geographical areas they serve are discrete. Their principals or presidents meet regularly with one another and intercollege conferences are organized regularly. In some quarters, the success enjoyed by community colleges, often under trying physical conditions and with lean budgets, is viewed with some uneasiness by the universities. Indeed, there is the suggestion that an unhealthy future rivalry will arise between universities and colleges in any contest for students and funds. On the other hand, the technical institutes enjoy an invariably good public image, in part because their programs are specific, readily understood, and directly connected to employment.

Between the community colleges and the university sectors the links are loose indeed. Virtually the only point of regular contact between the universities and the colleges is the agency or committee, in Alberta the Alberta Council on Admissions and Transfer,[57] established to deal with these problems. Parity of esteem, the latent ambition of most colleges, underlines a basic characteristic within the network: the existence of a pecking order among institutions, a circumstance which does not facilitate interinstitutional mobility of students or the development of clear-cut statements of institutional mission.

On one point there is general agreement: the institutions are not directing enough attention to the task of establishing and maintaining cordial and sympathetic relationships with their respective constituencies. Whatever the realities, an unflattering stereotype of the university does exist and this image is a basic point of reference for many people.[58] Its negative features, according to a Saskatchewan study,[59] picture an undisciplined student body, poor administration, an intellectual ghetto of self-serving academics (many of them foreign and with an antireligious bias). In the public mind, the university has not satisfactorily resolved issues of admission, adequate counseling, and effective teaching, nor accepted its accountability. In the main, taxpayers' participation in institutional affairs is limited to membership on boards of governors or occasional consultative committees. While the colleges appear to root themselves enthusiastically in their social environment, the universities tend to perceive themselves—how is problematic—as national institutions.

Whatever the accuracy of this popular image, there seems little doubt that all institutions could profit from a carefully developed and sustained attention to public relations (in the best sense of that term) which would go beyond a mere distribution of press releases and similar activities to the active coopting of citizens in institutional concerns. The regard in which each of the elements of the network is held, and thus its capacity to mobilize citizen support and political influence toward the attainment of its ends, is determined in the main by three factors: how well its role is understood; clear evidence of its contribution to society; and public confidence in its approaches and methods.

In each of the provinces of western Canada except British Columbia, the significance of higher education has been recognized by the emergence of a government department devoted exclusively to postsecondary education. There is little evidence in any of the provinces of any formal linkage between the school system and the network of postsecondary institutions. Whatever influence the school system exerts is limited to the character of the product it turns out. (Currently, the universities blame the schools for the alleged functional illiteracy of a proportion of high school graduates, while the schools blame the universities for the inadequate preparation of teachers.)

A new feature of higher education in western Canada which warrants comment is the recent development of productive, cooperative regional relationships among the western provinces and between these provinces as a group and agencies elsewhere in Canada. These are illustrated in interprovincial agreements to centralize veterinary training at the University of Saskatchewan, dental nursing at Regina's Wascana Institute, and nuclear technology and audiology training at the Red River Community College. Three of the western provinces have contracted with the University of Waterloo in Ontario to centralize the training of opticians.[60]

Evaluation

Finally, in this examination of the networks of higher education in the western provinces, we turn now to the logical end step—the evaluation of the product.

This can be stated briefly: in any sophisticated sense, comprehensive evaluation of the network does not exist. The apparent lack of effective evaluation is due to the sheer difficulty of the task, the inherent indifference of institutions to the rigors of the market place, and the lack of clearly defined and articulated goals. Little in the literature of higher education yet serves to support evaluative efforts. Moreover, it might well be considered naive to suppose that systemwide cooperation in the effort could be secured.

Nevertheless, within institutions, if largely on an ad hoc basis, infrequent attempts at evaluation are made: departments and faculties occasionally undertake such studies; research relating to particular facets of institutional effort is commissioned; the judgments of reputable international agencies, such as the OECD, are provided periodically; opinions of professional organizations are sought or proffered; accrediting organizations provide useful comparisons on how work is carried out elsewhere; and infrequent official investigations into administrative, organizational, or financial issues are both revealing and helpful.

Summary

The principal, obvious feature of higher education networks in the four western provinces is their recency. The majority of the institutions were, indeed, nonexistent as few as a dozen years ago. Public demand for expanded access to higher education and for alternatives to the university in postsecondary education prompted their creation; in some instances, institutions emerged as a result of growing demands for adult education. Within the community college sector particularly, the diversity of the institutions is striking.

In all of the provinces except one, the network features a university intermediary body, two of them very new. At the same time, the evidence clearly indicates that a single, provincewide organization would be unacceptable. Much of the change which has taken place in the four networks, in their short lifespan, has sprung from public enquiries and broad consultation with the electorate. Certainly, the charismatic leadership of university presidents has played an important role in the development of the network. The colleges—much less in the public eye, seemingly more malleable and accepting of government policy—are, in all of the provinces save one, a joint responsibility of local governing boards and government with the latter as dominant partner. In general, the evolution of the controlling agency, whether government, department, or intermediary, appears to foreshadow a shift from resource-allocator to resource-allocator-coordinator to resource-allocator-coordinator-planner. What are now still networks of disparate institutions appear to be growing toward full-fledged systems.

While the general purposes and individual institutional roles are reasonably well-understood at a rudimentary level, articulated network or institutional goals are more the exception than the rule. The educational product of the institutions is left largely in the hands of a special interest group: the teachers.

The degree of sophistication in planning varies. In particular, the task of harnessing the resources of the network to manpower needs appears to be a difficult and perhaps impossible task. Efforts to coordinate research needs with research capacities other than on an informal basis are limited; increasing attention, however, is being given to matching adult education needs to the capabilities of the institutions in the network.

Predictably, especially since it has been introduced so recently, the degree to which government control is accepted varies widely; however, no evidence suggests that there has been a damaging intervention into higher education. Both within the network and within institutions, power is widely diffused, and this has mixed consequences. Though the intermediary agencies are a recent phenomenon, the principles which determine their effectiveness are readily apparent; the essential element is, as in all human affairs, mutual trust. This ingredient is not universally evident with respect to the institutions' view of politicians, who ultimately hold the purse strings. The unionization of faculty can confidently be predicted as a major emerging influence on higher education administration. Finally, despite the temptation to regard the structural status quo as permanent, it is more prudent to regard the structure of control of higher education as dynamic, perhaps indeed, likely to follow a cyclical pattern, one continuously shaped by political, economic, and social change.

The expansion of the network has led to a host of new relationships among its component elements. Within the university sector, cooperative approaches to the solution of interinstitutional problems and to the exploration of societal needs are by no means routine. Substantial, well-planned efforts on the part of the institutions to interpret themselves to their constituents and to cultivate public support (and gain political influence) would return substantial dividends. In this respect, the recent emergence of productive, cooperative relationships among provincial networks is especially significant.

Acknowledging that the available tools are still scarce and the process difficult, efforts to evaluate the output of the network and its control agencies are few and far between. Yet, at present, one cannot conclude that the institutions are other than highly productive. Indeed, elements of the network exhibit a vitality and a fundamental solidity which has, nationally and internationally, earned them an enviable reputation.

Yet caution is warranted. As to the adaptability of higher education and, thus, of the likely relevance of its product to the future, not all speculation is optimistic:[61]

> The postulates are these: that man's emergence and survival have depended upon his appropriate use of technology; that

the future will not accommodate projections of our current style of technology; and that the establishments of education are unable to redirect our expectations and uses of technology. The problem is thus one of helplessness in forging a technological style for a felicitous habitation of the planet....

Our future lifestyles, and perhaps our survival, depend upon acquiring and developing a knowledge of technology that is appropriate to the individual and his immediate environment. The question, for which I have no answer, is how we may become educated for this new enterprise.

FOOTNOTES

1. British Columbia, *Report of the Commission on University Programs in Non-Metropolitan Areas,* W. C. Winegard, commissioner (Victoria, B.C.: Department of Education, 1976).
2. George Woodcock, "Playing to the People," *The Canadian* (January 8, 1977), p. 4.
3. University of Saskatchewan, *Report of the Committee on the Role of the University of Saskatchewan within the Community,* T. H. McLeod, chairman (Saskatoon: The University of Saskatchewan, 1971), p. 2.
4. Manitoba, *Post-Secondary Education in Manitoba,* report of the Task Force on Post-Secondary Education, Michael Oliver, chairman (Winnipeg: Queen's Printer, 1973), p. 5.
5. John B. Macdonald, *Higher Education in British Columbia and a Plan for the Future* (Vancouver: The University of British Columbia, 1962).
6. British Columbia, *Report* of the Winegard Commission, p. 6.
7. A new colleges and provincial institutes act, in preparation in mid-1977, would change all this.
8. John D. Dennison *et al., The Impact of Community Colleges: A Study of the College Concept in British Columbia* (Vancouver: B.C. Research, 1975).
9. British Columbia, *Towards the Learning Community,* Report of the Task Force on the Community College in British Columbia (Victoria: Queen's Printer, 1974), pp. 10-11.
10. Prior to 1975, an Academic Board established under the Universities Act, 1963, comprising members of the senate of each university and three members appointed by government, functioned as an advisor with these powers: "...to collect, examine, and provide information relating to academic standards, and to advise the appropriate authorities on orderly academic development of universities...and of colleges...by keeping in review the academic standards of each; and...to report on any matters respecting aca-

demic standards and development in higher education, as may be from time to time required by the minister of education." From the beginning, however, the board was denied that secretariat which would have allowed it to play a proper and significant role in education.

11. British Columbia, *Report* of the Winegard Commission, p. 7.
12. Duncan D. Campbell, *Those Tumultuous Years* (Edmonton: The University of Alberta, 1977).
13. Commission Sponsored by the Canadian Association of University Teachers and the Association of Universities and Colleges of Canada, *University Government in Canada*, Sir James Duff and Robert O. Berdahl, commissioners (Toronto: University of Toronto Press, 1966).
14. G. R. Maddocks, *A Comparative Analysis of Approaches to Planning Development in Post-Secondary Education*, Research Studies in Post-Secondary Education No. 23 (Edmonton: Alberta Colleges Commission, 1972), p. 97.
15. J. M. Small, *College Coordination in Alberta: System Development and Appraisal*, Research Studies in Post-Secondary Education No. 18 (Edmonton: Alberta Colleges Commission, 1972).
16. Gordon Campbell, "Some Comments on Reports of Post-Secondary Commissions in Relation to Community Colleges in Canada," *The Canadian Journal of Higher Education*, Vol. V, No. 3 (1975), pp. 55-68.
17. *Ibid.*, p. 57.
18. Alberta, Commission on Educational Planning, *A Choice of Futures*, Walter H. Worth, commissioner (Edmonton: Queen's Printer, 1972).
19. Observation suggests that, in manifestation of public will, constraints on the mobility of students among institutions may be eased and present institutional barriers to the acceptance of informal and experiential learning lifted.
20. Quoted in University of Saskatchewan, *Report* of the McLeod Committee, p. 70.
21. *Ibid.*
22. J. W. T. Spinks, *A Decade of Change: The University of Saskatchewan 1959-70* (Saskatoon: The University of Saskatchewan, 1972).
23. Saskatchewan, The University of Regina Act, S.S. 1974, C. 119, as am.; The University of Saskatchewan Act, S.S. 1974, C. 120, as am.; and The Universities Commission Act, S.S. 1974, C. 118, as am. (Regina: Queen's Printer).
24. R.F.E. Harvey, *Middle Range Education in Canada*, Quance Lecture in Canadian Education, 1973 (Toronto: Gage Educational, 1973), p. 13.
25. Saskatchewan, *Report of the Minister's Advisory Committee on Community Colleges* (Regina: Department of Continuing Education, 1972), pp. 7-8.
26. The committee, like other investigative bodies before it concerned with education and social affairs, tapped the opinion of the whole population of the province through public hearings conducted in fifty communities.
27. Gordon Campbell, "Some Comments...in Relation to Community Colleges...," pp. 57-58, 62.
28. Manitoba, Universities Grants Commission, *First Annual Report for the Year ending March 31, 1968* (Winnipeg: Department of Youth and Education, 1968).

29. But, as Berdahl shrewdly observes, "The power to reallocate and eliminate programs is seldom exercised because past experience has shown that such moves have unfortunate political repercussions, stirring up controversy and even leading to the agency's decision being overturned.... Powers to reallocate programs are little used during periods of rapid expansion, but should a severe recession or depression occur, this function of coordination might well become central." Robert O. Berdahl, *Statewide Coordination of Higher Education* (Washington, D.C.: American Council on Education, 1971), p. 15.
30. Manitoba, *Post-Secondary Education in Manitoba*.
31. *Ibid.*, p. 39.
32. *Ibid.*, p. 41.
33. *Ibid.*, p. 42.
34. *Ibid.*, p. 43.
35. R. W. Jackson, *Human Goals and Science Policy*, Science Council of Canada, Background Study No. 38 (Ottawa: Science Council of Canada, 1976), p. 113.
36. Reference to a model of a full-blown system, that in the state of Utah in the United States is helpful. Initial sections of a 1969 Act creating this system suggest its obvious unitary character:

    Section 2. Purpose of act—centralized direction, master planning—single board to govern higher education.

    It is the purpose of this Act to afford the people of the State of Utah a more efficient and more economical system of high quality public higher education through centralized direction and master planning providing for avoidance of unnecessary duplication within the system, for the systematic and orderly development of facilities and quality programs, for coordination and consolidation, and for systematic development of the role or roles of each institution within the system of higher education consistent with the historical heritage and tradition of each institution.

    The purpose of this Act is to vest in a single board the power to govern the state system of higher education and within the board's discretion to delegate certain powers to institutional councils.

    Section 3. State system of higher education—component units designated.

    The state system of higher education shall consist of the state board of regents, the University of Utah, the Utah State University of Agriculture and Applied Science, Weber State College, Southern Utah State College, the College of Eastern Utah, Snow College, Dixie College, Utah Technical College at Provo, Utah Technical College at Salt Lake and such other public post high school educational institutions as the legislature may from time to time create.

    G. Homer Durham, *General Policies of the Utah State Board of Regents: Governing the Utah System of Higher Education* (Salt Lake City: Office of the Commissioner of Higher Education, 1976), p. 13.

    The extraordinarily comprehensive range of operating policies in this system, set out by its Board of Regents in this 222-page manual, is instructive.
37. The mixed attitude of academics toward goal delineation is aptly illustrated by Young, who holds that: "universities that choose a 'role and goals' that are any more precise than 'the acquisition, storage, and dissemination of knowl-

edge and the pursuit of excellence in an atmosphere of free enquiry' are asking for trouble"; and Entwistle *et al.*, who argue that "the need for a systematic sifting of these concepts is long overdue. Rigorous linguistic analysis would contribute to the removal of confusion and to the construction of a logical framework of concepts within which agreement on the objectives of higher education could be sought." Peitchinis of the University of Calgary makes this urgent plea:

> It is simply imperative that we indicate what we are, what we can do, what we must do, and what resources we need to do the things that must be done. Failure to set goals and objectives, and failure to plan, will be an open invitation to eager government bureaucrats to do it; failure to cooperate, coordinate and rationalize within provincial jurisdictions will be an open invitation to bureaucrats to embark upon the formulation of policies designed to achieve such purposes; and failure to take a firm stand, in concert, on the vital role of direct federal participation, will weaken further the federal position and strengthen creeping provincial parochialism.

See: Walter D. Young, "Proposals for Planning too Time Consuming," *University Affairs* (July 1975), pp. 6-7; N. J. Entwistle, L. A. Percy, and J. B. Nisbet, *Educational Objectives and Academic Performance in Higher Education* (Lancaster: University of Lancaster, Department of Educational Research, 1971), pp. 16-23; Stephen Peitchinis, "Ivy Still Blocks the Light in Academia," *University Affairs* (September 1975), pp. 6-7.

38. Paul J. Gordon, "Characteristics of Organizational Species," paper for Course W501/502 at Indiana University, 1974, mimeographed.
39. The activity which absorbs most of the universities' energies is the training of paraprofessional and professional manpower; according to one observer this task was not imposed on them but evolved as a consequence of narrow specialization in individual disciplines. See: Stephen Peitchinis, "Ivy...in Academia."
40. Duncan D. Campbell, *Adult Education as a Field of Study and Practice: Strategies for Development* (Vancouver: The Centre for Continuing Education, University of British Columbia, and The International Council for Adult Education, 1977).
41. Canada, Statistics Canada, Education, Science and Culture Division, *Advance Statistics of Education, 1977-78* (Ottawa: Statistics Canada, 1977), p. 18.
42. Stefan Dupré, "Problems of Changing Growth Rates," *The Changing Conditions within the Universities*, Proceedings of the Annual Meeting, Association of Universities and Colleges of Canada, 1976, Vol. II, pp. 45-52.
43. A perception of the role of the governmental bureaucracy in the U.S. with respect to higher education is instructive. There, the intent of the bureaucracy is to "minimize the degree of controversiality in the planning process and its results; reduce possible alternatives to matters of choice of resource allocation; limit the planning process to those parts of the educational services and functions strictly controlled by [government]; exploit as fully as possible the powers, prerogatives, and responsibilities given to [it]...understate as much as possible the full role of the government in the determination of the future course of educational policy and even minimize it in the eyes

of the general public." "OECD Report on Britain: IV, 'British planning is at a watershed. Its capacity to cope with new pressures is still to be seen,'" *The Times Higher Education Supplement* (May 5, 1975), p. 11.

44. These are: the courts (which in recent years have decided a number of issues of staff policy); the visitor (who, one discovers from *The Universities Act, 1966*, has the authority "to do all those acts which pertain to visitors"); the minister of advanced education and manpower; the Department of Advanced Education and Manpower; the Board of Governors; the General Faculties Council; the Deans Council; faculty councils; department councils; the Senate; the Association of Academic Staff; and the Association of Non-Academic Staff. In addition to these, standing in lateral but significant relationship, are professional councils, the Alumni Association, The Universities Coordinating Council, and a host of other advisory and consultative committees.
45. Paul V. Grambsch, "Conflicts and Priorities," *The Troubled Campus*, edited by G. Kerry Smith (San Francisco: Jossey-Bass, 1970), p. 102.
46. Walter H. Worth, "From Autonomy to System: A Provincial Perspective," *Library Association of Alberta Bulletin*, Vol. 5, No. 2 (April 1974), pp. 64-65.
47. By way of illustration, the evidence suggests that the Universities Commission in Alberta was stripped of its credibility in large part and subsequently disbanded because private representations from those in the province's two rival cities were not deflected by government.
48. While in three of the four provinces, university intermediaries are constituted, it is important to note that two have functioned for fewer than eighteen months while the experience of the other is a matter of ten years. In Saskatchewan and British Columbia, the full impact of the intermediary in the power structure has yet to be felt.
49. An OECD report cautions against "tendencies toward unchecked bureaucracy and overstaffing" and notes the opinion that "some provincial authorities go too far in their attempts to control institutional decisions, particularly in Alberta and Quebec." OECD, *Reviews of National Policies for Education: Canada* (Paris: OECD, 1976), p. 82.
50. Alvin Toffler, *Future Shock* (New York: Random House, 1970), pp. 122-23.
51. Arthur Cohen, *Dateline '79: Heretical Concepts for the Community College* (Beverly Hills, Calif.: Glencoe Press, 1969), p. xix.
52. Principal among these is *Program Coordination—Policy, Guidelines, Procedures, 1974* (which carries the prefatory note, "Instructional programs in the Alberta system of advanced education will be coordinated to ensure the availability of effective education experiences and to avoid unwarranted duplication of effort in institutions"); *Research and Planning Studies, 1974* (in which is outlined the basis for the provision of government support to research facilitative of advanced education development); and *Further Education—Policy, Guidelines and Procedures, 1975* (which sets out the rationale for supplementary financial support to adult education).
53. Colin Mackay in an interview, "Where will universities stand in the provincial queue as they compete for funds?" *University Affairs* (February 1977), p. 8.

54. In Manitoba, a forecast of needs for the quinquennium, 1977-78 to 1981-82, prepared by the universities, has led to the preparation of a five-year "rolling plan" which has still to gain the acceptance of the universities, the Universities Grants Commission and government.
55. James A. Perkins, "The Distinctive Role of Universities in Systems of Higher Education," *Tenth Congress of the Universities of the Commonwealth, Report of Proceedings, 1968* (London: The Association of Commonwealth Universities, 1969), p. 40.
56. W.A.S. Smith, "A Comparative Study of Coordinating Structures for Systems of Post-Secondary Education," mimeographed (Lethbridge: The University of Lethbridge, circa 1971), p. 9.
57. This council (parallels for which exist in the other provinces), established in 1974, reports to the Department of Advanced Education and Manpower, which subsidizes the council's work of effecting transfer arrangements in a broad range of categories: university transfer programs, diploma, certificate, and other specified programs; special interinstitutional arrangements; and individual assessments.
58. Illustrative of public dissatisfaction is this editorial opinion: "[The preoccupation of secrecy of the Board of Governors has] resulted in much dissatisfaction and in much criticism of the board, on the part of the press and the public—indeed on the part, also, of students and faculty members of the university who were likewise kept in ignorance of the board's proceedings...a quite improper and quite unacceptable way of running a great public institution like the U[niversity] of A[lberta], that uses millions of dollars of public money, and whose business is both of interest and of importance to the general public." *Edmonton Journal* (March 17, 1975).
59. University of Saskatchewan, *Report* of the McLeod Committee, pp. 6-11.
60. IPCUR (Inter-Provincial Committee for University Rationalization) was organized by the western university presidents in 1966, originally as a subcommittee of the Prairie Provinces Economic Council. Though its successes in concrete terms were few, it paved the way for the establishment of its successor, WC-PSCC (Western Canadian Post Secondary Coordinating Committee), whose members comprise the ministers responsible for higher education in each of the four provinces. There is also a voluntary Committee of Western Canadian University Presidents which has a part-time secretariat.
61. J. Gordon Parr, "Prisoners of Inappropriate Technology," *Change* (April 1977), pp. 8-10. See also Ernest L. Boyer and Martin Kaplan, "Educating for Survival: A Call for a Core Curriculum," *Change* (March 1977), p. 22.

SUMMARY AND COMMENT
Edward Sheffield

Canada is a land of great distances and great diversity. Its geography varies from coastal plains to lofty mountains. The climate is suitable for the growing of fruit in one region and is frigid the year round in another. Some regions are rich; some poor. Canada's peoples are of many colors and many tongues, although two language-groups predominate — English and French.

It is a nation created by compromise and held together, tenuously, by further compromises. As a federation it is subject to interregional tensions and centrifugal tendencies. Each of the ten provinces has constitutional responsibility for education — a responsibility it chooses to exercise itself, with minimal regard for the interests of the whole nation. Little wonder, then, that Canada has systems rather than a system of higher education; little wonder that national goals for higher education have not been articulated.

Nevertheless, Canadians have much in common, and they discover this particularly at times when their way of life seems to be threatened by influences from elsewhere, especially from the United States. What is more, although Canada's economy in the mid-seventies shares the decline of most industrialized nations, it is really a country of rich resources, one of the most affluent in the world. Its future depends more than anything upon the ability of its people to get along with each other.

Any attempt to generalize about higher education in Canada must begin with a disclaimer. There will be at least one exception to almost every statement that can be made. As is evident, it is difficult even to generalize about the four eastern or the four western provinces, let alone all ten.

System Design

The principal institutions of postsecondary education in Canada are universities, institutes of technology, and community colleges. Universities range in size and complexity from a few with less than 1,000 students, providing first-degree courses in the liberal arts, to half a dozen multiversities enrolling more than 20,000 students and providing programs in arts, science, and the professions, leading to the baccalaureate, the master's degree, and the doctorate. Institutes of technology, normally operated directly by provincial government departments, provide practical programs of work-oriented courses, leading to diplomas. There were more of these before the advent of the community college, but the numbers now are small and they are found mostly in the western provinces. In the sixties a new type of institution made its entrance on the Canadian scene: the community college. There are now more such colleges than there are universities although the colleges still enroll only about half as many students. Their programs tend to be job-oriented, but some offer courses from which students may advance to, or transfer into, a university program. As their name implies, community colleges are especially responsive to the needs of the local community.

Altogether, these institutions offer a bewildering array of courses, from the most practical to the most esoteric, undertaken on a full- or part-time basis, for credit or no credit, in institutional settings or at a distance, and using an increasingly wide range of instructional techniques and media. The characteristics of the students also vary. While the majority are fresh from secondary school, increasing numbers of students are enrolled in correspondence courses, or are working and attending night school, or are retired and attend adult education classes. The latter clearly indicate the trend toward lifelong education programs.

Most of the universities in the central and eastern provinces were established as private institutions affiliated with churches, but in recent years almost all of these have come within the public systems and are financed, at least in part, by government. Most of the universities in the western provinces were originally created by the provincial governments although a few church-related colleges were established.

With respect to the development of institutions, several features deserve special mention. For many years the colleges have tended toward affiliation with the larger universities—thus creating minisystems of university families. Out of such groupings, new independent institutions have evolved, indicating the success of their tutelage. Two of the country's community college systems are of particular interest.

In the province of Quebec, during the educational reform of the sixties, a continuum of educational institutions beginning with a six-year primary school and followed by a five-year polyvalent (comprehensive) secondary school was created. For students choosing to study beyond the secondary level a single type of institution is provided—*collège d'enseignement général et professionnel* or CEGEP (college of general and vocational education). This public institution provides two-year general courses intended to prepare students for entry into a university (but, in fact, many students do not go beyond the CEGEP) and a three-year vocational program designed for students planning to go directly into the labor force. The CEGEP is the only route to the university. One of the notable features of this kind of institution, sandwiched between the secondary school and the university, is that any tendency for it to aspire to university status is effectively checked.

Another system of community colleges, of a quite different sort, is that recently established in the province of Saskatchewan. These are really programs, rather than institutions, designed to meet the need for adult education—determined on a community-by-community basis. These programs are not centralized and usually operate out of rented, rather than permanently owned, establishments.

Institutional Governance

A typical university governing board is composed of a slight majority of community representatives (in most provinces some or all of these are appointed by the provincial government), faculty of the university, students, and support staff; usually there are more teachers than student representatives on the board. The authority of such governing bodies, representative of the various estates within and without the university, has recently been challenged by the appearance of faculty unions. Although this trend is recent, by 1977 nearly one-third of the university faculty in Canada were members of unions. The agreements negotiated by the unions have tended to concern not only matters of remuneration but also aspects of working conditions — such as appointment of teachers, conditions of tenure and promotion, work load, and sabbatical leave — in fields formerly dealt with by the governing boards.

It is too early yet to measure the impact of the faculty unions. It is obvious, though, that what had previously been a collegial relationship between teaching and administrative members of the universities is now becoming an adversary relationship. On the other hand, negotiations between the two are now much more systematic: the rules of the game have been specified and codified, and that, generally, is considered to be an improvement.

Two other observations should be made with respect to faculty unions and governance. The first is that students, who had recently won seats on governing bodies, are excluded from the bargaining process, so they have lost influence. The other stems from the fact that individual universities have limited freedom to bargain with staff because the bulk of the universities' funds come from the provincial governments. It seems likely, therefore, that faculty groups will soon be cooperating on a provincewide basis to bargain directly with their provincial governments.

The nonuniversity postsecondary institutions in Canada have quite different governing structures. Institutes of technology are, for the most part, run directly by the provincial department of education or postsecondary education. Most community colleges have boards of governors composed of representatives of their local communities, but these tend to be primarily government appointees and usually do not include either staff or students. Among the exceptions are the CEGEPs of Quebec and Holland College in Prince Edward Island, in which staff and students do take part in the governing bodies. Another feature of the community colleges is that most of them draw upon the expertise of employers and occupational groups, which serve as advisory committees, one for each of the training programs offered by the college. (These committees vary in their effectiveness.) Unionization of college staff is almost universal and provincewide bargaining is the rule rather than the exception.

Institution-Government Relations

Of the ten provinces, six have government departments with responsibility for all levels of education, including postsecondary education. The other four have special government departments for higher education. In the case of the former, however, it is usual for the department of education to include a division concerned with postsecondary education. In the latter, it is not uncommon to find separate divisions for the universities, the community colleges, and adult or continuing education.

Intermediary bodies have become relatively common since the early sixties, especially with respect to university education. They tend to be modifications of the British University Grants Committee model and are found in five individual provinces, and one region comprising three provinces. The regional experiment is worth noting. About ten years ago, the three small eastern provinces of Nova Scotia, Prince Edward Island and New Brunswick undertook another in a long series of studies on the possibility of forming an economic and political union. The chief outcome was the creation of a Council of Maritime Premiers and a Maritime Provinces Higher Education Commission. The commission advises the three provincial governments regarding their support of higher education and also plans and coordinates the various institutions' programs so that they may operate as parts of a regional system. Another noteworthy item in the history of intermediary bodies is that the province of Alberta abolished two such organizations—one for university education created in 1966 and one for college education created in 1969—and replaced them with a government agency, the provincial Department of Advanced Education and Manpower.

As is obvious from the previous chapters, government influence over the operations of postsecondary institutions has increased steadily over the past two decades, and a simple correlation is observable between that increase in influence and the increase in public expenditure on postsecondary education. Until recently the pressure has been focused primarily on rationalizing the courses offered with the facilities available. However, with the formation of the joint federal-provincial Committee on Financing University Research in 1976 and passage of the federal Scientific Activities Act in 1977, government attention has been turned to the universities' research activities: here, for example, is a recent statement by the minister of state for science and technology:[1]

> The goal of all university research must continue to be excellence assessed by the peer review system.... I have said,

however, that the era of all university research being motivated solely by the desire to expand the frontiers of knowledge is passing. Research in the universities is now multifaceted, and increasingly the stimulus for research will be coming from outside the university. But we cannot expect, as a nation, that university research will be able to contribute fully to national issues if we do not define what the research objectives are with respect to those issues and what opportunities there are for university scientists and scholars to get involved.

Management

Planning

The locus of planning differs for the various types of postsecondary institutions. The universities, being autonomous, are responsible for their own planning, although they are subject to some prescription from the intermediary body or the provincial government. The provinces of Quebec and Alberta are closest to having system-wide planning. In Quebec, such planning has been going on for a number of years with the cooperation of the individual universities, the intermediary body (Council of Universities), the voluntary association of universities (Conference of Rectors and Principals), and the Division of Higher Education in the Ministry of Education. The goal is to identify the strengths and directions of the various universities in the system, to eliminate needless duplication, in short, to adhere to the principle of what is called "complementarity." Although the terminology used in the province of Alberta is different, and the bodies involved are fewer (principally the universities and the Department of Advanced Education and Manpower) the same concept is being implemented. Universities are being urged to define their roles and the government department both prods and supports them in this endeavor.

On the other hand, manpower planning in Canada is a relatively primitive art. In each of the provinces and at the national level there are government departments responsible for manpower training and supply, but their activities seem to be more reactive than directive. Indeed, most discussions of manpower planning lead either to the conclusion that students should be free to make their own choice, without guidance in the direction of manpower needs, or that new attempts at manpower planning must be initiated soon. Meantime, there is a mismatch between the supply of graduates from postsecondary education and the demand for their services in the job market. Currently this is especially noticeable with respect to newly trained teachers and to Ph.D. graduates, although engineers, geologists, and chemists have also been affected.

Another aspect of manpower planning has to do with the supply of teachers and research workers for the universities, which is also related to personnel management. The situation created by the almost wholesale recruitment of staff in the sixties is that these teachers and research personnel are now growing old. Add to this fact that little recruitment is currently taking place and it becomes evident that a complex problem exists. For one thing, there are few opportunities for new Ph.D. graduates to enter the profession. Consequently there is a temptation to restrict the enrollment of graduate students, which could produce a serious shortage of potential faculty members in the future.[2]

On the whole, planning for higher education in Canada is inadequate at all levels—institutional, provincial, and national. The information systems that do exist tend to be both complex and burdensome. Projections of enrollment, for example, are undertaken spasmodically. Too much planning is directed toward local needs and immediate problems.

Funding

Decision making with respect to budgets and the allocation of funds centers on the provincial governments. Each of them, with the blessing of the legislature, decides how much money it can allocate and, therefore, how much it must raise by way of taxes and other sorts of revenue. The division of funds between the subsystems of universities, institutes of technology, community colleges, and so forth, is a decision normally made in the name of the minister of the department concerned with postsecondary education. While, in the past, intermediary bodies have advised the government with respect to the total sums needed by the institutions, their advice is increasingly sought with respect to the allocation of funds to individual institutions of the subsystem. In fact, this task has been specifically designated to some intermediary bodies; others simply advise the government on what they consider to be appropriate allocation—normally keeping in mind both need and equity. As might be expected, the most important system decisions relate to financial and political matters.

It is usual for universities to receive block grants, frequently related in part to the number of students enrolled at different levels and in different faculties (weighted formulas are still in use in some provinces) and to be free to make their own allocation of funds within the institution. (A notable exception is to be found in Quebec where transfers from one budget category to another are not permitted by the government.) The institutes of technology are more often dealt with on a line-by-line basis; in other words, the financial administration is centered in the provincial department responsible for the institutes—in the bureaucracy. The community colleges fall somewhere between the two other types of institutions, with less freedom to make their own budgetary decisions than the universities, but with more freedom than the institutes of technology.

With respect to allocations, we should add that in the past four or five years governments have been much less generous with grants for postsecondary education; institutions of higher education are experiencing a steady state—for which they have no preparation and little liking. They have been growth-oriented for so long that they tend to behave as if the current decline in activities and funds were temporary. It is not.[3] They must accept that fact and learn how to cope with it.

Traditionally, the universities have been in charge of admission procedures, and they consider this freedom to be fundamental. However, their autonomy is tempered in those provinces in which the government has decreed that graduates of the community college should be admitted automatically, on application, to the university of their choice. The principle of automatic admission, subject to certain limitations and to a diversity of interpretations, exists in the articulation of the CEGEPs and the universities in the province of Quebec and, although not on quite such a universal scale, with respect to the transfer of students from certain programs in the community colleges to appropriate programs in the universities in the provinces of British Columbia and Alberta.

The nonuniversity institutions also control their own admission procedures. This is a less exact process in the community colleges than in the universities because "open admission" is characteristic of many college programs. By this is meant that students who are mature—for example, those who have already spent several years in the labor force—may be admitted to college programs even if they have not previously completed a formal secondary school course of studies. There are, however, some technical courses in the nonuniversity institutions for which acquisition of specific knowledge is required. Most universities also have "mature matriculation" provisions. Relatively small numbers of students take advantage of them on a full-time basis, but in institutions such as Athabasca University and Atkinson College of York University—both of which specialize in serving adult, part-time students—enrollment figures are impressive.

Members of faculty are selected by the institutions they serve. In several of the community college networks, the teaching staff must meet certain standards determined by the government—usually the minimum requirement is a master's degree—although even in such settings the requirement is frequently waived, particularly for an applicant who has had industrial experience which is considered to be more relevant to his teaching responsibilities than the attainment of a degree. One example of governmental control over the qualifications of teaching staff is the classification system which applies to the CEGEPs in the province of Quebec and determines the teacher's place on the provincial salary scale.

Another form of governmental direction in the selection of faculty concerns the rising proportion of non-Canadians engaged as members of university faculties. The governments of several provinces have made it quite clear that they want this trend reversed. In addition, the government of Canada has recently modified its immigration laws—to require an institution to clearly demonstrate that it was not able to hire a Canadian citizen or a landed immigrant.

Although a good deal of discussion has taken place with respect to the control of undergraduate curriculum in the universities, most of the real work in this realm has occurred at the graduate level. Provincial governments have power to withhold support of new graduate programs—by refusing to count students in unauthorized programs when the annual claim for the provincial grant is calculated for the university—and in some provinces they exercise this power. It is much more difficult, of course, to phase out a program than to prevent the introduction of a new one, and the record clearly shows that this is so.

The community colleges' curriculum is much more closely supervised by government. In the province of Ontario, for example, a proposed new program of studies must go through a number of evaluative stages before it is eventually approved by the Ministry of Colleges and Universities. There is even more centralized control of curriculum in the province of Quebec, which has a formal mechanism, centered in the ministry's Division of College Education, for determining the curriculum for the whole network of CEGEPs. However, the division actively consults with college staff before making its decisions.

It is generally conceded that it is appropriate for the government to make the ultimate decision with respect to the creation of new postsecondary institutions. Government, in turn, may receive proposals for new institutions from interested groups, either community-based or representing one of the professions. It may seek recommendations regarding the need for new institutions and their siting from the intermediary bodies. Even more frequently, however, the decision to establish a new institution is made on the basis of the recommendation of an ad hoc commission, usually one which has reviewed the total postsecondary education scene within a province.

Coordinating Bodies

An intermediary body modeled on the British University Grants Committee is found in many of the provinces. Such bodies are usually representative of the community at large, although they may include staff from the postsecondary institutions as well. One significant difference between two groups of intermediary agencies in the Canadian provinces is that those in the provinces of Quebec and Ontario are advisory with respect to the allocation of funds to the universities, while those in the Maritime provinces and Manitoba, Saskatchewan, and British Columbia enjoy delegated authority with respect to such allocation.[4] In no case, however, is the intermediary empowered to determine the total amount to be allocated to the universities. This is the government's prerogative. The province of Newfoundland has no intermediary agency; it has but one university, and its relations with government are direct. The province of Alberta is also without an intermediary. As has been reported, it once had such a body for the universities and one for the community colleges—both of which had the delegated authority. Evidently the government felt that it could coordinate postsecondary education more effectively if it eliminated the intermediary component.

So far, we have discussed university intermediaries. There are no intermediary bodies which operate between institutes of technology and government in the western provinces. However, in Ontario, the Ryerson Institute of Technology relates to government through the university advisory body. The community college of Prince Edward Island is affiliated with the Maritime Provinces Higher Education Commission, but the community college in New Brunswick is not. There is an intermediary body for the community colleges in Ontario (the Ontario Council of Regents for Colleges of Applied Arts and Technology) but no such college intermediary operates in the province of Quebec (although one has been suggested), nor in the provinces of Manitoba, Saskatchewan, and Alberta. An academic board deals with academic matters for the community colleges of British Columbia but, with respect to the allocation of resources to the colleges there, there is no intermediary.

From what has been said it may appear that the intermediaries in the Canadian provinces tend to be concerned primarily with the allocation of recources to the universities and colleges. That is indeed the case. Their mandates normally include reference to the control of curriculum, particularly the addition of new programs, and most intermediaries do play that role to some extent. In addition, most of them are expected to engage in system planning, but they have had minimal success.

Even when the intermediary agency is nominally advisory and does not have delegated authority, it is influential, both with respect to government policy and with respect to the operation of the universities or colleges. In general, however, Canada's experience with intermediaries is good. They provide governments with expert advice and, at the same time, temper the harshness of sometimes embarrassing political decisions. They provide the institutions with a channel for information and consultation and a feeling that they are understood even if they are not wholly satisfied.

In general, also, it can be said that although the institutions of higher education in Canada have circumscribed autonomy in political and fiscal terms, this does not seem to have had adverse effects on their basic functions: teaching and research. The teacher and the student are still free to pursue their scholarly activities as they choose.

The voluntary associations of universities or community colleges (never both in the same association) provide additional coordinating mechanisms. To the extent that the government's advisory agency is strong and influential, the institutions are more likely to organize their own collective bargaining agency. There is a limit, of course, to the degree to which a voluntary association can discipline its members, but there are many things on which they can agree, particularly when they are responding to a government initiative, or seeking to lead the government in new directions.

Innovation

In Canada, the establishment of an ad hoc commission of inquiry, usually but not always sponsored by government, is the customary first step in bringing about innovation. In the past twenty-five years, many major changes in systems of higher education can be traced to just such bodies.

A Royal Commission on National Development in the Arts, Letters, and Sciences recommended direct federal grants to universities, and these were instituted. It recommended the creation of a Canada council for the encouragement of the arts, letters, and humanities, and this was established; it recommended a national program of assistance to students and, although not quite in the form proposed, this too was instituted. A Royal Commission of Inquiry into Education in the Province of Quebec proposed a total reorganization of education within that province. The commission's recommendations were not implemented overnight, but they did result in what has been called the "quiet revolution" in Quebec.

Although a Royal Commission on Education and Youth in Newfoundland was ignored for a good many years, its recommendation to expand university facilities on a regional basis was implemented. One of the chief effects of the Maritime Union Study was the creation of a regional system of higher education for the provinces of Nova Scotia, New Brunswick, and Prince Edward Island. Earlier, the Royal Commission on Higher Education in New Brunswick recommended that the number of "university families" in that province should be reduced from six to three; the recommendation was enacted and set the system on its way to a more stable and equitable financial future. A commission of inquiry in British Columbia was responsible for the decentralization of the university subsystem and prompted the creation of the community college subsystem. A Commission on Educational Planning in Alberta led directly to the abolition of intermediary bodies for postsecondary education, and to the adoption of a plan for provincewide all-level coordination. The Saskatchewan system, too, is the result of recommendations of ad hoc commissions—especially, one set up to investigate community colleges and another to examine universities.

Not all such inquiries bring about change. The Commission on Post-Secondary Education in Ontario engaged many people for many hours at great cost, but no legislation resulted directly from it and things have gone on very much as before. Perhaps that judgment is not quite fair, since there is an increased interest in lifelong education throughout the province, although this might have occurred anyway. Two other efforts which seem to have produced few results are the Royal Commission on Education, Public Services, and Provincial-Municipal Relations in Nova Scotia and the Manitoba Task Force on Post-Secondary Education. On the whole, however, the ad hoc commissions of inquiry have proven to be effective, especially at the provincial level. There have been suggestions from time to time that another national study of higher education should be undertaken. When Canada finally agreed, after repeated suggestions from the Organization for Economic Cooperation and Development, to have its national policy for education examined by an outside group, it did so only by agreeing that there should be an examination of educational policies which would take no account of the constitutional problem. However, a recent study by the Organization for Economic Cooperation and Development stressed the fact that the reason Canada had no national goals for education lay in its Constitution. It seems, therefore, that neither the federal government nor the provincial governments are likely to sponsor a new national inquiry into higher education, at least for some time.

On the subject of innovation, mention should be made not only of fundamental changes in system structures but also of new types of institutions, new programs, new methods of teaching and learning. At present, ingenious schemes have been proposed for the extension of learning facilities—to the outports of Newfoundland, for example, to the fishermen of Nova Scotia, to the Indians of northern Manitoba, to the farmers of Saskatchewan, to the inmates of penitentiaries, to people who are homebound. There are variations on the British "open university" idea and the American "university without walls:" the Télé-université of the Université du Québec, the Ontario Educational Communications Authority with its own educational TV network, Athabasca University for Alberta adults, and British Columbia's university centers which serve the sparsely populated interior of the province.

Nor should the significant contributions of key individuals be overlooked. John B. Macdonald broke the monopoly of the provincial university in British Columbia and introduced the community college to that province and, indeed, to the country. John J. Deutsch designed the modern system of the Maritime region. Alphonse-Marie Parent was chairman of the inquiry which led to the "quiet revolution" in educational structures and processes in Quebec. Douglas T. Wright formalized relations between universities and government in Ontario. Walter H. Worth brought the Alberta system into a new era of coordination.

All of these men were academic administrators. There are three politicians who also belong on any list of innovators in the field of higher education: Jean Lesage, who was premier of Quebec at the time of the Parent Commission inquiry; William G. Davis, premier of Ontario, who deserves credit for reorganizing the government's role in postsecondary education and for introducing that province's system of colleges of applied arts and technology; and Alexander B. Campbell, long-time premier of Prince Edward Island, who took the bold decisions that brought order to postsecondary education there.

Effectiveness

One of the problems in discussing the effectiveness of the provincial system or systems of higher education in Canada is that it is difficult to identify what criteria should be applied. There is general agreement that the system should provide opportunities for postsecondary education for all those who desire such education and have the ability to profit from it. As has also been pointed out, the system is obviously expected to provide trained manpower, to discover new knowledge, and to offer individuals opportunities for self-development.

The institutes of technology and community colleges seem to have fairly clear-cut goals. The former are single-mindedly devoted to the preparation of trained manpower and to providing their students with marketable skills. The community colleges also have a unique purpose; although their role is rather more diffuse than that of the institutes of technology, they have a strong sense of responsibility to their immediate communities. Accordingly, the best of them are oriented toward lifelong education and the extension of formal and informal educational opportunities throughout the provinces, in both rural and urban areas.

The university has much more difficulty in defining its role, although it has been playing it for nearly a thousand years. Indeed, it may be said that the university has a split personality. The university for most academics, and a few students, is concerned with the exchange of ideas and the enhancement of civilization. The other role the university plays is that of a utilitarian institution which provides vocational (usually called professional) training (usually called education) to help students further their careers. Laymen think it odd, to say the least, that members of the academic community do not stress this aspect of the university. They sense irrelevance and arrogance in the utterances of university spokesmen. In truth, of course, the university performs both of these roles, and it would be far more productive if those who differ in their perspectives of the university would cease trying to convert each other and instead come to recognize the duality of the institution and the legitimacy of both of its roles.

There are enough postsecondary institutions throughout Canada today to meet the needs both of students and of employers. The distribution is not perfect but it has improved greatly since the creation of the community colleges. There have been successful efforts to modify entrance requirements, to take account of the special talents of people who have had unconventional school careers, and there has been increasing effort to provide for recurrent education. Although the cost of attending institutions of higher education is not the only factor which determines whether a student will or will not enroll, most of the provinces have relatively generous student aid programs, and these are complemented by a national student loan program. Nevertheless, studies in Canada, as elsewhere, reveal that, in spite of efforts to change the situation, the majority of students in postsecondary institutions come from the more affluent socioeconomic groups, even in those institutions which are devoted to adult education. Although this is a matter of much concern, it seems likely to continue.

The universities provide the chief medium for research, there being few research institutes in Canada which are not within the universities themselves. The provincial governments are showing some interest in the support of research, and even in directing it toward what they deem to be their priorities, but for a long time the chief support for research has come from the federal government. No body of researchers, of course, is satisfied with the amount of money provided. Most good research proposals, unless they are extremely costly, can be funded and are, but the number of proposals made is limited by the fact that relatively few scholars are engaged in full-time research, especially in the humanities and social sciences.

The question of what role the institutions of higher education should play with respect to social policy has been given much attention in Canada. It is generally thought that the university should be devoted to training analysts rather than coaching advocates of particular points of view. Accordingly, although there are social reform groups within university and college faculties and student bodies, it is normally quite clear that they are acting for themselves rather than for the institution of which they are members.

These remarks represent, for the most part, generalizations about higher education in the provinces. Any assessment must take account also of the national perspective, to which we now turn.

National Perspective

In the mid-sixties the OECD reviewed the training of and demand for high-level scientific and technical personnel[5] and found that Canada had no national policy for education. It concluded that:[6]

> Better coordination is needed at two levels, not only to relate the programs of the provinces to each other and to those of

the federal government but also to link the programs in one broad policy sector to the policy aims in another sector when these sectors are interdependent....The latter need is illustrated by the almost watertight separation that seems to exist between economic planning and forecasting on the one hand, and educational planning and forecasting on the other....

According to the OECD, the consequences of the dispersal of responsibility among the provinces, "have been not merely to restrict central authority but to inhibit federal action and to impede program planning in the provinces themselves."

Ten years later there was another, more comprehensive, OECD review of education policies in Canada.[7] Again the OECD found no national policy for education: "Canada has trodden out its own path, with an array of exceptionally active programs for vast quantitative expansion and significant qualitative change of the education system that are, however, derived from no explicitly stated, overall national conception of the country's interests." Referring to higher education in Canada as an "enterprise," the investigators observed that "Canadian educational development has exhibited in its rapid growth a high degree of entrepreneurial risk-taking behavior, as well as openness, flexibility, and the capacity for improvisation. The comparison might be a little less favorable to Canada, only if one thinks of the spirit of coordination, cooperation, and rationalization that is also demanded of modern, large-scale entrepreneurs."

At the national level, some planning does take place—for example, with respect to resource allocation among the provinces, to measures designed to equalize educational opportunity, to the supply of and demand for highly qualified manpower, to the support of research, and to the promotion of national unity. Decisions made at the provincial level tend to concern the spending of federal funds. With respect to programs and projects, prior consultation with the provinces is necessary; the federal role tends to be to persuade and support. Thus the government's influence in this area is restricted. One may well wonder how this could be, when the government of Canada bears more than half the costs of postsecondary education and research. It does have indirect and sometimes subtle influence on the development of the "system," but the state of federal-provincial relations renders the central government much less powerful than its potential would indicate.

In the summer of 1976, David Munroe wrote for this ICED study:

> It is obvious that some order must be established in higher education, that some elements of a system are essential, yet this has so far been impossible on a national scale.
>
> Objections come from both sides. University leaders, long accustomed to act independently, still claim the right to control admission policies, the level of student fees, the conditions of graduation, and the internal administration of their budgets. Governments, for their part, wish to establish equality of opportunity, mobility between institutions and provinces, a fair distribution of financial resources, and a reasonable balance between qualified graduates and manpower needs. Efforts in recent years to come to terms on these issues have not been noticeably successful, whether they have resulted from direct federal intervention, federal-provincial consultation, interprovincial cooperation or interinstitutional action.
>
> Yet, the forces of expansion, diversification, coordination and long-range planning have become so strong that it is inevitable some sort of system will emerge. With expenditures rising at the rate of 15 percent or 20 percent a year, with the public demand for education steadily increasing, with ten provincial authorities operating independently, with modern technology opening new channels of access to new knowledge, the nation cannot long continue to tolerate discrimination and waste. Educational and political leadership must devise some structure within which future educational policy can be designed and implemented.

There are two possible approaches to assessment of Canada's "national system" of higher education. One would be to measure, or attempt to measure, the extent to which the Canadian government has achieved its objectives related to higher education—for example, the six listed in our first chapter. Generally the results are discouraging.

- *Cultural development.* Canadian culture is threatened by that of the United States. Canadians still seek identity.
- *National unity.* There is tension among the regions, and the province of Quebec has recently elected a government whose declared intent is to take that province out of the Canadian federation.

—*Economic growth.* Canada is basically a rich country, but currently the economy is sluggish and the rate of unemployment is high.
—*Equality of opportunity.* Although there is free movement of students from one province to another and the overall participation rate is high, "there is still wide inequality in participation—and hence probably in accessibility—at the postsecondary level"[8] and postsecondary education opportunities for working adults are inadequate.
—*New knowledge.* Although support of research is moderately satisfactory, many of the nation's basic problems are not being systematically investigated.
—*International responsibilities.* Canada's external aid programs seem to be effective, but at home concern about numbers of foreign staff and students is increasing.

Of course, these matters are related only in part to higher education and there are many other factors involved as well. Evaluation of the system on this basis can only be impressionistic.

The other approach is to try to evaluate the system as a system—to judge the structural features rather than the outcomes. Does it have the elements of a national system of higher education? Are they articulated? Coordinated? Do the interested parties communicate with one another? Do they cooperate? Does the system work? Here, too, the result is discouraging, but some recent improvements can be noted.

The provincial governments have new resources and additional autonomy as a result of the 1977 rearrangement of fiscal relations with the federal government. What is perhaps most significant from the point of view of the system is the existence and new sense of responsibility of the Council of Ministers of Education. Though the council will probably not create an interprovincial system, through it the provinces can, if they will, communicate as one and cooperate with the other sectors. In fact, the council has decided to pursue the latter course. It must be careful, however, not to usurp the prerogatives of its members, each of whom is politically responsible to a provincial constituency and not to estrange any of its members by appearing to yield to federal influences or to tolerate federal interference.

The federal government, too, is attempting to improve its internal coordination in the fields related to higher education, notably by defining coordinating roles for the Ministry of State for

Science and Technology (MOSST) with respect to research, technological development and the supply of highly qualified manpower, and the Department of the Secretary of State (SOS) for postsecondary education. However, MOSST and SOS are finding it difficult to gain recognition of their coordinating roles, both among federal government departments and agencies and from the public at large. Recognition has also been impeded by constant internal reorganization within MOSST and SOS. Passage of the Scientific Activities Act of 1977 should help to strengthen MOSST, but the new Federal-Provincial Fiscal Arrangements Act of the same year is vague in its assignment of functions to SOS in the field of postsecondary education.

However desirable improved internal coordination at the federal level might seem to be, from the point of view of the provinces it could go too far. Development of any agency which could be seen to assume the role of a federal office of education would spark a negative reaction from the Council of Ministers of Education and reverse the current trend toward cooperation.

Because of the widespread use of the intermediary body in provincial systems, one might wonder why there is not a government advisory body with respect to postsecondary education. This has been suggested tentatively from time to time, but the recent constitutional history of Canada runs counter to creation of such a federal agency. If the government of Canada has no ministry of education, how could it justify the appointment of a body to advise it on such matters? Thus runs the argument. One important implication of this situation is that the academic community has an opportunity and a responsibility to assume advisory roles (whether invited or not) which might otherwise be played by a government-appointed agency. Indeed the academic community should direct its advice not only to the government of Canada but also to the provinces. One would hope, however, that it could rise above the level of a glorified fund-raiser.

Unfortunately, the academic community—what we have called the third sector—is far from being able to act collectively. National associations representing research interests, notably SCITEC, the Social Science Federation of Canada, and the Humanities Research Council of Canada work fairly well together, but the Royal Society of Canada, which might be expected to be an active participant in policy making, shows little interest. The organizations representing what one might call administrative interests—the associations of universities, of university teachers, of community colleges, and of students—tend to compete rather than cooperate. If the academic community does not act collectively on those occasions when a single united voice is needed, it will not be able to play its role in relations with the other two—the governmental—sectors in the national "system." It will not effectively express its interests and it will not fulfill its potential contribution to policy formulation.

It must be acknowledged, however, that there are more occasions when each group within the academic community will want to proceed independently, especially with respect to matters within the area of its own special interest. The pragmatic approach suggests, therefore, that each association should be encouraged to gather its own strength for its own purposes, and that groups of associations should learn how to pool their strength when the challenge or the opportunity is general.

Among the national organizations, the Association of Universities and Colleges of Canada should be the leader. In order to play that role, however, it needs renewed commitment from the university presidents. The AUCC might also benefit from reorganization as a federation of provincial or regional associations—in recognition, long delayed, of the provincialization of higher education, and as a way of drawing on, as well as contributing to, the resources of such associations. And the AUCC may decide it would be wise to reorder its priorities, stressing, for example, identification of issues, analyses of available data, staff, and commissioned research on nationwide problems in higher education, and the provision of information services, not only for member institutions or associations but also for governments and the public.

So the elements of a national system exist, even if in a relatively unrefined state. The stuttering which is characteristic of communication among the sectors has been recorded, as has been the hesitancy with which they engage in cooperative activities. The balance of relationships is delicate and calls for sensitive participation by all parties.

If higher education in Canada seems to be fragmented, it is because Canada itself suffers from the same disability. Nevertheless, the governments of Canada and the provinces, the universities, institutes of technology, and community colleges do provide a wide range of educational opportunities for a variety of students. The enterprise is uncoordinated and consists of many subsystems rather than a single, unified system, but at the same time its decentralization enables it to be responsive to regional needs. In spite of its structural shortcomings, it serves Canada tolerably well.

FOOTNOTES

1. Honourable Hugh James Faulkner, minister of state for science and technology, in the debate on third reading of the Government Organization (Scientific Activities) Act 1976, in Canada, *House of Commons Debates*, Vol. 120, No. 136 (June 3, 1977).
2. This is documented by Max von Zür-Muehlen in "The Canadian Universities in a Crisis," prepared for the workshop of the Science Council of Canada on "Optimization of Age Distribution in University Research," Ottawa (June 11-12, 1977).
3. See, for example: Canada, Statistics Canada, Education, Science, and Culture Division, *Advance Statistics of Education, 1977-78* (Ottawa: Statistics Canada, 1977), especially pp. 9-23.
4. For a discussion of types of intermediary agencies, see: Edward Sheffield, "Organization for the Control of Systems of Higher Education," in Barbara B. Burn, ed., *International Perspectives on Problems of Higher Education: Access, Systems, Youth and Employment*, (New York: International Council for Educational Development, 1977).
5. Organisation for Economic Co-operation and Development, *Training of and Demand for High-Level Scientific and Technical Personnel in Canada*, Reviews of National Policies for Education (Paris: OECD, 1966).
6. On another occasion J. Stefan Dupré and colleagues were to speak of "the clash of grand designs" — those of educationists (provincial) vs. economists (federal) — and of "the two solitudes of education and economics." See: J. Stefan Dupré *et al.*, *Federalism and Policy Development: the case of adult occupational training in Ontario* (Toronto: University of Toronto Press, 1973).
7. Organisation for Economic Co-operation and Developoment, *Reviews of National Policies for Education: Canada* (Paris: OECD, 1976).
8. Canada, Department of the Secretary of State, Education Support Branch, *Some Characteristics of Post-Secondary Students in Canada* (Ottawa: Minister of Supply and Services Canada, 1976), p. 89.

SELECTED BIBLIOGRAPHY

In addition to the documents listed here, most of the agencies mentioned in the previous pages issue annual reports which are excellent sources of recent information.

Items followed by an asterisk are available in both English and French.

Canada

Association of Commonwealth Universities. *Commonwealth Universities Yearbook*, Canada section, especially the introductory article on "The Universities of Canada." London: The Association. Annual.

Association of Universities and Colleges of Canada, Commission on the Financing of Higher Education, Vincent W. Bladen, chairman. *Report of the Commission.* Toronto: University of Toronto Press, 1965.*

Association of Universities and Colleges of Canada, Research Division, J. F. Houwing and A.M. Kristjanson. *Composition of Governing Bodies of Canadian Universities and Colleges, 1975.* Ottawa: The Association, 1975.*

Bonneau, Louis-Philippe, and J.A. Corry. *Quest for the Optimum: Research Policy in the Universities of Canada.* The Report of a Commission to Study the Rationalisation of University Research. Ottawa: Association of Universities and Colleges of Canada, 1972.*

Burn, Barbara B., et al. *Higher Education in Nine Countries: A Comparative Study of Higher Education Abroad.* A general report prepared for the Carnegie Commission on Higher Education. New York: Mc-Graw-Hill, 1971. Chapter 5.

Campbell, Gordon. *Community Colleges in Canada.* Toronto: Ryerson/McGraw-Hill, 1971.

Canada, Department of the Secretary of State, Education Support Branch. *Some Characteristics of Post-Secondary Students in Canada.* Ottawa: Minister of Supply and Services Canada, 1976.*

Canada, Royal Commission on National Development in the Arts, Letters and Sciences. *Report.* Ottawa: King's Printer, 1951.*

Canada, Secretary of State and Ministers of Education of the Provinces. *Review of Educational Policies in Canada.* Submissions to the Organisation for Economic Co-operation and Development. Toronto: Council of Ministers of Education, Canada, 1975*

Canada, Senate Special Committee on Science Policy, Hon. Maurice Lamontagne, chairman. *A Science Policy for Canada.* Ottawa: Information Canada. 1970-1974.*

Canada, Statistics Canada, Education, Science and Culture Division. *Education in Canada: A Statistical Review.* Ottawa: Statistics Canada. Annual*

Canada, Statistics Canada, Education, Science and Culture Division, in cooperation with the Association of Universities and Colleges of Canada. *Universities and Colleges of Canada.* Ottawa: Statistics Canada. Annual.*

Corry, J.A. *Universities and Governments.* Quance Lectures in Canadian Education. Toronto: W.J. Gage & Co. Ltd., 1969.

Duff, James, and R.O. Berdahl. *University Government in Canada.* Report of a Commission sponsored by the Canadian Association of University Teachers and the Association of Universities and Colleges of Canada. Toronto: University of Toronto Press, 1966.*

Dupré, J. Stefan, *et al. Federalism and Policy Development: the case of adult occupational training in Ontario.* Toronto: University of Toronto Press, 1973.

Harris, Robin S. *A History of Higher Education in Canada, 1663-1960.* Toronto: University of Toronto Press, 1976.

Hodgson, Ernest D. *Federal Intervention in Public Education.* Toronto: Canadian Education Association, 1976.*

Hurtubise, René, and Donald C. Rowat. *The University, Society and Government.* The Report of the Commission on the Relation Between Universities and Governments. Ottawa: University of Ottawa Press, 1970.*

Konrad, Abram G., ed. *Clientele and Community: The Student in the Canadian Community College.* Willowdale, Ontario: Association of Canadian Community Colleges, 1974.*

Macdonald, John B. "Change and the Universities: University-Government Relations." *Canadian Public Administration,* Vol. 14, No. 1, 1970.

Macdonald, John B., *et al. The Role of the Federal Government in Support of Research in Canadian Universities.* Special Study No. 7, prepared for The Science Council of Canada and The Canada Council. Ottawa: Queen's Printer, 1969.*

Manzer, Ronald A. "The National Organization of Canadian Education." *Canadian Public Administration,* Vol. 11, No. 4, Winter 1968.

Meekison, J. Peter, ed. *Canadian Federalism: Myth or Reality.* Second edition. Toronto: Methuen, 1971.

Munroe, David. *Case Study on Alternative University Structure in Canada.* Paris: UNESCO, 1973.

——————*The Organization and Administration of Education in Canada.* Prepared for the Education Support Branch, Department of the Secretary of State, with the cooperation of the Education Division, Statistics Canada. Ottawa: Information Canada. 1974.*

―――――"Post-Secondary Education in Canada: A Survey of Recent Trends and Developments," in T.H. McLeod, ed., *Post-Secondary Education in a Technological Society.* Montreal: McGill-Queen's University Press, 1973.*

Organisation for Economic Co-operation and Development. *New College Systems in Canada,* by Cicely Watson. Paris: OECD, 1973.

―――――*Reviews of National Policies for Education: Canada.* Paris: OECD, 1976.*

―――――*Reviews of National Science Policy:* Canada, Paris OECD, 1969.*

Pilkington, Gwendoline. "A History of the National Conference of Canadian Universities, 1911-1961." Unpublished Ph.D. thesis, University of Toronto, 1974.

Ross, Murray G. *The University: The Anatomy of Academe.* New York, Toronto, etc.: McGraw-Hill, 1976.

Sirluck, Ernest. "Causes of Tightening Government Control of Universities." *Stoa: The Canadian Journal of Higher Education,* Vol. 4, No. 2, 1974.

Smiley, D.V. *Canada in Question: Federalism in the Seventies.* Second edition. Toronto: McGraw-Hill Ryerson, 1976.

Trotter, Bernard, A.W.R. Carrothers, *et al. Planning for Planning—Relationships between Universities and Governments: Guidelines to Process.* A study prepared for the Association of Universities and Colleges of Canada by its Advisory Committee on University Planning, A.W.R. Carrothers, chairman. Ottawa: The Association, 1974.*

Wilson, J. Donald, Robert M. Stamp and Louis-Philippe Audet, eds. *Canadian Education: A History.* Scarborough, Ontario: Prentice-Hall, 1970.

Atlantic Provinces

Association of Atlantic Universities. *Higher Education in the Atlantic Provinces for the 1970's.* Halifax: The Association, 1970.

Maritime Provinces Higher Education Commission. *Higher Education in the Maritimes—1976: An Overview.* Frederiction: The Commission, 1976.*

―――――*In Process: Three Year Regional Planning for Higher Education in the Maritime Provinces.* Fredericton: The Commission. 1977.*

―――――*Unique Regional Approach to Coordinating Higher Education.* Fredericton: The Commission, 1975.*

Maritime Union Study. *The Report on Maritime Union commissioned by the Governments of Nova Scotia, New Brunswick and Prince Edward Island,* John J. Deutsch, special advisor. Fredericton: Maritime Union Study, 1970.

New Brunswick. *Report of the Committee on the Financing of Higher Education in New Brunswick,* J.J. Deutsch, chairman. Fredericton: Queen's Printer, 1967.*

―――――*Report of the Royal Commission on Higher Education in New Brunswick,* J.J. Deutsch, chairman. Fredericton: Queen's Printer, 1962.*

Newfoundland and Labrador. *Report of the Royal Commission on Education and Youth*, Philip J. Warren, chairman. St. John's: Queen's Printer, 1967-1968.

Nova Scotia, Royal Commission on Education, Public Services and Provincial-Municipal Relations, John F. Graham, chairman. *Report.*, Vol. III. Halifax: Queen's Printer, 1971. Chapters 61-65.

Prince Edward Island. *Policy Statement on Post-Secondary Education*. Charlottetown: Legislative Assembly, 1968.

Quebec

Audet, Louis-Philippe. *Histoire de l'enseignement au Québec, 1608-1971*. Montréal: Holt, Rinehart and Winston, 1971.

Audet, Louis-Phillippe, et Armand Gauthier. *Le système scolaire du Québec: organisation et fonctionnement*. Second Edition. Montréal: Beauchemin, 1969.

Breton, Lise, et Jean-Luc Roy. *Le collège québécois: introduction bibliographique*. Montréal: Centre d'animation, de développement et de recherche en éducation (CADRE), 1976.

Daoust, Gaetan, et Paul Bélanger. *L'université dans une société éducative: de l'éducation des adultes à l'éducation permanente*. Montréal: Les Presses de l'Université de Montréal, 1974.

Dorais, Léo A. *L'autogestion universitaire: autopsie d'un mythe*. Montréal: Les Presses de l'Université du Québec, 1977.

Gingras, Paul-Emile. *La vie pédagogique des collèges, 1960-1970*. Montréal: Centre d'animation, de développement et de recherche en éducation (CADRE), 1969.

Hurtubise, René, rédacteur. *L'Université québécoise du proche avenir*. Montréal: Editions Hurtubise HMH, Ltée, 1973.

Locas, Claude. *La Réforme scolaire du Québec: bibliographie pour un bilan*. Quebec: Gouvernement du Québec. Ministère de l'Education, Direction générale de la planification, 1975.

McGill Journal of Education. Special Issue on Quebec Education, Vol. 7, No. 2. Fall 1972.

Québec. *Report of the Royal Commission of Inquiry on Education in the Province of Quebec*, Alphonse-Marie Parent, chairman. Quebec: Government of the Province of Quebec, 1963-1966.*

Québec, Conseil des universités. *Objectifs généraux de l'enseignement supérieur et grandes orientations des établissements*. Québec: Le Counseil, 1972-1976.

Québec, Ministère de l'Education. *L'enseignement collégial et les collèges d'enseignement général et professional* Documents d'éducation. 3. Québec: Le Ministère, 1967.

Québec, Superior Council of Education. *The College: Report on the State and

Needs of College Education, Jean-Guy Nadeau, chairman of the Study Committee. Quebec: The Council, 1976.*

Société royale du Canada, Académie des Lettres et des Sciences humaines. *Le Rapport Parent, 10 ans après.* Montreal: Ballarmin, 1975.

Ontario

Committee of Presidents of Provincially Assisted Universities [and Colleges of Ontario]. *Post-Secondary Education in Ontario, 1962-1970.* Report of the Presidents of the Universities of Ontario to the Advisory Committee on University Affairs. Toronto: The Committee of Presidents, 1963.

Committee of Presidents of Universities of Ontario, Presidents' Research Committee. *From the Sixties to the Seventies: An Appraisal of Higher Education in Ontario.* Toronto: The Committee of Presidents, 1966.

Davis, William G. "The Government of Ontario and the Universities of the Province," in *Governments and the University.* The Frank Gerstein Lectures, York University, 1966. Toronto: Macmillan, 1966.

Fleming, W.G., *Ontario's Educative Society,* Vol. IV: "Post-Secondary and Adult Education." Toronto: University of Toronto Press, 1971.

Hansen, B.L. "The Balance between Economic Efficiency and Political Rationality: A Description of Planning for Ontario Universities." *Educational Planning,* Vol. 2, No. 2, Oct. 1975.

Harris, Robin S. "The Evolution of a Provincial System of Higher Education in Ontario," in D.F. Dadson, ed., *On Higher Education: Five Lectures.* Toronto: University of Toronto Press, 1966.

Ontario, Commission on Post-Secondary Education in Ontario. *The Learning Society: Report of the Commission,* Douglas T. Wright, chairman (succeeded by D.O. Davis). Toronto: Ministry of Government Services, 1972.*

Ontario, Commission on Post-Secondary Education in Ontario. *The Ontario Colleges of Applied Arts and Technology.* A study prepared for the Commission by Systems Research Group Inc., Toronto: Queen's Printer, 1972.

Ontario, Ministry of Colleges and Universities. *Horizons: A guide to educational opportunities in Ontario beyond the secondary school level.* Toronto: The Ministry. Annual.*

Ontario Council of Regents for Colleges of Applied Arts & Technology. *Guidelines for Governors—Colleges of Applied Arts & Technology.* Toronto: Ministry of Colleges and Universities, 1975.

Porter, John, Bernard Blishen, *et al. Towards 2000: The Future of Post-Secondary Education in Ontario.* Toronto: McClelland and Stewart, 1971.

Sheffield, Edward F., ed. *Agencies for Higher Education in Ontario.* Symposium Series/3. Toronto: Ontario Institute for Studies in Education, 1974.

Smyth, D. McCormack. "Some Aspects of the Development of Ontario Colleges of Applied Arts and Technology." Unpublished M.Phil. thesis, University of Toronto, 1970.

Stewart, Edward E. "The Role of the Provincial Government in the Development of the Universities of Ontario, 1791-1964." Unpublished Ed.D. thesis, University of Toronto, 1970.

Trusz, Andrew R. "The Activities of Governmental Education Bodies in Defining the Role of Post-Secondary Education Since 1945: A Comparative Case Study of the State of New York and the Province of Ontario, 1945-1972." Unpublished Ed.D. dissertation, State University of New York at Buffalo, 1977.

Western Provinces

Alberta, Commission on Educational Planning, Walter H. Worth, commissioner. *A Choice of Futures: Report of the Commission.* Edmonton: Queen's Printer, 1972.

British Columbia. *Report of the Commission on University Programs in Non-Metropolitan Areas,* W.C. Winegard, commissioner. Victoria: Department of Education, 1976.

————*Report of the University Government Committee,* Walter D. Young, chairman, to the Hon. Eileen Dailly, minister of education. Province of British Columbia, May 2, 1974. Victoria: Department of Education, 1974.

————*Towards the Learning Community: Report of the Task Force on the Community College in British Columbia,* Hazel L'Estrange, chairman. Victoria: Queen's Printer, 1974.

Dennison, John D., Alex Tunner, Gordon Jones and Glen C. Forrester. *The Impact of Community Colleges: A Study of the College Concept in British Columbia.* Vancouver: B.C. Research, 1975.

Macdonald, John B. *Higher Education in British Columbia and a Plan for the Future.* Vancouver: University of British Columbia, 1962.

Maddocks, G.R. *A Comparative Analysis of Approaches to Planning Development in Post-Secondary Education.* Research Studies in Post-Secondary Education No. 23. Edmonton: Alberta Colleges Commission, 1972.

Manitoba. *Post-Secondary Education in Manitoba.* Report of the Task Force on Post-Secondary Education in Manitoba, Michael J. Oliver, chairman. Winnipeg: Queen's Printer, 1973.

Saskatchewan. *Report of the Minister's Advisory Committee on Community Colleges,* Ron Faris, chairman. Regina: Department of Continuing Education, 1972.

————*Report of the Royal Commission on University Organization and Structure,* Emmet Hall, chairman. Regina: Department of Continuing Education, 1973.

Saskatchewan, University of. *Report of the Committee on the Role of the University of Saskatchewan within the Community,* T.H. McLeod, chairman. Saskatoon: The University, 1971.

Sirluck, Ernest. "University Presidents and the Politicians." *Canadian Journal of Higher Education,* Vol. 7, No. 1, 1977.

Small, J.M. *College Coordination in Alberta: System Development and Appraisal.* Research Studies in Post-Secondary Education No. 18. Edmonton: Alberta Colleges Commission, 1972.

Worth, Walter H. "From Autonomy to System: A Provincial Perspective," *Library Association of Alberta Bulletin,* Vol. 5, No. 2, April 1974.

DIRECTORS OF COUNTRY STUDIES

Australia
  Bruce Williams, Vice-Chancellor and Principal, University of Sydney.

Canada
  Edward Sheffield, Professor of Higher Education, Chairman, Higher Education Group, University of Toronto.
  Sponsor: Higher Education Group, University of Toronto.

Federal Republic of Germany
  Hansgert Peisert, Professor, Zentrum I, Bildungsforschung, University of Konstanz.
  Sponsor: University of Konstanz.

France
  Alain Bienaymé, Professor of Economics, University of Paris-Dauphine IX.
  Sponsor: Secretary of State for Higher Education.

Iran
  Abdol Hossein Samii, Director, Imperial Medical Center of Iran.
  M. Reza Vaghefi, Dean, School of Economics, University of Tehran.
  Sponsor: Reza Shah Kabir University.

Japan
  Katsuya Narita, Director of First Research Department, National Institute for Educational Research.
  Sponsor: National Institute for Educational Research.

Mexico
  Alfonso Rangel Guerra, General Director of Higher Education, Secretaria de Educacion Publica.
  Sponsor: Asociacion Nacional de Universidades e Institutos de Ensenañza Superior.

Poland
Jan Szczepański, Professor, Institute of Philosophy, Warsaw.
Sponsor: Institute for Higher Education Research.

Sweden
Bertil Östergren, Adviser, National Board of Universities and Colleges.
Sponsor: National Board of Universities and Colleges.

Thailand
Sippanondha Ketudat, Secretary-General, National Education Commission.
Sponsor: National Education Commission.

United Kingdom
Anthony Becher, Professor of Education, University of Sussex.
Jack Embling, Former Deputy Under Secretary of State, Department of Education and Science.
Maurice Kogan, Professor of Government and Social Administration, Brunel University.
Sponsor: Leverhulme Trust.

United States
John R. Shea, Carnegie Council for Policy Studies in Higher Education.
David D. Henry, President Emeritus, University of Illinois at Urbana-Champaign.
Lyman A. Glenny, Center for Research and Development in Higher Education, University of California, Berkeley.
Sponsor: International Council for Educational Development.